The Voice of Government

The Voice of Government

EDITED BY

RAY ELDON HIEBERT
Professor and Head, Department of Journalism
University of Maryland

CARLTON E. SPITZER
President, Public Affairs Communications, Inc.
Washington, D.C.

John Wiley & Sons, Inc.
New York · London · Sydney · Toronto

Library of Congress Catalog Card Number: 68-55335
SBN 471 36755 9
Printed in the United States of America

Series Preface

In a democratic society there is no more important principle than the people's right to know about their government and its obligation to keep the people informed. The role of the press and communication in the governing process has been important since the earliest days of the nation.

In the modern mass society of an international power, communication between government and people through a complex and often instantaneous means of transmission has vital implications and consequences. The explosive impact of the mass media on the political and governmental process has brought about changes in politics, public administration, and international relations.

The interrelationship between government and communication has many new dimensions that must be explored and understood. The "Wiley Series on Government and Communication" was conceived to probe and provide greater understanding of those new dimensions.

Some of the books in the series deal with the way in which governments (local, national, and international) communicate with the people, either directly or through the press and mass media.

Other books in the series discuss the way in which the people, usually through the press and mass media, obtain information from government.

Finally, some of the series books deal with the problems that arise at that intersection of society at which government and people meet through the media. These are problems of the social, economic, legal, and political implications of the communication process when dealing with government, the problems of restriction and censorship, of distortion and propaganda, of freedom and national security, and of organization and technology.

Certainly the future of democracy may depend to a large extent on the success with which we understand and deal with the problems created by the relationship between government and communication in a new age.

RAY ELDON HIEBERT
Series Editor

Acknowledgments

The editors would like to acknowledge their debt to countless colleagues who have contributed ideas, suggestions, critical appraisal, and hard work to this book. Special gratitude is due to John W. Gardner, former Secretary of the Department of Health, Education, and Welfare; John Leslie, Director of Information, Department of Labor; Harold Lewis, Director of Information, Department of Agriculture; Richard Fryklund, Deputy Assistant Secretary for Public Affairs, Department of Defense; Herbert J. Kramer, Director of Public Affairs, Office of Economic Opportunity; Irving Goldberg of HEW; Roy Hoopes of HEW (a chapter author who made many other special contributions to the book); Lawrence Hogan, lecturer at the University of Maryland; Thomas Kraner, former editor of the Public Relations Journal; and secretaries June Evans of HEW, Patricia Robinson of Public Affairs Communications, Inc., and Elaine Williams and Margaret Markfield of the Journalism Department, University of Maryland. The editors gratefully acknowledge their special indebtedness to John M. Sullivan, former Washington editor of John Wiley & Sons, Inc., now Director of Publications for the Atomic Energy Commission.

Contents

xii CONTENTS

The Voice of Government

Introduction

RAY ELDON HIEBERT
PROFESSOR AND HEAD
DEPARTMENT OF JOURNALISM
UNIVERSITY OF MARYLAND

How does the federal government communicate its plans and programs? With what voice does it speak to the people? How, as government grows bigger each day, does it manage to transmit all the vital information so necessary to maintain our complex society? Anyone concerned with these questions will find answers in this book, whether he is a private citizen anxious to be informed about government, a student of political science, public administration, journalism or communication, or a participant in the public information process.

"Information, its communication and use, is the web of society; it is the basis for all human understanding, organization, and effort." So says John Diebold, one of the prophets of our newly computerized age, in his book, *Beyond Automation*.

Indeed, we live in the age of an information explosion. Never before in history has man possessed so many facts, and he is presently producing new data at such a rapid rate that the world's current knowledge will be doubled in about 20 years. Never before has man possessed such enormous ability to communicate, either on a personal basis facilitated by an efficient postal system, vast telephone network, superhighways, rapid rail lines, and supersonic jets, or on a mass basis through newspapers, magazines, books, radio, television, and motion pictures. At every turn we are bombarded with messages.

Because information is essential to all human understanding, it is the key to power. Those who have knowledge have strength and wield influence.

In totalitarian societies, where power is concentrated in the few at the top, communication is usually regarded as a chief instrument of state. The channels of information and the media of communication are closely guarded and carefully controlled by the leaders in order to maintain and strengthen their positions.

In the Soviet Union, for instance, the manufacture and distribution of information is regarded with the same awe and respect that Americans have for the minting of money. In Russia it is the right of the state alone to distribute information, as in America it is the right of the government alone to print dollar bills. A man charged with privately publishing a newspaper in Moscow would be subject to the same sort of penalty as an American caught counterfeiting money.

3

In democratic societies, where power is diffused among the many, free communication is regarded as the province of all men. The guarantee of free speech and free press is written into the American constitution, and the media of communication have become a fourth branch of government, guarding against a concentration of power in any of the other three.

Traditionally in America the government has been restrained from participating in the communication process. The privately owned mass media do not want competition from the government, and the people do not want to feel that government controls the information they get. Suspicion of propaganda and fear of brainwashing have often interfered with the government's efforts to spread information. But this situation has changed remarkably since World War II.

Today there is new recognition that in a mass society government often exists mainly to produce information for the benefit of its citizens. Many government programs are established for the sole purpose of developing knowledge through research to produce a better society. Without communicating this knowledge to the people, such efforts would be worthless.

In addition, government information practices have become increasingly professional and responsible. Most public information officers today acknowledge that effective communication is two-way communication. The information officer listens to his audience as sensitively as he speaks to it. He seeks to incorporate the attitudes, ideas, and feelings of the people into programs and policies in order to make them effective. There is greater participation by the information officer in the program and policy function; he feeds information back to the government as much as he passes government information to the people. And in this way, the information officer plays an important part in allowing the people to participate in policy and program formulation. He allows the democratic process to continue in spite of a monolithic, mass society.

In the early days of the American nation the founding fathers believed that this role could be assigned to the press alone. They felt that if the press were free from government control, it could provide the people with all the facts they needed to form their own opinions and participate in the governing process. Today we realize that in spite of increased mass communication facilities, it is economically impossible for the news media to do all the work caused by the information explosion—ferreting out all the facts on all fronts and communicating them effectively to all the people. Even if there were enough well-trained and dedicated news reporters, researchers, and editors to do this, there would be increasing need for government information officers.

Thus in a sense responsible and professional government information officials have taken on many of the duties of the press. They have taken upon themselves the obligation to be objective, to be fair, to see and communicate both sides of all issues, to be the advocate of their audiences as well as their employers. And in doing so, they do not weaken their message; they enhance it and make communication effective. There are many indications that the Soviet Union does not communicate very effectively with its citizenry, for although the government has total control of the information process, there is little feedback mechanism to *involve* the people in that process.

This does not mean to say that in the American system, with responsible government information officials, we no longer need a private and free press. Even if newsmen cannot do the full job of reporting the facts, their presence serves as a constant guarantee of responsible public information.

Public information, like public relations in its best sense, means involving both parties, sender and receiver, in the communication process. It means relating one to the other, to the extent that one changes and shapes the other, in a constant and mutual act.

Today America is regarded by the free world as a leader in developing legitimate public information programs and policies. Almost every country of the world now has an information office modeled on American practice. In most countries the information function is served by a "ministry of information" at the cabinet level, usually one of the highest executive positions. (In the United States there is as yet no cabinet-level information official, although the President's press secretary plays an increasingly important role.)

Naturally, not all government information practice is perfect, and not all of it is responsible. There are still many officials who, given the chance, would use the public information man to further their own political causes, to enhance their own reputations, to cover up their own iniquities, to satisfy the greed of their own ambitions. But a corps of increasingly professional public information men is developing: they pay heed to their own profession's ethics and win approval from their colleagues, not their bosses.

It must be sadly admitted that many public information officers still are, in the words of one of our contributing authors, Henry Scharer, the "stepchildren of bureaucracy." They have been given second-class standing to do a front-line job. Their function has not been neglected, for few public officials, political or bureaucratic, fail to understand the importance of public communication; nearly all insist on a large publicity budget and try to get the best information man they can find. It does mean, however, that too often the public official is more interested in having a press agent than in providing effective communication. He is all too often concerned about keeping his information man subservient, not allowing him to participate in program and policy formulation, not interested in his professional or ethical responsibilities.

For these reasons, among others, there have been few treatises on public information in the federal government. Discussion of the subject has been neglected, the function itself often hidden. There have been several important book-length studies of the subject, but none that is current or has dealt with its theory and practice in a useful way from the practitioners' viewpoint. (A complete bibliography of works on public information is given at the end of this book.)

This book deals with public information of the federal government, but there is much here that pertains to the city, county, and state levels, too, and to other national governments as well.

The authors represent a wide variety of governmental and professional background. Included here are members of both the executive and legislative branches of the federal government. Authors are from such executive agencies as the White House, State Department, Defense Department, Treasury Department, Department of Health, Education, and Welfare, Commerce Department, Department of Housing and Urban Development,

Social Security Administration, Veterans Administration, National Aeronautics and Space Administration, Agency for International Development, and several Presidential commissions and committees.

The judicial branch is not represented because, with only a few exceptions, it does not provide the public with information. The Supreme Court has only one man in its public information office, and his activities are extremely limited. Most agencies of the judicial branch have traditionally held that any public communication of their work would only serve to unbalance the scales of justice.

The authors are among the best professionals in the field today. All of them have had intimate contact with the public information function. A few who are no longer actively engaged in government have the added advantage of extra independence and the perception of hindsight.

Each author, of course, speaks only for himself and describes only the operation that he himself has been a part of. No man knows everything about all branches of government or practices all techniques of the field. No two departments or agencies are alike, and none perform the public information function in the same way. But the spectrum represented here indicates the breadth and variety of level and experience in the field, and out of these specifics certainly generalizations can be achieved.

The purpose of this book is to increase the understanding of the process of public information, particularly for those engaged in the work and for young people recruited for the field, but also for the citizen who needs to know how the government operates in order to take his rightful place in society.

1. Public Information in Perspective

PUBLIC INFORMATION IN PERSPECTIVE deals with the background and history, philosophy and social role, size and scope, and future potentials and problems of public information in government.

The first chapter in this section, "Communication in a Democratic Society," is appropriately the work of the head of one of the largest government executive departments with one of the largest public information staffs.

Wilbur J. Cohen, Secretary of the Department of Health, Education, and Welfare, has been intimately involved with the federal government since the early days of the New Deal, when he served in President Franklin D. Roosevelt's Cabinet Committee on Economic Security and helped draft the original Social Security Act. He has been connected with almost all legislative developments in the social security and public assistance programs since 1934, and has been closely associated with the recent medicare, medical school, and education legislation.

A graduate of the University of Wisconsin, he served as Professor of Public Welfare Administration there from 1955 to 1961, and he served as Assistant Secretary and Undersecretary of HEW before being appointed Secretary by President Johnson in March 1968.

The second chapter, "Future Problems and Prospects," was written by a man who has had more to do with investigating public information than any other man.

Congressman John E. Moss (Democrat from California) is

9

chairman of the regular Subcommittee on Foreign Operations and Government Information in the House of Representatives; in this post he has won nationwide acclaim for his investigations into news supression and government information activities. In 1963 he received the John Peter Zenger Award of the New York State Society of Newspaper Editors for furthering the access to government information for a free press. In 1960 he was awarded the Sigma Delta Chi Professional Journalistic Award for his "magnificent fight, 1955 through 1960, in behalf of the American people's right to know about government." These are but a few of the many awards and recognitions that he has been given for his work in government information.

Congressman Moss has served in Congress since 1948, has been Deputy Majority Whip since 1961, and serves on a number of other key House committees as well.

The third chapter, "Information Activities Today," was written by *Arthur Settel,* Director of the Office of Information and Publications for the U.S. Bureau of Customs in the Treasury Department.

Mr. Settel has had a varied career in many phases of mass communications, public relations, and government information. A graduate of the Columbia University School of Journalism, he worked as a foreign correspondent during the thirties, and, after military service in World War II, he became director of public relations for the Office of the U.S. High Commissioner in Germany. He worked with Edward R. Murrow on the Person to Person show at CBS, and then became director of public relations for KLM Royal Dutch Airlines before joining the Customs Bureau. He is the author of two books on Germany.

BACKGROUND AND PHILOSOPHY . . .

Communication in a Democratic Society

WILBUR J. COHEN, SECRETARY
U. S. DEPARTMENT OF HEALTH,
EDUCATION AND WELFARE

"The basis of the government being the opinion of the people, the very first object should be to keep that right."

Thomas Jefferson

PATRICK HENRY is usually remembered for his moving address to the Virginia legislature in which he said "Give me liberty or give me death." But to students of the Democratic process, he is also remembered as the man who said, in effect: Give us information, or we will lose our liberties. Government officials, Henry said, must be prevented from "covering with the veil of secrecy the common routine of business, for the liberties of the people never were, or never will be, secure when the transactions of their rulers may be concealed from them."

There is little doubt that the men who founded our country were aware that information and government go hand-in-hand. As they did in so many other areas, they showed remarkable foresight about the need for the people to know what their government is doing and the importance of the people approving the government's actions. So important is information to the governing process today that many of the new nations emerging from the nineteenth-century colonial empires have ministries of information presided over by cabinet-level officers. The ministers of information in the new countries are usually the "nation builders" in charge of informing the people what the government is doing and why, and encouraging them to increase their own contributions to the society in which they live.

The founders of American democracy realized that the people had the right to know everything about the operation of the government—not just what federal officials wanted them to know. They conceded, in Patrick Henry's phrase, that "such transactions as relate to military operations or affairs of great consequence, the immediate promulgation of which might defeat the interests of the community," should be denied to the public. And the writing of the Constitution, in their opinion, was an affair of such consequence. They decided that the day-to-day debate that took place at the Constitutional Convention should not be released piecemeal and discussed in every tavern in the land, so they took a pledge of secrecy. This helped set a precedent—that the day-

13

to-day discussion among officials leading up to the formulation of policy is not necessarily public information.

However, the founding fathers insisted that every other aspect of the nation's business should be made known to the people. The writers of the Constitution clearly foresaw that without information, democracy would not function and the people would not be free. But the founding fathers carefully refrained from creating an official information system. Instead, the function of informing the people about the government was left to the free press. And it is often said that the genius of the American system stems in part from the healthy tension between a free press and the men responsible for conducting the people's business.

It must be remembered, though, that the founding fathers created the Constitution in the aftermath of a war against an oppressive government. They were also molded in a climate dominated by the eighteenth-century fear of governments whose authority rested on "divine right" rather than a mandate from the people. They created a government for an eighteenth-century country that was essentially agricultural, rural, under-populated, and anxious to have a minimum of foreign entanglements, and for a people who understandably feared government and believed essentially that government services should be kept at an absolute minimum. Under such conditions, a free press was capable of providing the people with the vital information about their government that the people needed.

By the middle of the twentieth century, however, the country created by the founding fathers had undergone profound changes. The 13 states rimming the Atlantic Ocean had grown to 50 states, one of which was halfway across the Pacific, nearly 6000 miles from the nation's capital. America was now essentially urban and industrial and contained nearly 200 million people, of which several millions were illiterate and approximately 30 million lived in poverty. It also had endured a major economic depression and two World Wars, had developed staggering military capability, had emerged as the leader of the free nations in a cold and sometimes hot war, and was preparing to send expeditions out into space to explore the universe.

Most important, the government was spending huge sums of

the people's money to conduct their business, especially to improve social and economic conditions and maintain the security of the free world. Obviously, the expenditures of such vast sums and the administration of hundreds of complex programs needed the continuing support of the people, and to gain this support it was essential that the people be completely informed about their government's activities. By mid-twentieth century, informing the public about the activities of the government was a big job—one that the press, despite the fact that it had experienced a communications revolution and developed, in Douglass Cater's phrase, into the "fourth branch of government," could not do alone.

Confronted with a vast, sprawling government undreamed of by the founding fathers, the press today has its hands full just performing the basic functions envisioned by Jefferson, Henry, Madison, and the other framers of the Constitution: keeping an eye on the government and reporting to the people how their elected and appointed officials were conducting the nation's business. In fact, so vast and complicated is the operation of the federal government today that, in the opinion of many students of the fourth estate, the press would find it virtually impossible to perform even this basic function without the assistance of the growing army of government information officers. As James McCamy said in his classic study of *Government Publicity* (published in 1939): "Probably the best argument for the government publicist, in fact, is that he is essential to even the minimum adequate coverage of events in Washington. The glut of occurrences each day in the vast, chaotic web of Federal administration simply could not be followed by newspaper staffs unless they were enlarged many times their present size."

In one study of the information activities of President Franklin D. Roosevelt's Administration, it was estimated that the government's information program provided each Washington newspaper and wire service bureau with the equivalent of ten additional reporters. Arthur Krock has said that no newspaper could have covered the activities of the NRA, for example, without the NRA press office acting as an auxiliary.

That was 30 years ago. The activities of the federal government have increased manyfold since FDR's time, and although the Washington news bureaus have also been enlarged many times, students of the Washington press corps agree that it would still be impossible to cover government activities efficiently without the aid of the government's information offices.

There has been a lot of talk in recent years about "managed news." Every administration since George Washington's has understood the importance of informing the people—preferably in a favorable light—about the activities of the government, and many early administrations employed members of the press and newspapermen to write for them or to handle relations with the press. Andrew Jackson has been accused by at least one historian of being "the first President who ruled the country by means of the newspaper press." And it was Abraham Lincoln who said: "In this and like communities public sentiment is everything. With public sentiment, nothing can fail. Without it, nothing can succeed. Consequently, he who moulds public sentiment goes deeper than he who enacts statutes and pronounces decisions."

It is often said that "managed news" began with FDR, but Lincoln waited for two months to find the right moment for releasing the Emancipation Proclamation. Later he wrote: "Finally came the week of the battle of Antietam. I determined to wait no longer. The news came on Wednesday that the advantage was on our side. The Proclamation was published the following Monday."

Although professional newspaper men had been employed by many early administrations, the idea of a government agency employing a newspaper man to handle its press and public relations apparently did not occur to anyone in Washington until around 1910. In that year, "some member of a Congressional Committee," as William Rivers wrote in his book, *The Opinion Makers,* "looking into the operations of the Census Bureau were startled when the director confessed that 'for about six months now we have had a person whose principal duty is to act as what might properly be called, I suppose, a press agent.' " His name was Whitman Osgood, a former reporter, and his title at the Census Bureau was Expert Special Agent.

The thought that a government agency should have a "press agent" was no more popular on Capitol Hill in 1910 than it is today, and three years later Congress passed a bill specifying that "no money appropriated by this or any other Act shall be used for the compensation of any publicity experts unless specifically authorized for that purpose." This Act is still on the books, which is one reason among many that the government thinks and acts in terms of public information, not publicity.

From 1913 until 1932, Congress was relatively successful in resisting the expansion of the government's information services. But in 1932, President Franklin D. Roosevelt was elected with a clear mandate from the people to launch programs designed to lift one-third of a nation out of poverty and the whole country out of an economic depression. The economic recovery program launched by Roosevelt and carried on by President Harry S Truman gave the government a new role—that of spending millions and then billions of dollars of the people's money to ensure the Nation's social and economic security. With these new responsibilities, it was absolutely essential that the people be given a maximum of information about their government's activities: (1) so that they would know how to take advantage of the many programs available to them, and (2) so they would have enough information about the programs and about the efficiency of the administration administering them to approve or disapprove when they went to the polls.

Another landmark in the evolution of public information in our democratic society occurred in 1941, when the United States entered World War II. Just as it was essential to the democratic process that the people be completely informed about the vast sums of money their government was spending on economic and social programs, it was equally essential that, within the bounds of national security, they be completely informed about the even greater sums the government was spending on national defense. And, unfortunately, the need for huge national defense appropriations did not end with World War II. The Cold War has necessitated a continuation of a large, complex defense establishment with, if anything, a greater need for a large and efficient information program. The threat to the nation's security during World War II was obvious; the threat to our security has not always been as obvious during the Cold War, which has meant that the government has had to increase its efforts to explain the requirements of national security in a complex and changing world.

In the twenty years from 1932 to 1952 the explosion of governmental activities at home and abroad necessitated a corresponding increase in government information programs. By the end of the Truman Administration, there were 3632 government employees classified by Civil Service as "Information Specialists" or "Editors," plus numerous public affairs officers working as special assistants to Cabinet officials or even as Assistant Secretaries. In the first four years of the Eisenhower Administration, the information specialists in the government nearly doubled. The increase continued during Eisenhower's second term and as William Rivers has pointed out, Christian Herter, who, as a member of Congress, had been critical of the size of the government information program under Truman, later, as Eisenhower's Secretary of State, presided over one of the largest information programs in the federal government.

Today, fifty-seven of the sixty major government agencies have information programs. A 1967 Associated Press survey reported 6858 information specialists. Not surprisingly, the departments with the greatest number of information officers are Defense and Health, Education, and Welfare; Defense has almost 3000, nearly half the government total, and HEW has over 600.

The government's information programs cost money; HEW's information budget for fiscal 1967, for example, was $7.8 million. It is difficult to say precisely how much all the government information activities cost, but it is nowhere near the figure of $425 million a year which the Associated Press reported in its 1967 survey. An estimated $200 million of the AP figure was spent on public relations by the firms having contracts with the government. The government's expenditure on information is closer to $225 million annually, with perhaps another $125 million spent by the Government Printing Office producing publications for the government's information programs. This compares to the $353 million which the AP survey said Congress and the Judiciary spent on its public information programs during the same period.

Because of the sensitivity many people—in Congress, in the press, and in many walks of life—have to the excesses of modern advertising, image building, "Madison Avenue," and hucksterism, there is considerable criticism of the federal government's information program on the grounds that it is "public relations," a term still unmentionable around government offices and officially forbidden by law. It is time to dispense with this semantic nonsense. Government agencies today must be extremely sensitive to public opinion; they must report the nature and availability of their programs financed by the people, and they have no choice but to practice public relations—effective two-way communication—twenty-four hours a day, 7 days a week.

However, government information programs are not public relations in the popular and often erroneous sense of the phrase. They explain programs and services. And explaining the government's programs to the people who must pay for them is as essential in a democracy as developing the programs and carrying them out. As J. A. R. Pimlott wrote in his book, *Public Relations and American Democracy:* "Modern Administration would come to a standstill if government could not constantly speak to the people as individuals and in and through the different groups to which they belong. It must do so mainly through the mass media."

Today we are in the midst of a peaceful revolution which is bringing about profound changes in American society. This revolution is taking place in civil rights, health care, education, social welfare—in almost every phase of our daily lives. There is a heightened social awareness and a new sense of responsibility on the part of the American people. This is accompanied by— in fact, is partly the result of—increasing national wealth and an increased ability to cope with old and new problems. We are no longer content to coexist with poverty. As President Johnson said in his historic Howard University speech: "It is not enough just to open the gates of opportunity. All our citizens must have the ability to walk through those gates."

However, to help the millions of people living in poverty, the aged, the handicapped, the underprivileged children—all those Americans who are not enjoying the fruits of the world's most affluent society—through the gates of opportunity calls for an information program undreamed of by the framers of our Constitution. And considering the increasing number of programs designed to help people and the greater number of people in need of help from these programs, the government needs to expand and improve its information programs, not curtail them. Last year, several HEW information officers spent three days living and working in the poverty areas of Baltimore. One of them reported that he "found not one piece of HEW program information material in use or on display, nor any worker or client who recalled seeing or using any." He commented further: "Judging by observation and conversation with health and welfare clients—confirmed by workers—publications, newspapers, radio and TV do not reach the Baltimore poor. Word-of-mouth from a neighbor, minister or block leader is the common channel."

Obviously, we must make greater effort to reach the recipients of our economic, social, and medical programs in cooperation with state and city officials. At the same time, we must redouble our efforts to make certain that the great majority of Americans who are living in comfortable circumstances and paying for the government's antipoverty programs are getting their money's worth. Almost as important, we must make certain that they know they are getting their money's worth and that they are confident the billions of dollars we are spending to improve the economic and social conditions of America are being spent wisely and efficiently.

This presents a different set of challenges. Just as the HEW officials who spent three days living and working in the slums of Baltimore found that information about programs available to them has not always reached the poor, surveys show that we have not always been successful in informing the taxpayers about the programs for which they are paying.

One problem in reaching busy citizens with information about their programs is that people generally want to read what's going on in the world in terms of what's wrong, not what's right. Most readers assume that the government is doing the things it is supposed to be doing and do not particularly want to read about them; what they are interested in reading about is how the government is *not* doing its job, or the things government is doing that it should not be doing. President Johnson alluded to this fact when he commented that the press never seems to print any good news.

Another problem in reaching the busy American is the communications explosion itself. The average American is bombarded daily with newspapers, magazines, television, radio, movies, direct mail, blimps, airplanes, door-to-door and telephone salesmen carrying messages. Almost everyone is trying to get his attention and using the most professional, up-to-date techniques to do it. To compete not only with the increased amount of information coming at the busy American from all sides, but with the highly professional products put out by the nongovernmental communicators, the government must improve its communications media—its press releases, magazines, movies, brochures and pamphlets. Recently, the Office of Economic Opportunity produced a short film about VISTA called "One Year Toward Tomorrow." It was good enough to be shown in movie theaters all over the country, then on nationwide television. It was also good enough to win an Academy Award as the best documentary of 1967. All the government information efforts could be as effective as the OEO film. Most of the government agencies have dramatic stories to tell that concern every American. The activities of the federal government are paid for by the taxpayer and he should be told about them in a way that will not put him to sleep. This is difficult enough under the best of circumstances because once legislation is passed and an administrative agency established, the actual carrying out of many government programs is simply not a very exciting business to most people.

Most information officers in government today are aware of the need for improving the quality of information activities, publications, and films. But they have run into some resistance. As long as the government produces publications which end up by the thousands in basement warehouses, read by no one, not even officials of the sponsoring agency, then no one seems to mind. But as soon as the government publishes or produces an information product that is good enough to command attention, someone yells competition!

In improving the quality of its information programs, the

government *is* attempting to compete with the communications industry—but not for the advertising dollar or the subscription dollar per se. The government is competing for the reader's or viewer's time. If the government information officer wants to catch the busy American's attention, he *must* turn out a professional product that is as attractive, exciting, and compelling as all the other communication products on the market.

As McCamy pointed out, there is an assumption that the press and the press alone is the unimpeachable guardian of the public interest. But this is not always the case.

The press in America is an essential element in the democratic process, but the government information officers are just as concerned about giving the public information it needs to know as are the members of the working press. Down through the years, many students of the government information program— in the Congress, the academic community, and the press—have attacked the government's information programs and have questioned whether they are necessary. But equally honest and intelligent men have lamented the failure of the press at times to do its job in informing and protecting the public and have emphasized the essential role of government information in our society.

Today's information officers, as much as anyone in government, are aware that a program must have the support of the public for it to succeed and this usually means that it must be reported widely in the press.

As Douglass Cater has said, public information "effects not only men and politics but the fundamental balance of government itself." The press is a quasi-official fourth branch of government and just as every major government agency today must have highly trained officials to handle its relations with the legislative branch of government, so must it have highly skilled men to handle its relations with the fourth estate. Paul Hoffman has said that the Marshall Plan would never have succeeded without the support of the press, and certainly the success of many government programs have hinged on the extent to which the working press understood and supported them.

A knowledgeable and informed people supporting the activities of their government is the hard-rock foundation of a democracy. As James Madison wrote: "Knowledge will forever govern ignorance. And a people who mean to be their own governors must arm themselves with the power knowledge gives. A popular government without popular information or the means of acquiring it is but a prologue to a farce, or a tragedy, or perhaps both."

PUBLICITY VERSUS PRIVACY . . .

Future Problems and Prospects

CONGRESSMAN JOHN E. MOSS
CHAIRMAN, HOUSE SUBCOMMITTEE
ON FOREIGN OPERATIONS
AND GOVERNMENT INFORMATION

THE Great Society is here to stay. This certainty poses a problem for those who believe that access to government information is basic to the proper functioning of a democratic government. Whether the Great Society is labeled with that name or some other; whether it is led by President Lyndon B. Johnson whose administration adopted the "Great Society" tagline or by his successors; whether it is administered by the Democratic or Republican Party—or by some future, yet unnamed political group—the social and technological progress which is the hallmark of the Great Society is here to stay. Improved living conditions for all members of the society are a certainty for the future, but it is by no means as certain that the governmental organism which assures this future will be able to solve government information problems as competently as it will solve social problems.

If the Great Society of the future is to bear any resemblance to the democratic society of today we must

· improve the techniques for transmission of information from the government to the public,

and

· draw a clear and effective line between information about the government and information about the individual which happens to be in possession of the government.

As government inevitably plays a larger part in the workings of the society and the life of the individual—and as the individual, with a better education, plays a larger part in government —current and accurate information about what the government is planning and doing becomes an absolute necessity. There must be an effective flow of information from the government to the public if we are going to maintain a society based on both the consent and the participation of the governed.

At the same time, as the benefits of the Great Society increase —as social and physical ills are cured and a better standard of living is extended throughout the world—the government will need more effective information about the individual. It will need information easily stored, readily retrieved, and effectively collated. It will need, in essence, all of the facts now available about the individual and his social groupings— and much, much more—in a computerized data bank. It will need this informa-

27

tion, scientists tell us, if the government is to do an effective job.

But this is the point at which efficiency and democracy may clash—the point at which the achievement of the good life may become less important than the preservation of the democratic ideal. The clash is inevitable unless the planners of today set up government information guidelines for the programmers of tomorrow.

Before considering the future needs for a government information system which will assure a flow of public information, it is necessary to look at the system now in being. In 1947 a study was published that became the major topic of conversation at journalism schools and newspaper conventions. It was titled "A Free and Responsible Press: A General Report on Mass Communication: Newspapers, Radio, Motion Pictures, Magazines, and Books." It was called, familiarly, the Hutchins Commission Report, named for the chairman of the Commission on Freedom of the Press, Robert M. Hutchins, who was then Chancellor of the University of Chicago.

Twenty years after publication of the report, the *Columbia Journalism Review* asked a number of experts in the communications business to assess the current worth of the Report's recommendations. One fact stands out: those answering the *Columbia Journalism Review*'s query concluded that there had been progress—ranging from insignificant to substantial—in putting into effect the recommendations of the Hutchins Commission Report *except* the recommendation that the government improve its domestic information procedures.

The Hutchins Commission urged 20 years ago that the government "inform the public of the facts with respect to its policies and of the purposes underlying those policies." The only important development in this field—except for the creation of the United States Information Agency and related organizations to tell the U.S. story abroad—has been action to permit access to government information. Two laws have been enacted to remove *negative* restrictions which federal agencies applied when the press or the public sought information. Little has been done to improve the *positive* flow of government information.

In 1963 the Government Information Subcommittee of the House of Representatives surveyed the federal government's positive information activities and the survey was updated in 1966. A digest of these surveys indicates the government attitude toward its duty to inform the public.

1. There were 4617 Federal employees whose principal duties were in public information; their salary costs were estimated at $33 million, an average salary of slightly more than $7000 a year. Almost half of the government's public information workers (2302) were employed by the Defense Department.

2. Of the 50 important government agencies, only the State and Defense departments have an Assistant Secretary in charge of their public information activities; this important job is under a lower level functionary in all other agencies.

3. In 1963 one-third of the major government agencies did not permit their top public information expert to participate in discussions leading to major policy decisions; by 1966 one-sixth of the agencies still kept information officers out of policy discussions.

4. The public information offices of Cabinet-level agencies handled 4¼ million inquiries from the public in 1963 and spent 1¼ million man-hours doing the job; almost the same amount of government employee time was spent answering inquiries from 535 members of Congress, their staffs and committees. The top government agencies spent about the same amount of time preparing original material to tell their stories to the public as they spent preparing material originated by the agencies for presentation to the Congress.

An economy-minded Congress might look with disfavor on the expenditure of $33 million in salaries for public information employees. This is, however, a minuscule percentage of the $127 billion spent to finance the federal government—a much smaller percentage than is spent by every Representative and Senator out of his office staff allotment to get his story across to the people back home.

The job of informing the public of the facts with respect to government policies and of the purposes underlying those policies—the job which the Hutchins Commission urged the government to do 20 years ago—cannot be done at all well if the public information function is not at a top administrative level. The job of a government information officer is to advise those running his agency of the probable public effect of agency actions. He must know what is going on in his agency so he can intelligently answer inquiries from the press and the public and can prepare adequate material to explain the agency's actions.

He often finds himself in an administrative no-man's land; the public expects him to put his agency in the best possible light and often regards the end product of the public information officer's job as propaganda. The administrative officials running an agency are regularly harassed by their own public information officers who are trying to do a good job—to tell the public more about the agency's activities and to fight against the normal attitude of bureaucratic experts who feel they can do a better job if the public is not peering over their shoulders. They are top technicians in their fields and they often speak a technical language which is difficult to translate into public terms without losing important nuances and shades of meaning. They usually resent a public information officer's prying in the name of the public's right to know. The employee with the public information assignment thus often finds himself not quite trusted by either the public or the agency.

The top public information officer of a government department needs the administrative muscle provided by a position as an Assistant Secretary. He must be able to speak in the name of the head of the agency, both to the public and to the agency technicians. He needs the administrative power to back up his employees when they seek out the facts of the agency's operation. He most certainly should be in on all agency discussions which will result in major policy decisions, for he must be prepared to explain those decisions to the public and to help put out the fires that will be caused if the decisions are not accepted by the public.

As more people participate in government—for this will be an end product of better education and better government—there must be more factual information disseminated about government, by government. The present rate of expenditures on government information—about 18/100,000 of the federal budget—must become more realistic; the salary of the average government information worker must be higher than the present $7000 level. Meeting the informational needs of members of Congress certainly is an important function of the executive agencies; it is a necessary part of the business of government. Just as necessary, however, is the informing of the general public. The two functions are way out of balance when as much government effort is spent to inform 200 million citizens as is spent informing 535 Congressmen.

One side of the cloudy crystal ball indicating the future of government information is the necessity to improve the transmission of information from government to the public. The other side is the necessity to draw a clear line between public access to information about government activities and public access to information about the individual which the government happens to have in its possession.

This line between privacy and publicity was implicit in the ideas of the founders of our democratic society. Basic to the system set up nearly 200 years ago was the principle that people who are going to govern themselves must know what their government is planning and doing. The First Amendment to the Constitution was an effort to keep open a channel permitting the flow of information about the government to the public and permitting the transmission of public opinion to those who hold the power of government. By prohibiting laws abridging freedom of speech and freedom of the press, the Constitution keeps a channel clear. But it neither guarantees that information will be available to flow through that channel to the public nor requires the government to publicize every bit of information it collects about the members of the society it governs.

In 200 years the federal government has enacted two laws designed solely to make available information about government activities. Neither of these laws requires the government to invade the realm of privacy by disclosing information it collects about individuals. Neither law requires the government to disclose intimate personal details about individuals which the public does not need to assess the actions of its government. The laws merely guarantee public access to the type of information which citizens must have to participate in the workings of government.

One law, enacted in 1958, clarified one of the first bills passed by the Congress when it granted department heads the authority to keep the records and maintain the property of their agencies. This old "housekeeping" statute gradually was twisted into a claim of authority to keep secret the records which the government officials really only had the power to "keep." The 1958 amendment stated that the records-keeping law was not authority for secrecy.

The other law which took effect on July 4, 1967, spelled out the types of government records which need not be disclosed to the public. It granted any person the right of access to all other government records and provided for court enforcement of that right. The careful consideration which the authors of this law gave to the right of privacy is indicated by the fact that six of the nine categories of government records which are exempt from disclosure are based on considerations of privacy. Some of the exemptions protect business or corporate privacy, such as those governing disclosure of bank records. Some of the exemptions guarantee the privacy necessary for internal government operations, such as those governing disclosure of investigatory files. One exemption specifically protects information which, if disclosed, would be a clearly unwarranted invasion of personal privacy.

Balanced against the two laws designed to make information available to the public are more than 100 laws restricting access to certain types of government information. Many of these laws are based on the need to protect personal privacy. When the techniques of information search and retrieval through computerization are applied to government files, additional laws may be necessary to protect specific items of private information held by the government.

Alan Westin, in his monumental study of the conflict between privacy and freedom in a technological society, reports that the federal government already has on hand 100 million punch cards and 30,000 computer tapes digesting information about our society and the individuals in it. To put this information into a computerized data bank would take about five years and cost $3 million according to the Budget Bureau's review of a proposal for a National Data Center. Presumably then, by pressing a button, all of the government's knowledge about any of its citizens would be instantly available.

The types of information already available in the government's electronic records ranges from business details on the purchase of corsets and the payment of corporate income taxes to personal details on the results of school achievement tests, on military service, on work habits, and on social security or retirement plans. Add to this the intimate details recorded during thousands of tests on the polygraph machine, the so-called "lie detector," given to potential government employees by the Central Intelligence Agency and the National Security Agency. Then add the government files filling millions of square feet of warehouse space. When all of this information is filed in an electronic government data bank, computerized comparison and analysis can dredge up a type and a volume of government information about private individuals which has absolutely no relation to the people's right to know the facts of government. The very existence of this wealth of information, in a form to be readily retrieved and used, may pose a threat to the flow of necessary government information unless a very precise line is drawn between the public need to know the facts of government and the private need to maintain the sanctity of the individual.

The difference between public information and private information is clear, although it may be difficult to perceive in individual cases. When a particular fact or a category of information is collected by the government it does not automatically become a public record which must be disclosed to permit the citizens to assess the actions of their government. For instance, names and addresses of individuals who qualify for payments under the social security insurance program are not public records merely because they are in a government filing cabinet. This personal information is not needed by the public to determine how well the Social Security Administration is administering the program.

Names and addresses of government contractors, on the other hand, should be a matter of public record along with all details of the contracts after deleting the military security, foreign policy, or other sensitive details which can be withheld by law. This is a record of government action; access to the information permits the public to decide whether the action was proper.

The line between publicity and privacy will become even more important in the future as the facts of an individual's life from the cradle to the grave are stored in a computerized government records center. The social progress of tomorrow will depend partly upon the scientific techniques of today, including the technique of computerized information storage and retrieval. But the fruits of science must not be gathered at the cost of individual freedom.

In a series of hearings before a House of Representatives Subcommittee, Congressman Cornelius E. Gallagher of New Jersey discussed the problems of "Computerized Man," pointing out that this future citizen of the Great Society may well be stripped of individuality and privacy. Information about all aspects of the citizen's life can be collected in a master government memory system which, by the use of a push-button telephone, will disgorge details on how he did from nursery school to graduate school, the results of personality and aptitude tests he took over the years, what his job compensation was, his efficiency ratings, his health record, and his record of brushes with the law including minor traffic tickets.

The collection and collation of these details for some official use is bad enough, for its interchange between government agencies would strip an individual of the civilized veneer which helps make possible the interaction between individuals in a democratic society. Worse, however, is the possibility that these private details might become available—intentionally or by electronic or human error—outside the government.

Every past mistake of every citizen, every minor omission or misunderstood event which came to the attention of every government jurisdiction from the rural police officer to the federal personnel officer, would be permanent evidence filed in an electronic data bank and instantly available for official eyes or, possibly, unofficial ones. This is the situation which led Alan Westin to warn of a potential "records prison . . . capable of controlling destinies for decades."

Justice and mercy are elements of the human personality just as they are elements of a society of men whose government is based on the will of the majority tempered by the rights and needs of the minority. Man forgets many trespasses of his fellow man, and he forgives others, but computers do not forget and they are incapable of forgiving. A government with a computerized dossier on each of its citizens would not necessarily be a government without justice and mercy, but it could be and it may be if present trends continue.

An indication of the wind blowing in that direction is the serious reception given to the ideas of Canadian philosopher Marshall McLuhan. Whether his contention that the "medium is the message"—that the electronic gadgets transmitting information have a greater effect on society than the content of the information—is a logical argument or a great spoof as his detractors claim, his ideas have been taken seriously by many writers and thinkers. The next step, according to the McLuhan cult, is to transfer our consciousness to the computer.

The potential danger of this development was emphasized by Charles S. Steinberg, a CBS Vice President, who warned that the technological extension of consciousness proposed by McLuhan means that "man becomes serf to the computer." If McLuhan is to be taken seriously, Steinberg warns, "the transference of consciousness to the computer can only mean a total abandonment of ethics and an abdication of value judgments. What we confront is a new theology in which the computer resolves—or explains away—all the moral dilemmas of modern man."

Less articulate reactions to the computer takeover range from the urge to fold, spindle, and mutilate the punchcards which are the individual's contact with the machine to serious proposals for laws that would prevent the gathering of information by the federal government. The preventive approach to the solution of future government information problems is not practical, for it will be necessary to gather and computerize information about the social and economic conditions of individuals to achieve the programs which will make this a better world for those individuals.

It is possible, however, to achieve a balance between broad dissemination of information about government plans and programs and the narrowest possible dissemination of government-held information about the individual. It is possible to improve the government's techniques for informing the public and, at the same time, collect and computerize information about members of the public without that information, itself, becoming a public record. In recent years there has been a fight to remove restrictions on access to government information. That fight has been largely successful. Efforts now must be devoted to a system designed to keep the public informed about public matters—and to keep private matters private.

NATURE AND SCOPE . . .

Information
Activities Today

ARTHUR SETTEL, DIRECTOR
OFFICE OF INFORMATION
AND PUBLICATIONS
BUREAU OF CUSTOMS
U. S. TREASURY DEPARTMENT

G OVERNMENT information covers an infinite variety of subjects. Facts about welfare, education, health, safety, air and water pollution, and even art once came from state, county, city and private sources. But today the federal government provides information about all of these subjects and many more. Citizens in all parts of the country may still debate whether this federal involvement is inevitable or desirable, but it is a fact of American life.

The chief concern of most cautious observers is the sweep and the depth of government information programs in the executive branch, excluding the legislative and judicial press information operations.

They are sobered by the extent of the individual's personal involvement with government, from the moment of birth to final demise and burial, from the instant one opens his eyes in the morning to the second he closes them at night. The air one breathes; the water one drinks; the car one drives; the clothing one wears; the job one has; the company one keeps; the stock one buys; the product one sells on the marketplace; the floor one walks on are all regulated, taxed, timed, tried, controlled, or conditioned to some extent by government.

Society has grown so complex and interdependent that the centralization of government appears to be necessary to survival; in fact, modern man looks to government for protection against a wide range of man-made and natural enemies: against disease and pestilence; against fraud and infringement; against trespass and incursion. He looks to his government for guidance and leadership in creating a better life and in the march toward equal opportunity. And in all of this ferment, there is one vital element of key importance—communications.

Take as an example the field of health and welfare, which aims at enhancing community living and solving problems of life and death: effective communications are essential to the effective functioning of any health operation. Disease prevention and rehabilitation depend on public understanding; without it, government's vast programs would fail.

As citizen involvement with government grows, it becomes increasingly essential that the public information programs be strengthened and accentuated.

There are in the United States about 1750 daily newspapers;

20,000 magazines and house organs; 6000 radio stations; 700 TV channels; 2 major press associations; 3 major radio-television networks; tens of thousands of newsletters, trade journals, and a miscellany of other media of information, serving an exploding population that exceeds 200 million persons.

These media constitute a vast and intricate network: a maze of communications linking federal, state, and local governments and the general public; linking organizational entities and their own various special publics; linking our country and the rest of the world. This network exists because it is needed and because it is demanded by the American people.

Commercial public relations, which has become a $2 billion industry in the United States, is estimated to have 110,000 practitioners in this country and thousands more throughout the world.* Considering the vast expansion in the size and influence of the United States in world affairs, it is not surprising that the federal government's communications has grown proportionately.

The scope of government information reflects the broad range of United States programs in peace-keeping, world trade, moral and ethical leadership, technology, and science research. The following are a few selected programs and policies under the broad federal umbrella, illustrating the close tie between an action program and its supporting information apparatus.

Foreign policy affects all of us. It may be said that it is everybody's business. Our safety and that of our families, our jobs and our earnings, our security, our future and our hopes are all locked to our government's foreign policy. Can we protect ourselves from a devastating nuclear attack? Can we depend upon our allies to act with us in defense against attack? How can we best employ our national resources in building a better world? What steps can we take to increase trade and raise the standards of living in the developing nations?

These are some of the reasons which demand extensive information programs, both at home and abroad, conducted under the aegis of the Department of State in the inter-related fields of foreign trade, aid to underdeveloped and emerging nations, and the assurance of self-determination for all nations.

The Department of State, which stage-manages America's

* Based on a *Fortune Magazine* study, Sept. 1967, pp. 98-101 *et seq.*

foreign policy as formulated by the President "with the advice and consent of Congress," maintains public affairs staffs not only in Washington but in every embassy around the world. It is their job to give the American people a report on the success or failure of foreign policy actions. Overseas, the Department of State is responsible for the delicate task of making our national policies understandable, if not always palatable, to our allies as well as our adversaries and, in addition, to the neutral nations which are often poised between hostility and alliance.

The Department's efforts to "promote the national interest through our relations with other governments around the globe" are mirrored in an around-the-clock public affairs program, manned by staffs who employ many media of information to transmit their story to the American people. Its Bureau of Public Affairs services the information media with a volume of material, issued through the printed and spoken word: briefings, booklets, brochures, exhibits, historial narrative, and guided tours. Virtually every national crisis in which the United States is involved requires the energies and skills of this bureau.

The Cuban crisis illustrates how the department attempted to meet its responsibility to the American people by keeping them up-to-date on developments after the invasion attempt. There were three official sources of information on the crisis—the White House, and the Defense and State Departments. The Assistant Secretary for Public Affairs, Mr. Richard Manning (currently editor-in-chief of *The Atlantic*), gave a succession of briefings for press, radio and TV, over a period of 12 days. His deputy assistant secretary and a team of three aides maintained 24-hour vigil at the department, and gave an estimated 500 interviews to correspondents, individually and in groups. The News Branch went on a 24-hour schedule to handle the enormous volume of queries. Attendance at the department's daily news conferences tripled. Arrangements were made for principal officers of the department to appear on all the major radio and TV networks to answer inquiries from the public. One public affairs officer appeared on six different TV shows. Meanwhile the Publications Division rushed pamphlets into print dealing with the background of the crisis, and the Public Correspondence Division was busy answering thousands of letters.

The Defense Department and the Armed Services which function under its control have the Government's largest communications system. There are a number of reasons for this complex information network, which includes the Army, Navy, and Air Force and provides support from top headquarters to battalion, company, and squad levels.

If for no other reason than the military accounts for the largest part of the national budget, around $80 billion in 1967, the Department of Defense must attach importance to its communications with the general public. The Department's responsibility for the defense of the country and the direct involvement of every American in one way or another in this responsibility makes good communications absolutely essential.

The average American citizen has strong personal reasons for wanting to know what goes on in the Department of Defense, whether it is a policy decision in the Pentagon or a battle in Vietnam.

Thousands of small communities which are located adjacent to military and naval installations have strong economic and social ties with the military. The prosperity of hundreds of cities and towns, communities large and small, frequently is dependent upon the proximity of the men in uniform.

A typical Army, Navy, or Air Force headquarters unit is rarely without a public information staff. Frequently there are divisions and branches, sections and subsections, specializing in radio, television, public speakers, mass circulation media, the trade press, and correspondence with the public.

Each information unit replies to inquiries from the press; handles correspondence from the public; performs research from Congress; works up flyers, leaflets, handouts, and giveaways; arranges interviews with responsible military functionaries; conducts briefings; maintains files and writes histories.

The military establishment has for years been conducting training courses for its information people. One of the best known of these is the Defense Information School at Fort Benjamin Harrison, Indiana.

Under the supervision of specialists from all over the country, the Defense Information School conducts 8- to 10-week long courses for radio and television specialists, news writers, feature writers, and others. Included are courses in proofreading, technical editing, the law of libel, services' newspaper operations, geography, international relations, research and oral communications, and United States history with special emphasis on the Cold War.

Some government activities are more popular than others and some programs are better understood and supported than others. For example, few citizens enjoy paying taxes, but almost all citizens understand why taxation is necessary. This understanding has resulted from great efforts by the tax collecting agencies to demonstrate both the need for funds and their logical and efficient allocation.

The public information elements in the programs of the Department of Health, Education, and Welfare *are an integral part of the operations of this department,* which would doubtless be ineffective without public information. For example, the Food and Drug Administration is deeply involved in warning consumers against harmful or useless products and misleading medical advertising.

Spurious scientific data which are contrived to lend authority to medical advertising was the subject of a publicity campaign by the Food and Drug Administration in 1967. It provoked a storm of opposition from pharmaceutical companies, but in the end the campaign forced acceptance of higher standards for medical advertising. The public was the beneficiary. Without a well-formulated supporting information program, the campaign would have failed.

The Patent Office, Geodetic Survey, Foreign Trade Bureau of the Department of Commerce, the Bureau of Labor Statistics, the Bureau of Census, the Smithsonian Institutions are among hundreds of government adjuncts designed to serve either the public at large, a specific public, or a number of specific public. Thus the information supervisor plays a key role, for the United States is a country of 200 million mostly literate people who insist upon an accounting from their government officials, reject government by "diktat," and are sensitive to the credibility factor.

The Bureau of Customs of the Treasury Department provides a splendid example of exciting diversity within a single agency of a large government department.

Chasing smugglers along the borders, on the east and west coasts, inland and overseas, is one of the Bureau of Customs most exciting occupations. It provides an unlimited source of spot news, features, and human interest stories.

Enforcement of the laws of some 40 other government departments is another Customs function which provides material for the information operation. By cooperating with Immigration and Public Health Service in baggage and personal inspections at ports of entry, Customs achieves a wider degree of media penetration than might otherwise be possible.

By enforcing the State Department's Neutrality Act, Customs is frequently engaged in running battles with illicit arms traffic users and abortive attempts by Cuban refugees to mount private wars and invasions of the Communist-controlled island.

In its historical perspective, the Bureau of Customs stands as a unique steeple among other federal entities. Herein lies one of its most valuable public relations assets: Customs revenue provided the U.S. Government with 80 to 99 percent of its income for 115 years; customs revenue collected during the nineteenth century paid for the Louisiana Purchase, for the area now known as Florida, for the wars of 1812, 1861, and 1898. Personalities such as Chester A. Arthur, Herman Melville, Nathaniel Hawthorne were employees of the Customs Service. History is a patchquilt of unique facts, many of them—including the Boston tea party and Prohibition—based on customs laws and regulations.

The activities of the service reach into virtually every nook and corner of the land. There are customhouses in more than 280 cities and towns and at ports of entry.

Customs is a major information assignment, comparable to that of any $3 billion corporation in scope and complexity. It embraces all of the elements of public relations counseling; public information services for the traveling public and for the business community (chiefly importers); service-wide and regional employee publications; and more. The various categories of information coming out of the Customs offices are:

1. General educational material—statistical data such as collections of revenue and expenditures of appropriated funds.

2. Specific technical material—revisions in the Customs regulations pertinent to specific trading communities such as importers of textiles.

3. Specific nontechnical material—data and regulations of interest to the huge traveling public (now numbering approximately 200 million persons arriving in the United States annually).

4. "Deterrent" material—news of antismuggling activities by the investigative arm of the Customs Service.

5. Notices in the Federal Register of impending rule making, inviting comments pro and con by the public.

6. Specialized publications—Customs hints for world travelers, both foreign visitors to the United States and U.S. nationals going abroad.

The Bureau of Customs, of course, is just one example of government agencies and their information opportunities. Every other department and agency has other categories and activities to be communicated.

The overwhelming power and scope of the U.S. government is reflected in the communications network which has grown up within it. It virtually is without frontiers. Its scope is that of the government establishment itself, which necessarily must touch upon the lives of every one of us. In my judgment the science of government information is in its infancy. It requires consummate skill, training, and experience, and it will continue to demand the best of all who are its practitioners.

2. Public Information Theory and Policy

PUBLIC INFORMATION THEORY AND POLICY deals with the developing concepts of government communication. Unfortunately, all four chapters in this section show that there is still a considerable gap between theory and practice in public information.

In theory, *Carlton E. Spitzer* says, the public information officer should participate in policy formation and be an integral part of the total government program. In practice he is too often last to be involved.

Mr. Spitzer, co-editor of this volume, was director of the Office of Public Information at the Department of Health, Education, and Welfare, under Secretary John W. Gardner. He is now president of Public Affairs Communications, Inc., a management consulting firm dealing largely with public affairs problems in government and industry. He was formerly a senior account executive at Hill and Knowlton, Inc., New York City, director of information services for American Cyanamid Company, and director of public relations for Wyandotte Chemicals Corp. He has been a consultant to government, lecturer, and author of many magazine articles.

In theory, *Henry Scharer* says, the information officer occupies a key position in the government hierarchy. In practice he is too often the stepchild of the bureaucracy.

Mr. Scharer speaks out of a long involvement with that bureaucracy. He began government information work in 1942 as a regional news director for the Office of War Information. After the war he joined the Commerce Department, serving for a time under Bruce Catton as Commerce news chief. He served as deputy director and became director of information for Commerce in 1962. Mr. Scharer started his career as a reporter and editor on New York and New Jersey newspapers, after attending the New York University Evening School of Journalism while working as a copyboy for the old *Morning World*. In 1967 he served as Acting Special Assistant to the Secretary for Public Affairs.

William Ruder maintains that, in theory, information is only effective when communication is two-way. In practice, however, the government has not set up sufficient mechanisms to insure a two-way flow of information.

Mr. Ruder is president of Ruder & Finn. Inc., one of the world's largest public relations counseling firms, and he also served as Assistant Secretary for Public Affairs in the Commerce Department under President John Kennedy. Together with his partner, David Finn, he has been credited with developing many new techniques and concepts in public relations and information. He has been a lecturer at Columbia and Harvard, is co-author of *The Businessman's Guide to Washington,* and is a consultant to the State Department, the Committee for Economic Development, and the Office of Economic Opportunity.

In theory, says *Samuel J. Archibald,* the government has a legal obligation to keep the people informed. In practice, there is still too much secrecy, but the new Federal Public Records Law of 1967 is a step toward progress.

Mr. Archibald had more to do with that law than any other man. For 12 years, from 1955 to 1967, he served as staff director of the Government Information Subcommittee of the House of Representatives, where he supervised the investigations and wrote the reports that led to the law. A graduate of the University of Colorado's School of Journalism, he worked for the Associated Press, United Press International, and the *Sacramento Bee* before going to Washington. He currently serves as executive director of the Fair Campaign Practices Committee and is a consultant to the Freedom of Information Center of the University of Missouri's School of Journalism.

INTEGRATING FUNCTIONS . . .

Information
and Policy

CARLTON E. SPITZER, PRESIDENT
PUBLIC AFFAIRS COMMUNICATIONS, INC.
WASHINGTON, D.C.
FORMER DIRECTOR,
OFFICE OF PUBLIC INFORMATION
U. S. DEPARTMENT OF HEALTH,
EDUCATION AND WELFARE

WRITING to his agency heads and assistant secretaries on December 21, 1965, six months after his appointment by President Johnson, then Secretary John W. Gardner said this about the information function in the Department of Health, Education, and Welfare:

"A sound information policy in the operating agencies cannot be built without the active interest and participation of the operating chief. He should include his public information officer in policy discussions. Only thus will the information program become an integral part of the agency's activities."

Former Secretary Gardner's memorandum also recognized the need to recruit new talent, and he stressed the creation of special programs for summer interns to attract outstanding young men and women to government information. He wrote: "We must be vitally interested in our recruiting and training programs because the future is not worth a nickel without them."

Secretary Gardner's memorandum was significant because public information is one of the most misunderstood and neglected functions in the executive branch of the Federal government, and the legislative branch has been largely to blame for this condition. Although some of the nation's most able communicators are in government, few have played a significant role in policy formation, and there has been a general lack of continuity between administration of government programs and the flow of information about them. It is a tribute to the ingenuity and resourcefulness of government information officers that so much good work is accomplished.

Fortunately, a more constructive environment for public information is evolving in the Congress and in the executive branch, bringing new emphasis on quality performance and integration of information activity with program planning and administration. But it will take patience and hard work to overcome more than a half-century of Congressional sensitivity—real and imagined—and timidity about the information function in the executive agencies.

In passing the Act of October 22, 1913, Congress prohibited the use of appropriated funds for "publicity experts" unless specified for that purpose. By this action, taken without serious debate, the Congress also inadvertently established an information underground of sorts. Many government agencies have created jobs of varying nomenclatures—usually special assistant —to accommodate speech writers, film experts, and others whose services were needed but could not be funded if properly labeled. Ironically, these *sub rosa* information specialists often draw higher pay than designated information officers performing similar duties. Low pay and low status (grades) for designated information workers are the result of critical Congressional attitudes, amplified and exaggerated by cautious comptrollers and personnel managers in the executive branch.

Congress appears to have applied its 1913 prohibition in the most constructive sense; namely, to defend against hucksterism in government and concentrate on the flow of factual information. But the premise needs intelligent review. A flood of legislation has been enacted in recent years to serve the American people, yet most information channels and techniques are still woefully inadequate, fragmented and unimaginative. People simply do not know about the services the Congress has made available.

The Freedom of Information Act, which went into effect on July 5, 1967, is a landmark in moving useful information to the people, and a tribute to the determination of Congressman John E. Moss of California and his colleagues. Some government agencies have responded to this Act by initiating programs to make materials and data more readily available to the public; not only in Washington, but in regional offices, State and municipal bureaus of every kind, and even storefront information centers in the ghettos of large cities.

Constructive new attitudes now evident in Congress indicate legislators now recognize that useful information, professionally presented and attractively packaged, is not propaganda; and drab, uninteresting, and usually unread materials paid for by public funds are surely not in the public interest. Today, government information efforts must be conducted on a professional level in order to compete for a share of the citizen's attention about things he should know or wants to know. Thus the effectiveness of a message is measured not only by its accuracy, usefulness, and good taste, but also its timing, relevance, and distribution plan.

Too many government messages have been written for internal applause rather than the audience. Significant improvement is not likely to be forthcoming until top level information talent in Washington dedicates itself to upgrading the information function throughout government. The chief weakness in government public information is its general lack of involvement in program planning.

Noninvolvement of information people when plans are first formed means that they must be "filled in" at the eleventh hour when a crisis breaks and all planning time is lost. Under these conditions, the best information talent cannot make an informed response.

Opinion surveys should be a vital element in planning; not simply to review what has been done (often to prove the correctness of past action or justify it), but to learn from experience, to analyze actual conditions, and to assess attitudes about government agencies and their programs. Surveys could help reduce the volume of overlapping publications throughout government and help agencies to concentrate on the really effective information projects.

Surveys are simply a part of good field intelligence. They force Washington bureaucrats to be responsive to what is really happening and being discussed in all parts of the nation.

As Senator Abraham Ribicoff, former Secretary of Health, Education, and Welfare, told a Wallingford, Connecticut audience on May 31, 1967:

"Our nation was founded on the single premise that the people make the ultimate decisions. I do not believe that the government has the right to hide the facts or misinform. But the best defense against secretive bureaucracy is in vigorous, enterprising reporters working for courageous, responsible newspapers."

Surely, the next best defense is in vigorous, enterprising government information officers working for courageous, responsible public officials.

Government public information officers can be as guilty of propagandizing narrow causes and clouding issues as any huckster on New York's Seventh Avenue, and usually with far more serious consequences. But only the foolish or misguided would participate in such schemes because they are doomed to failure. The whole system of government in America is open and fragmented. Employees in various agencies are not necessarily on the same side of all issues, although they may occupy the same offices. Leaking information is common practice. Public information workers cannot act merely as creatures of the Congress or spokesmen for the current administration. Their moves and statements are scrutinized and challenged by a skeptical press and critical private-interest associations of every kind. Memorandums and plans are sometimes prematurely reported to outside groups and to members of the Congress by employees who may be unfriendly with the trend of events. As one veteran Congressman observed, "I never ask an agency for a paper I don't already have."

Thus information officers and their peers must hold to the truth and remain faithful to the facts of any issue in order to survive. The government is commanded by circumstance to provide information, not propaganda. The real fear for America is not "managed news" but bureaucratic timidity. Fear of press criticism about the use of public funds for information has been one reason among many that government officials often have been passive about information needs.

However, the information lag—the difference between actual progress and what is known about it—is now so formidable and obvious that few editors or Congressmen would seriously criticize the executive branch for spending reasonable sums for staff and program to communicate effectively with the American people.

Information officers should insist on having budgetary control of information activities and participation in policy discussions so as to head off problems, prepare for unavoidable difficulties, and plan constructive efforts based on surveys and their personal knowledge of coming events.

They should arrange orientations about the information functions for noninformation managers in their agencies in order to improve internal cooperation. They should fight constructively for higher grades and greater recognition for deserving information workers. This is simply necessary if government is to get, keep, and encourage the talent it needs to ensure a well-informed public and the success of programs that depend heavily on information reaching people.

Information officers must provide continuing training opportunities for middle and top grade information personnel, recruit new talent, and establish trainee positions.

They must stress the need for surveys and evaluations to cut down on irrelevant materials and misguided effort.

They must improve communications with business: arrange briefings and other platforms for the exchange of information, offer thoughtful recommendations to the top officials of government, initiate new communications approaches, suggest new concepts for reaching illiterate and disadvantaged citizens, and provide a sense of objectivity in the preparation of testimonies and statements.

Finally, imaginative public information men and women can spearhead a positive attitude throughout government agencies regarding public information and the obligations of government in keeping all citizens adequately informed.

Government information specialists have the talent to accomplish these things. They simply need the will and determination.

Fear of Congressional sensitivity has deterred progress, clouded budgets as well as job titles, and fragmatized information activity. For example, Health, Education and Welfare's 600 Washington area (including the Social Security Administration at Baltimore and the National Institutes of Health at Bethesda) information specialists are located in 87 different offices and report directly to 90 different managers. (Nine regional information officers were added in 1967.)

The average information officer in government is confronted not only by a maze of contracting procedures and other administrative road blocks, but usually does not have budgetary control of his own function. The noninformation managers who hold the purse strings often have little knowledge of the information function or empathy for its practitioners.

These conditions breed serious problems. Contracting procedures often put creative decisions in the hands of employees who will never see the finished product and know little or nothing about information needs, graphic arts, or films. Such procedures must be revised to place the responsibility in information where it belongs. Present systems also permit large sums to be spent for films of questionable relevance and quality, and other costly projects, without the involvement of information officers. Grants for various information projects are also awarded with no review by information specialists. Thus the timidity about information expenditures expressed by comptrollers and contracting officers is confined mostly to money spent by designated information officers and their staff people; larger sums spent less wisely for information projects not under the surveillance of designated information officers too often catch comptrollers and contracting officers looking the other way.

"When Congress clears its throat to question a public information expenditure, comptrollers are already slashing the item from the budget," claims one veteran information officer, adding, "We have few champions for public information on the Hill or in our Department. We have to fight hard with what we have."

Until information officers are able to manage their own affairs, their programs are likely to flounder for lack of funds and talent; films and publications will continue to be contracted by non-information personnel for vague audiences which have never been surveyed to determine their interest; and elaborate reports of all kinds will be produced primarily as monuments to their authors.

In administering his own function, the information officer's goal should be to stimulate objective reporting, not increase the volume of handouts. His action should encourage and persuade writers, editors, publishers, and producers to visit Washington agencies, regional offices, and program sites in urban and rural areas.

Too often the Washington bureaucrat's insulation from people where they live (including the information bureaucrat) robs him of genuine understanding of local problems. And many grassroots volunteers take the sheltered position that they work only for their own agency, for their agency's cause, and perhaps for the overall good of their community; but solving national issues is somebody else's obligation.

It is possible, and even necessary, to involve people in a national effort where they live. Only in this way can the average citizen feel a sense of involvement in national affairs and the Washington bureaucrat a sense of involvement in local issues.

The role of information activity in bringing this about was

voiced on September 23, 1967 by the *Washington Post* in an editorial entitled "Publicity for a Constitution." Citing a dispute at Annapolis, Maryland, about the propriety of spending State funds to publicize the results of that State's Constitutional Convention, the *Post* commented:

"It would make very little sense for a State to spend more than a million dollars to get a new constitution drafted and then refuse to spend anything to acquaint the voters with what they are being asked to approve. The task of informing the public about the contents of the new constitution will be tremendous and the Convention ought not to underestimate this part of its job."

Neither would it make any sense for the Congress of the United States to enact laws for all the people and then restrict or inhibit the vital process of informing the people about its actions and their implications.

A discouragingly large number of information specialists have been numbed into accepting a subservient role to program managers rather than fighting for equal status in their organizations. They have become messengers for affluent program managers. Their principal job is to send out press releases after program managers have determined strategy and content. The press release is still an important element in the dissemination of information. But to limit action to a press release routine—a press release mentality about information—is to fall far short of the government's responsibility to itself and all citizens. First, information officers must be responsible for style and timing of releases. Second, they should stress more selectivity and less volume in news releases; more planning and following through; greater use of all media rather than comfortable routine with old favorites.

Public information officers are not simply spokesmen for their own government agency—accountable only to their peers—they are the voice of government itself, responsible first to the people. Their role is to be objective, not subjective.

Should a public relations man representing a commercial company distort the truth, the company's product sales may decrease, or its relations with the government may suffer, or its foreign investments may be adversely affected—all serious issues to the company, its employees, stockholders, and suppliers.

Should a government public information man distort the truth, the American people are deprived of information they should have in order for them to make judgments about the future of their country. So there is a vast difference in the scope of responsibility, although day-to-day problems may be similar.

Government public information, like industry public relations, is often clumsy, reactive, and paralyzed by controversy. Both industry and government are uncomfortable with controversy. Neither really understands that controversy can be a powerful asset and sometimes the only way to get front page attention for a positive program.

If government refuses comment at the moment of crisis and issues a careful statement a week later when other events are commanding headlines, a statement which likely appears on page 30, not page 1 (if it appears at all), government has lost, perhaps forever, its opportunity for effective rebuttal or explanation. Years later government may find itself defending allegations reported in the first story, its own belated comment never having registered on the public mind as anything more than a feeble defense.

As one industry company president cautioned his colleagues a few years ago when faced with an antitrust allegation:

"If we're not guilty, let's say so today. When a man calls you a sonofabitch on Monday you don't wait until Saturday to issue some feeble statement saying that your lawyers haven't yet studied how the man spelled sonofabitch. Either you are one or you aren't, and you better let the public know where you stand when they can still read your reply on the front page."

Most company presidents—and government officials—are not inclined to follow this advice. They still hide under desks, or on the golf course, when trouble strikes and reporters call. As a result, stories that might have appeared only once, stating both sides of the question, are strung out for days, with the side willing to talk with the media making its point time after time in the public mind.

Thus a mechanism for quick response is essential. Usually the only way this can be accomplished is to have the information officer participate in policy discussions and key meetings. When a crisis breaks, there is no need to "fill in" the information officer; he already knows the background and can act. That's his job.

When a qualified information officer is fully informed he can prevent problems. His sensitivity to developing issues can alert his agency to the need to change course or modify its position to avoid pitfalls and static in the media. That's also his job.

One of the government information man's chief obligations is to encourage constructive working arrangements with private industry. He cannot meet this obligation if he plays a passive role. Conversely, he cannot push his ideas into a vacuum. What he can do is set the stage for cooperation and generate interest among business and industrial groups by holding background briefings in various parts of the country on government programs, providing information on how they are funded, why some succeed, why some fail, and ways business and government can collaborate. State and municipal authorities and industry executives should take part in these briefings to illustrate by their presence the federal-state-local partnership with business and discuss ways to improve the administration of federally sponsored programs.

Cooperation between government and business is essential, but it can flounder on the misunderstandings of one or another of the partners. Government information people too often err in assuming that business interests are uniformly narrow and self-concerned. Business, in turn, too often underestimates the breadth and complexity of federal-state-local government activities.

One of the nation's largest corporations recently sent to Washington a rather pompous and uninformed young man whose mission was to analyze all government programs designed to help solve the crisis in American cities. He was given four weeks to accomplish his review and recommend a plan of involvement to his management. When questioned, the man could not say what his company was already doing through its community relations efforts to help meet human needs and coordinate the resources in the towns where the company's installations are established. Nor could he say what motivations prompted his management to send him on his mission. He was somewhat upset with the government people he met because, as he put it, "they could not spell out exactly how my company might inject itself into government activity, and I certainly don't have time to study hundreds of different government programs in four weeks."

Government information officers who welcomed the industrial missionary and applauded what seemed to be another constructive move toward industry-government collaboration were shaken by the superficiality of the man's approach and left wondering about the management people who had sent him.

This sort of encounter is unlike many sophisticated and effective programs, both formal and informal, now underway to relate industry-government interests for the common good. The Brookings Institution, the National Industrial Conference Board, the American Management Association, and more recently, the National Association of Manufacturers, have embarked on training and seminar programs for large numbers of business managers. More often than not government officials are participants in these sessions.

Informal efforts also have been successful, such as the ad hoc business-government dinner meetings which have been held in Washington seven or eight times yearly since 1964. The group has no title, no formal organization, no dues structure. Company presidents alternate in hosting the dinner discussions. Candor and informality are the key ingredients. Half the attendees are from business, half from government. Stereotyped misconceptions are erased and the men get to know each other as individuals. Sensitive issues which are difficult and sometimes impossible to discuss on-the-record are debated off-the-record. As a result, formal dealings between business and government have been improved. Such meetings could be held in any region, state, or city with similar success. All that is required is the initiative of one or two serious-minded public information or public relations men. That is how the Washington group was formed.

The need for further initiative by government public information officers in building rapport with business is clear when a large, respected company sends a young man to Washington to develop solid recommendations for collaboration with government in four weeks, rather than involving its top executives in government affairs on a continuing basis. There are 86,000 separate units of government in America. There are more than 200 federal programs in Health, Education, and Welfare alone. They might have given the young man five weeks.

The incident dramatizes government's responsibility in helping business to understand that social ills are complicated and of long duration. The competitive spirit cannot solve all of America's problems, for human needs respond best to the steady thrust of cooperative effort rather than the push-pull of competitive forces.

Although each tends to be condescending about the other, the trials of the government information officer are painfully similar to the woes of the public relations director in business. Both feel second-guessed by their colleagues and short-changed on budget. Both appreciate the need for candor and realism to communicate effectively with their audiences and maintain the respect of the media. And both have found it can be difficult to persuade their peers that candor is the best policy. Nobody wants to be wrong, and things do not always go right in anybody's business. There is sometimes a tendency to sacrifice candor for the half-truth; to cloud or ignore troublesome issues. At these times, it becomes quickly apparent whether the agency or company has an able public information professional or a messenger.

It is an obligation upon Washington officials to do away with the information messengers in government. New legislation enacted by Congress demands public explanation. Improvement of federal-state-local arrangements requires that briefings be held for media representatives in all parts of the nation. Government information officers must be fully informed and personally responsible for initiating and carrying out a wide range of communication activities.

Actually, information officers have often had the opportunity to influence policy. But they have not always recognized this opportunity.

The significant speech or testimony that results from good collaboration between writer and spokesman will be reported to a wide audience. The conventioneers who hear the speech first-hand, or the Congressional committee that listens to the testimony, are only the first reactors in a national response that can result from a well-known official making a statement of some importance in phrases that a good speech writer wrote to be quoted in the media.

The entire business of public information depends upon constructive collaboration between top officials and the information officers.

Support for the public information function in Washington and perspectives about it vary from agency to agency depending basically upon the attitudes of the Secretary and his top staff. Some Cabinet officers have demonstrated a constant concern for their own good press while largely ignoring the fundamental information needs of their agency. Other Cabinet officers have been comfortable in maintaining a passive posture—discouraging initiative in information activity and reacting to media interest only when pushed. The most effective Cabinet officers have stressed quality performance, adequate planning, and participation in policy.

In government as in business, the role of information in planning, strategy, and policy depends largely on the support of the boss. But support for public information in government can change abruptly from one Secretary to the next, even under the same Administration. The change of presidents in a large corporation can have a similar effect.

Representative Moss, Chairman of the regular Subcommittee on Foreign Operations and Government Information (which investigates, among other things, the withholding of information from the public), Ex-Secretary Gardner, and John W. Macy, Jr., Chairman of the Civil Service Commission, are leaders among a growing number of top officials in the legislative and executive branches of government who have helped to upgrade the stature and quality of information activity by their thoughtful actions and powerful support. They know that facts clearly presented help to build public trust in the federal government, the only government all Americans share. They also know that empty phrases do not register for long with the press or the public; and that ducking around sticky issues is a dangerous and silly game for any government agency to play.

The American people understand that agencies deeply involved in trying to solve major national problems did not create the problems. The people do hold the agencies responsible for reporting on their actions fully and regularly. Agency spokesmen should remember that Americans respond with strength and determination to discouraging news if the news is honestly presented and a course of action is outlined. But the American people, like good editors, rarely if ever forgive a lie.

A government information officer may have a difficult time applying this candid philosophy, but he has no claim to participate in policy formation affecting the American people if he is unwilling to try.

Congress today has much less difficulty sorting out legitimate information needs from propaganda campaigns. But too many veteran information people still lack confidence in themselves and their ability to upgrade their function. They fight ghosts in the closet and fail to come to grips with the reality of today's condition. Their attitudes have become inbred and subjective, oriented almost exclusively to The Hill, the White House, their boss, and the current editorial positions of the Washington and New York newspapers. Theirs may be a fascinating world, but it is not the one most Americans live in. Because their field intelligence is limited, their releases are used more as internal memorandums and news letters to constituent groups than communications for media consideration. They have fought for improvement in government information but grown tired.

In the words of one long-time Washington information bureaucrat:

"After you've taken your lumps for a few years fighting the good fight for excellence in information, you realize that you're a mere creature of the Congress and the current Administration, and a victim of second-class professionalism as defined by the Civil Service Commission. Your job is to survive. In the process, you do your best to look beyond immediate pressures, administer worthy activities, and produce useful materials."

There is a sharp—and healthy—change underway in the atmosphere of federal information programs. It is not too long ago that a federal information executive could safely instruct his staff that queries from press and public were to be answered only on a "need to know" basis.

Those days are over. This is not an era of the people's need to know, if such a restrictive concept was ever valid in the United States; it is an era of the people's right to know and desire to know. It is the job of the government information officer to respond to developing trends, anticipate public concern, and provide useful information, always protecting personal privacy and national security but opening all the doors and all the avenues he can and should open.

The government information officer must learn to listen. He should be both a catalyst, showing the way toward constructive independent action and collaboration, and an analyst, evaluating and reporting what has been done, what is currently under way, and what is likely to develop. When the information officer fills this role, he automatically and significantly participates in policy formation as he should. His voice at the conference table is equal to all others. His counsel becomes a part of strategy- and decision-making. His premise is that the American people must be kept informed; that it must be a recognized government policy to keep citizens fully informed. Candor and realism are the chief ingredients of this policy in order to dispel public mistrust of government and to create the kind of harmony and cooperation that this nation must have to survive. Helping to form this policy is the job of government information officers.

This policy can help federal agencies work more cooperatively with states and municipalities which carry out federally sponsored programs. Arguments against initiating communications from Washington to the regions have most often been based on the protection of states' rights and local initiatives. Experience shows, however, that good two-way communications usually result in mutually respecting federal-state-local partnerships and much more accurate intelligence on why some programs succeed and others fail. With local participation and feedback, those who draft proposed federal legislation and administer programs from Washington are more acutely aware of state needs and the problems a city may have in adopting procedures that looked reasonable on Independence Avenue, but proved impractical on Main Street, USA.

Information can be the key to how well federal programs are used. As Ex-Secretary Gardner said of HEW programs, "for these programs to produce the full benefit intended by the Congress, people must know what they are and how they can be used."

Local communities cannot take advantage of benefits they never heard of. Part of the answer, therefore, is to transfer information people from Washington to the regional offices of the major federal departments both permanently and on special assignments where they can better serve local media and constituent state agencies. Misunderstanding has come mainly from a lack of information and a lack of empathy for the problems of others. Cooperation on a regional basis—a multistate basis—does nothing to interfere with a state's prerogatives or a town's own design of its response to a federally sponsored program. Conversely, the presence of information people assures more accurate and helpful reporting locally and in Washington, and provides the kind of frank internal evaluation that makes Washington officials less inbred and more responsive to the needs of people where they live.

The presence of skilled information people in the regions also tends to reduce substantially the volume of institutional "facts and figures" releases from Washington, which may delight the working statisticians but do little to explain the worth of federally sponsored (and almost always state administered) programs in terms of human need and human achievement.

If federal-state-local partnerships are to be formed and accurately reported, a constant exchange of useful information on the local scene is essential. Providing platforms and avenues for this exchange demands that information directors have a voice in the formation of policy.

STEPCHILDREN OF BUREAUCRACY? . . .

Information in the Hierarchy

HENRY SCHARER, DIRECTOR
OFFICE OF PUBLIC INFORMATION
U. S. DEPARTMENT OF COMMERCE

THE importance of the career information officer in the government hierarchy has escalated in recent years, but he has not yet achieved the level of recognition and authority that his work merits or the interests of the government and the public require. His ascent up the ladder of bureaucracy has been slippery and fraught with hazard; his present perch is not secure, and there is always the possibility of a backslide to oblivion.

In a sense, the information man is a stepchild of the bureaucracy, constantly struggling for legitimacy. As the most visible point of public contact with the communications media, he is a ready-made scapegoat for his agency when policies or programs misfire—happenings that might not occur had he been consulted in the decision-making process.

The truth of the matter is that despite increasing acceptance of the philosophy of "Let the People Know," too many government officials mistrust the information officer. They may not admit this attitude, but buried in their bones is the subconscious fear that if they bungle their jobs the information man somehow will channel the juicy details to the news media—or to Drew Pearson. The information man would be more acceptable if he could conceal their errors of omission and commission from the pitiless glare of publicity.

To achieve status in the hierarchy, the information man has a job of educating his agency's high priests. In this effort, stressing the vital importance of open communication with the taxpayer, he can point to the constructive benefits that flow from public understanding and support of agency programs. At the same time, considering the nature of human vanity, he can cite the pleasing by-products of personal prestige and glory that accrue to doers of good deeds. Perhaps the most difficult phase of the educational effort will be to convince the official, particularly if he has not had previous public exposure and comes from the private sector of business or academe, that the news media are not conspiring to crucify him and that the information officer is not in cahoots with reporters, tipping and "leaking" unauthorized information about their work. Too many unsophisticated officials hold the information officer personally responsible for unfavorable mention in the press and feel he should be able, at their whim, to control, if not pre-edit, unfavorable items appearing about them in print or on the air.

69

Advised by his information man that a newspaper had learned of an impending appointment by the President of a key official, an agency chief instructed the information officer to "kill" the story. "Call the reporter and tell him to lay off," the official ordered.

When the information man demurred, pointing out that would be a fruitless and fatal exercise, the official invoked the mantle of his office. "I'll talk to his boss. Get me his name and number."

Fortunately the information man was able to reason the official out of his headstrong impulse—fortunately, because several other newspapers and broadcasters had the same "leak" and used it. Had the official been successful in plugging the dike at one point, he would have been overwhelmed by the other leaks and his personal prestige and that of his agency submerged.

Another top official firmly expressed the opinion that "85 percent of what appears in the newspapers is lies, 10 percent is suspect, and perhaps 5 percent is possibly true." Budging such dogma calls for considerable patience and skill on the part of the information man.

In addition to the job of education, the information man must cultivate his agency officials as sources of news. He encounters little difficulty, generally speaking, with the career specialists and personnel; they understand and accept, perhaps grudgingly, the function of the information officer more so than officials of temporary tenure whose interest in institutional imagery often takes second place to personal ambitions in their scale of priorities.

The information man represents the conscience of his agency— an ever-present goad and reminder for truth and propriety. But who loves a conscience?

Some officials talk too much about matters outside their ken. Most reporters and writers can spot this breed after a few utterances, discount what they say, and check the information man or other sources. These compulsive talkers, when they occupy high posts, pose a problem for the information man. At times they blurt out, without realizing it, significant bits of information. These premature disclosures, so dear to the heart of the enterprising reporter, can prove embarrassing to the agency and to the official, even where the latter manages to remember to ask that the news not be attributed to him. It is not difficult for these nonattributable stories to be traced directly to source by those who want to do so.

Without disturbing personal relationships with correspondents, the information man will have to disabuse the bureaucrat of the illusion that "nonattribution" and "off-the-record" declarations will safeguard him from embarrassing exposure absolutely. The device may be useful under special circumstances, but it is not foolproof and there is real question as to its desirability or efficacy.

Another area of difficulty for the information man seeking his place in the hierarchy is resentment of the information man's "second guessing" on public reaction to programs or policies which the information man has had no part in formulating.

Here lies the core of the problem. If the information can be made a part of the policy planning and formulating process, his knowledge of public attitudes could prove extremely helpful in increasing the prospects for success of agency programs. Although there is increasing awareness by intelligent and thoughtful officials of the value of the information man's input of ideas and advice, too many officials continue to regard him as an interloper and to patronize his presence at policy-planning sessions. If he is wise, the information man will speak up only when he has something of substance to contribute.

He must also inculcate the concept that the best "image building" of an agency and of its leaders—as well as the best politics—rests on an active program and not on synthetic press agentry devices, gimmicks, or special stunts. While circus-type drum beating can attract attention momentarily, the sound must swiftly give way to substance, or the agency, the official and the information man will soon find themselves trapped in a yawning chasm of credibility. News cannot be manufactured or manipulated for long. Officials in government for a brief stay, during which they may hope to prepare for future political ventures or rapid advances up the corporate ladder, may find this a hard lesson to accept. Their impatience puts an added burden on the shoulders of the information man.

The struggle of the information man for status is not unique

—it occurs throughout the career professional service. But it is more acute where the information officer is concerned.

If he is to make a maximum contribution to his agency and to the public, he should be close to the top, a member of the inner staff group listening in and contributing to policy formation. Some of the least informed people in government, alas, are the information officers. Too often, they must develop parallel lines of communication both within and outside government to obtain needed knowledge to function. Bureaucrats justify their practice of keeping the information man in the dark—"If you don't know, you can honestly plead ignorance to reporters." But a conscientious information man is not cut out to be an utter ignoramus. Information that is not ready for release because it is incomplete or classified is safer with him, as a rule, than with officials with loose tongues who lack experience in dealing with the media.

Most agencies and the Congress recognize the need for an informed public and for an information function, and although the funds provided vary from agency to agency, a fair-minded observer has not much cause for complaint.

But adequacy of funds, of course, does not guarantee a proper niche for the information officer. His predicament is often complicated by the fact that he is layered by a political appointee, generally under the title of special assistant for public affairs or public relations. This is known as a Schedule "C" appointment, the "C" standing for "confidential" but usually meaning "political." Where this appointee functions solely on the political level, handling chores a civil servant may not handle, he is often a help rather than a hindrance to the career officer. If, in addition, he assumes the job of press-agenting for the chief of an agency, that is all to the good. The complication is that the special assistant usually intrudes in operations and displaces the information man in the policy councils of the agency.

This is a reflection of the dichotomy of government service at the upper levels where the goals of an agency and of its political officials do not always coincide. The interests of sound and efficient administration suggest that more attention be given this problem by the powers that be. Public information is a continuous function of government; it should be recognized as such, and the perennial political appointee should not be grafted on the information function. From the standpoint of government continuity there are few career persons with greater value to agency and public than the professional information officer.

Until the system is changed, it is perhaps better to have a political appointee handle special chores of a personal and confidential nature for the boss, and let the information man function on behalf of the institution. At its worst, the current system attempts to use the information operation for partisan purposes; at best, it provides central direction and coordination of information activities, relating them to administration objectives and generating needed financial support at top levels for its operations.

Unfortunately, there appears to be a ceiling on the level to which career information officers can aspire. That is, unless they forsake civil service habiliments, becoming ardent political partisans in the process. They may then hope for a Presidential appointment as assistant secretary for public affairs, or membership on a commission, or they can run for public office.

Relations with Congress is another area in which the information officer operates, either directly or through a Congressional liaison officer in his agency. Where requests from the Hill come directly to the information officer, as many do, he should cue in the Congressional liaison officer, a member of the hierarchy.

One aspect of Congressional relations can be irritating to the career information officer—the increasing tendency to provide selected Congressmen with exclusive information regarding their districts, such as a grant of Federal funds for a local project or a procurement contract. The choice of Congressmen to receive these news morsels in advance of public release is obviously made on a political basis. The practice, which is growing, creates problems for the information man, who bears the brunt of outraged calls from those not among the chosen. This is not a happy situation for the information officer whose standard states that news is in the public domain and available to all. It is a political reality that Congressional good-will is vital to an agency, but should freedom of public information be compromised in the process?

In his relations with the White House, the information officer will have frequent dealings with the President's press office. In recent years, the tendency has grown for agency officers to advise the White House in advance of news releases they are scheduling, so that the press secretary can have the option of first look. This is particularly true when news at the top is thin, or the White House press corps is on an out-of-town assignment with the Chief Executive and the news lions must be thrown a bone. It is also true when diversionary material is sought in attempts to de-emphasize negative developments in national affairs and to feed public hunger for more palatable fare.

Release of agency news at the White House level gives the information man an opportunity for prime attention; he could not ask for a better launching pad. Most of his agency's news, however, will not be suitable for White House release, and he will find his batting average quite low. But the contacts he will make with the White House staff will stand him in good stead when he seeks guidance on a sensitive issue involving his agency. He is fortunate indeed when the White House press office is manned by professionals who are accessible and responsive to his needs.

It is clear that the information man faces many challenges and problems in the daily performance of his professional duties, but if he is dedicated to his agency and to the public, he will accept and recognize them as opportunities to help elevate the quality of government.

In so doing, he will earn the respect and confidence of those with whom he deals. At the same time, he will deepen and broaden his own knowledge of government and become doubly valuable to agency and taxpayer.

In sum, the information man has not quite made it, but despite some dragons to be slain en route, he is on his way to a proper place in the government establishment.

RECEIVING AS WELL AS SENDING . . .

Information as Two-Way Communication

WILLIAM RUDER, PRESIDENT
RUDER & FINN, INC.
FORMER ASSISTANT SECRETARY FOR
PUBLIC AFFAIRS
U. S. DEPARTMENT OF COMMERCE

THERE are several perspectives within which one can view the public information function in government—at all levels. Several of the criteria used to support the necessity for the function are rather objective.

For instance, government produces a great outpouring of data. This data is useful to the private sector, to the individual citizen, and to the corporation. It must be made available to the potential user. Government also has a responsibility to send information which articulates policy and conveys material concerning rules, regulations, and limitations to its constituencies. And there are all of the bands in the total spectrum of files, data, background, and testimony that in effect are public property and about which the public has a "right to know." This access is almost a question of Constitutional right and must not be frustrated by the bureaucrat.

Within a second perspective—undoubtedly a less objective perspective—there are other perfectly legitimate damnds which contribute to the indispensability of effective public information operations in government.

For instance, we might look at the need of any administration at any level of government to create an informed public that knows and supports its programs. There is also the understandable requirement that the politician make capital of those actions and programs which he initiates and advocates for the benefit of his constituents. This is part of the lifeblood of the political process. And finally, there is perhaps the overriding consideration of insuring that the public derives maximum use of government services and benefits. If the government is to use public monies to make services and benefits available, it is only sound economics—and sound democracy—that the services and benefits reach the intended recipients and are fully used. Information is a critical factor in achieving these goals.

But within either of these perspectives, the objective or subjective, most of the communications techniques utilized involve only one-way sending. They do not involve any receiving. They do not involve any real communications in the true sense of the word. I use the word communications in terms of two parties sending and receiving to each other—understanding each other's positions—and having an impact on one another—not merely going through the motions. Most government information sends only. Some of it receives, but receives only responses to very specific questions and even then only on a highly mechanical, unthinking, unresponsive basis.

This has several consequences. First, the public official develops a proprietary point of view towards his function, its relationship to public information and to the public's right to know. All too often he learns to feel that the less light shed on any given subject, the better. The less real public debate, the less said until something is *fait accompli*—then the less chance there is of something going wrong. The fewer the number of variables, the more certain the outcome. These are political axioms.

A second point that follows this is that the public official tends to feel that he can handle information so that he can use it as a tool to manipulate public support—or to neutralize public involvement and controversy. None of this is healthy. But the public official is a human being and he, like the rest of us, would dearly love to be able to accomplish his work under the least difficult conditions and with a minimum of what, in his eyes, might be looked at as unproductive effort. But this contravenes the democratic process.

So in my view there is a "second half" of the public information function in government. And it is the half that involves the establishment of techniques for receiving messages and for eliciting the sending of messages to the government by the nongovernmental sources—individuals and institutions. It is not just enough to try to listen. One must actively go out and seek messages. When this happens you can create real two-way communications.

To illustrate, consider the situation in which listening is not enough—but involving soliciting what has to be listened to requires the development of mechanisms through which information can flow. An individual cannot stand on 42nd Street and Broadway and talk to his government. We have to make it possible for him to do it easily and effectively.

We have our own bosses in government to contend with. The top government man is a political animal. Since he is a political animal he must contend with the politician's conceit that "he's in touch with the people." True, a good politician has an intuition about the public, but this does not mean that he's in a dialogue with them. And from a substantive programming standpoint we must be in dialogue. The politician's instinct is no substitute for it and we must, each of us, convince our top administrator that this is a truth.

We must train our employees in each government agency by using all of the tools at our disposal through the behavioral sciences. The employees must be trained to seek feedback, to elicit and solicit sending. The employee must be trained to listen.

Additional training and mechanisms are required so that the employee will be able to feed back what he hears, to feed back what he learns and knows, to faithfully transmit ideas, reactions, and mood. This does not just happen. Training and mechanisms are required.

A structure must be developed that literally and physically takes the government agency and removes it from its office— removes its from behind its desk and puts it out in the field in face-to-face contact with its constituency. This must be done in many different ways, in many different places. New interfacings must be created between the government agency and the public. And it is the responsibility of the information officer to help design them.

The United States is possibly the most organized country in the world. The 100 largest voluntary organized groups (the American Legion, the National Council of Churches, etc.) together aggregate in membership more than twice the total population of the country. Each of these organized groups is a complete organism of its own. Each organism has its own communications patterns, techniques, and facilities already set up and in motion. The government agency must engage its own communications gear into this incredibly effective, viable, and larger gear of organized group life in America. Because these groups have such effective internal communications, they also represent one of the most effective sources for feedback and two-way communications at the government information officer's disposal.

Finally, there is the technique of professional surveying. Somehow or other this is done largely at the political level—and not paid for by the government. On the one hand you have the political opinion poll that is handled privately, and on the other hand you have the incredibly broad information-gathering process of the Census Bureau. In the middle you have good, objective measuring technique available to tell a government official how much of his operating program is understood by the public or by his special constituency—to advise him as to what misconceptions are abroad concerning his program—and to give him feedback on a valid, objective basis as to what kinds of changes, improvements, and refinements would better serve the public and how the public evaluates the benefits of the effort. If government is to be responsive and sensitive to the ultimate, this kind of professional surveying—reaction-getting—is crucial.

I admit that there have been some experiments with some techniques for creating new interfacings and two-way dialogue. The Kennedy Administration experimented with local meetings between government and businessmen—and most particularly between government officials and senior citizens prior to the passage of the Medicare legislation. But most of these were really not two-way communications. They were only more dramatic ways of handling one-way communications. The government was sending, not receiving.

The Office of Economic Opportunity is possibly the one single government agency that is doing the largest amount of experimentation in this field now. The whole concept of the Community Action Program is designed around pulling in the community —involving it, listening to it, working with it, and creating a dialogue with it.

And this brings me to my final point. Up to now, I have written about two halves of a program. When these two halves are put together correctly, a total of more than one is created.

This happens when the public—or a segment of it—is involved in feeding information, judgments, frustrations, attitudes into its government. This process effects programming. This process changes the substance.

To me this is one of the great and ultimate beauties of democracy. There is a dynamic relationship between the public and the government. The information officer who can permit these dynamics to gain traction is the information officer who facilitates the most democratic technique I know of for creating optimum programming by way of the interaction between the government and the constituency.

The great problems that recently have been identified cannot be solved unless the public participates in deciding that they should be solved—and in thinking through the alternate directions of solution. The problems of environmental pollution, of urban decay, of mass transit, of unequal employment opportunity, of utilizing human resources, of harnessing genetic advances, of conserving national resources, of improving public education, of controlling world population, and of eliminating world starvation are not susceptible to solution by the spending of money alone. There must be a public commitment to their solution. There must be a public commitment to the answer chosen from among all those existing. The government at whatever level at which it operates must learn to engage itself into the dynamics of the community so that the community will have the will to solve these problems and make the necessary commitments. All the government can supply are the funds and they are not enough to do the job alone.

The concept of two-way communications has in my opinion emerged as a fundamental requirement for solving the frontier problems which now govern the question of survival of our economy, our social fabric, and our political institutions as we know them. The new category of combined social, physical, and economic problems needs a base of two-way communications from which we can all move to make progress.

In short, I see communications as the basis for solving many of the new problems of government and politics. In addition to this, I believe it provides the new basis for program assessment, for understanding current needs, for determining future action, for clearing up misunderstandings and misinformation, for identifying and predicting future roadblocks, for creating escape valves for blowing off steam, for achieving public commitment to objectives, and for creating a momentum through which the public can make a contribution to programming.

In conclusion, I think that the information officer is crucial to the government process. Furthermore, I derive tremendous satisfaction from earning my livelihood in a field part of whose contribution is to "minimize conflict." And anytime anything that I personally can do in this tense world of ours to make a contribution to minimizing conflict—then I can be proud of the way I earn a living.

THE RIGHT TO KNOW . . .

Information and the Law

SAMUEL J. ARCHIBALD, EXECUTIVE DIRECTOR,
FAIR CAMPAIGN PRACTICES COMMITTEE
FORMER DIRECTOR
HOUSE SUBCOMMITTEE ON FOREIGN OPERATIONS
AND GOVERNMENT INFORMATION

THE document read like part of the script from a Batman episode. It was as wild and improbable as the mad scientist's scheme which Batman and Boy Wonder foil just before the closing commercial—but there was one important difference. It was an official government document: it was classified as a military secret and it was in the files of the Central Intelligence Agency.

The document was nearly 20 years old when a Washington newspaper reporter heard rumors about it, and he complained to the Government Information Subcommittee of the House of Representatives that the secrecy stamp was no longer necessary. The Subcommittee's investigators interviewed John S. Warner, legislative counsel for the CIA, who explained that during World War II scientists working for the Army were given the job of developing highly concentrated fluid which had a disgusting odor of human feces. The psychological warfare plan was to spray it on Japanese villages or to put it in capsules which could be slipped into the pockets of Japanese officers in occupied China.

The CIA lawyer did not know whether the smelly chemical actually had been used, but he did know it was still classified as a military secret. He explained the secrecy stamp was still on the old document outlining the chemical process because there was a good chance that CIA operatives could use the chemical—maybe they had been using it recently.

"Suppose we're at an international conference," the CIA lawyer explained. "Some of the delegates are our friends and some represent the 'other side.' Suppose our agent slips a capsule in the hip pocket of a representative of the 'other side.' He sits down, and from then on he doesn't smell too good. Well, the rest of the delegates aren't going to like his smell. They won't like him, and they won't like the program he is pushing."

Although the whole thing sounded like a television spy extravaganza, the secrecy stamp seemed justified. If that was the kind of operations the CIA was running, the less said about it the better.

And there the matter lay for about a year until one of the government's top cloak-and-dagger scientists wrote an article for a national magazine which has the reputation of paying the highest prices in the business for magazine articles. His article told of some of the dirty tricks he had concocted—including every detail in the old document which the CIA lawyer had said must be kept secret. He even added one more detail the CIA lawyer had not told subcommittee investigators—the project was titled, "Who, Me?"

CIA officials blandly explained to the subcommittee that the man who had written the magazine article knew which gadgets and gimmicks in the CIA's arsenal were valuable, and if he wanted to lift the secrecy stamp from the "Who, Me?" project, he had the authority. But he had not exercised that authority when a newspaper reporter asked about the project nor when a subcommittee of Congress asked. He had waited until he wrote an article for a high-paying magazine.

The CIA's expert on dirty tricks had violated no law by publicizing an interesting bit of government information on his own terms, but he had added one more case to the hundreds of examples of improper government secrecy which proved the necessity for a new Federal public records law. The case was one of many which exposed the government's attitude toward the people's right to know the facts of government.

The new federal public records law which became effective on July 4, 1967—the 191st anniversary of the Declaration of Independence—was designed to change a growing government attitude that the public should be told only what the bureaucrats want them to know when they want them to know it. The new law expressed the spirit of Thomas Jefferson every bit as much as the document he drafted 191 years before the law was enacted. It guaranteed the rights of man in a democratic society every bit as much as did the courageous actions of the men who pledged their lives, their fortunes, and their honor to establish that society.

The law states that all public records are available to any citizen. It sets up nine categories of government documents which can be withheld to protect the national security, to insure individual privacy, or to permit the efficient operation of government. And it states that any person who feels he is wrongfully denied access to a government record has the right to go to court and get an immediate ruling on government secrecy.

This law most certainly carries out the intent of those men in

Congress assembled who created a fledgling nation based on the idea that all governments derive their just powers from the consent of the governed. It carries out the ideas of John Adams, who warned that a people who mean to be their own governors must arm themselves with the power of knowledge. And it carries out the ideas of Thomas Jefferson, who would not hesitate to choose a system that develops an informed and knowledgeable people over a system that promises only efficient government.

Excessive government secrecy is not a new problem, but it is a problem which grew bigger as government grew bigger. Neither is government secrecy a partisan problem—in Republican administrations and in Democratic administrations there have been those bureaucrats who equate national security with their own job security, bureaucrats whose theme song is: "When in Doubt, Don't Give It Out," bureaucrats like the CIA scientist who regard government records as their private property.

Careful investigations of the growth of government secrecy were carried out for ten years before the federal public records bill was introduced in Congress. A few of the results of the investigations were dramatic—for instance, the disclosure that public opinion polls which the United States Information Agency purchased from private contractors in foreign countries were classified as national secrets when they were sent to the United States. The investigations uncovered a secret order sent to U.S. officials early in the Vietnam conflict telling them to keep reporters from writing critical stories about the Vietnamese government and to keep the reporters from reporting the extent of U.S. involvement in the war.

Some of the facts disclosed by the Congressional investigators showed how ridiculous the government censors can be. They disclosed monkey business at the Pentagon when the fact that we were using monkeys in space research was classified as a military secret. And they disclosed a secrecy stamp on a report about a modification of the bow and arrow.

But most of the secret dealings of the government uncovered by the Congressional investigations related to routine, day-to-day administrative actions—not in the headquarters in Washington but in the bureaus and branches of federal offices throughout the country. For instance:

· The Forest Service denied the request of a small Colorado newspaper to make public the names of persons granted permits to graze cattle in a national forest.

· The Civil Service Commission refused to make public the results of an investigation into a rural mail carrier test given in a midwestern town.

· The Defense Department refused to identify the local military installations where liquor is sold to servicemen by the bottle.

· The General Services Administration refused to disclose the amount a federal agency was paying to rent office space in an eastern town.

· The Public Housing Administration refused to make public a report on irregularities in the operation of a housing authority in a Pennsylvania county.

· The Interior Department kept secret an order designed to prevent mineral exploration in part of a western state proposed for a national park.

It is the routine government secrecy that is immediately affected by the federal public records law, for it shifts the burden of proof that secrecy is necessary from the citizen to the government. The law is the end product of careful legislative and political planning and the most important parts of the product are those provisions which take the decisions on access to government records out of the hands of secrecy-minded bureaucrats who have the most to gain from secrecy.

It is really two laws. Sections (a) and (b) are public records laws requiring hundreds of government agencies to explain how they operate and to publish the orders, opinions, policy statements, manuals, and instructions that are the end product of their operations. Section (c) is a freedom of information law, requiring public records to be made available upon request and permitting a court test of government secrecy. Section (e) applies to both the public records and freedom of information parts of the law, spelling out those categories of government records which are not necessarily public property. Sections (d) and (f) are special sections, one requiring all votes of multiheaded government regulatory agencies to be put on record and the other protecting the special congressional right of access to Executive Branch information.

The public records section requires every government agency —and that includes the boards and bureaus and divisions of all departments—to publish in the Federal Register a description of its operations, explaining how it does business and how the public can find out about its routine activities. This is not significantly different from the Administrative Procedure Act, which the law amended, but one provision forces the agencies to honor the publication requirement by stating that an agency's operations cannot "adversely affect" any person if the agency fails to publicly explain its operations.

The same sort of sanction is in the second section of the law. While the first section requires a published explanation of *how* each agency operates, the second section requires disclosure of *what* the agency does.

As the federal government has expanded its activities to solve the nation's expanding problems, the bureaucracy has developed its own form of case law, embodied in thousands of orders, opinions, statements, and instructions issued by hundreds of agencies. This is the material which must be disclosed under the second section of the law.

To help the public cut through this paper jungle, the law requires each agency to publish an index of all important material issued after the July 4, 1967 effective date. Guidelines issued by the Department of Justice suggest that the indexes also should reflect past administrative actions that have become precedents for future rulings.

The court enforcement provision of the new law applies only to the "availability" section, not to sections (a) and (b), which require publication or disclosure of routine administrative actions. Any person denied access to a public record has the right to ask the district court to rule on the propriety of the refusal with the burden of proof resting on the agency.

This does not mean that every reporter and inquiring citizen must be accompanied by a lawyer, for very few of the requests for access to public records will end up in court if the inquirer insists on his right to know. Nearly every government agency, following a suggestion in the Department of Justice guidelines on administration of the federal public records law, has set up a system for appeal of an initial decision against disclosing government records. The appeal—backed up by the threat of possible court action—forces the problem of whether to disclose a particular document up through the bureaucracy to a level where some political thought is given to the decision. Technical experts at the bureaucratic levels of federal agencies resent the public peering over their shoulders. They are doing a good job—most of them—and they are technicians who find it difficult to translate their expert knowledge into general terms. They resist, therefore, reporters' prying for news stories or interested citizens whose inquiries interfere with the efficient working of a government program. But top level government administrators realize that there is more to the job of governing than technical expertise. They are more likely to recognize the propriety of public disclosure or the potential damage to their department if a court rules against secrecy.

There still are plenty of excuses for government secrecy, most of them built into the federal public records law itself. The built-in excuses are the nine categories of government records the law exempts from public disclosure.

Some of the nine categories spell out restrictions for which there was no previous statutory authority; others merely restate the old law, making it clearer.

Exemption Number One grants the President statutory authority to protect secrets "in the interest of national defense or foreign policy," an authority heretofore exercised only under the President's general powers flowing from the Constitution.

Exemption Number Two clarifies the law protecting operating manuals and rule-of-thumb handbooks which government employees follow to carry out inspections or spot audits. It also applies to government negotiations in purchasing transactions.

Exemption Number Three covers all documents that are already withheld from the public under other specific statutes— documents such as personal income tax records or military plans.

Exemption Number Four covers "trade secrets and commercial and financial information obtained from any person and privileged or confidential." The Department of Justice guidelines spend more time discussing this exemption than any other restriction. They point out that the language is muddy. It could cover three categories—trade secrets, commercial or financial information, and privileged or confidential information. However, the information might have to satisfy all three categories to qualify for exemption. The guidelines leave the decision up to the agencies, suggesting they attempt to follow the Congressional intention, but the guidelines do not clarify that intent.

Exemption Number Five covers staff memos and letters protected to permit the free exchange of ideas and to prevent "premature disclosure." This exemption from disclosure is based on a government contention that memoranda from government staff assistants will be completely frank only if they are protected by the cloak of secrecy. This exemption, along with Exemption Number Two, clarifies the 1946 law which permitted secrecy about all "matters of internal management." And there is a saving clause.

The memoranda exempted from disclosure are those "which would not be available by law to a private party in litigation with the agency"—that is, internal memoranda which would not be disclosed routinely through the discovery process in a court suit against an agency. This is a minor grace note whose importance may well depend upon court interpretation.

Exemption Number Six protects files which, if disclosed, would constitute a "clearly unwarranted" invasion of personal privacy. It covers, for instance, the details of personnel files and medical files.

Exemption Number Seven restricts access to "investigatory files compiled for law enforcement purposes." So far such files—FBI files or Secret Service files—have been protected under the broad "public interest" restriction or under the old "housekeeping" statute which gives agencies the general power to regulate the use of their files.

Exemptions Number Eight and Nine restrict access to special types of business information which probably would be adequately protected under the "commercial and financial" cover of Exemption Number Four. But special interests were able to convince the Congress to add Exemption Number Eight protecting government information about financial institutions and

Exemption Number Nine protecting information which oil company geologists must file with the government.

After the federal public records law was enacted, doomsayers in both the press and the bar expressed the fear that it would be almost useless because the nine exemptions from public disclosure granted too much authority for secrecy. But the critics forgot the broad authorities for secrecy which were in the old law repealed by the new federal public records law—a 1946 statute spelling out administrative practices of federal agencies. That old law also said that government records are public property, but it added that any government official could withhold any government document "for good cause found." Certainly, if disclosure of a particular document might embarrass a government official —might, conceivably, cause him to lose his job—he would certainly find "good cause" to withhold it. Instead of this broad blanket of secrecy, the federal public records law limits restrictions to nine specific categories and it requires secrecy-minded bureaucrats to prove to their bosses the necessity for each restriction. And the top officials are answerable to the courts.

In the first six months the new law was in operation, a dozen cases were filed in Federal District Courts and two of them were settled.

In the first case decided under the new federal public records law, a corporation charged with unfair labor practices demanded access to all of the evidence in the National Labor Relations Board's investigative files, but the NLRB contended the evidence should be given to the corporation only after the witnesses had testified on direct examination. The court held that disclosure of the investigative files prior to the NLRB hearing was *not* required by the new law.

In the second case in which there was a court decision, the judge ruled that the information requested should be made public. The federal district court judge in Colorado granted access to the Interior Department's reports on a group of mining claims, rejecting the government's contention that the reports were "internal memorandums" or "investigatory files."

Two other court cases filed under the law in the first six months resulted in the disclosure of public records even though the judges did not issue decisions. After a California labor relations consultant filed a suit demanding access to all NLRB files in the area, the agency directed all of its offices to make public a daily docket identifying the labor relations matters filed in the offices —the material that the California consultant really had been trying to get anyway. A case filed in the District of Columbia demanded access to a manual telling Defense Department employees how to audit contractors. As a result of this case, the Defense Department manual was split into two volumes—one with all of the general information which is a public document, the other with auditing tolerances and other details which, the Department argued, it should keep confidential.

Some of the first court cases filed under the act had little more than nuisance value. For instance, a resident of a federal prison filed suit to gain access to his pre-sentencing report and another man filed suit against the Immigration and Naturalization Service to force them to disclose the whereabouts of his alien wife. But most of the first court cases seeking federal records were based on broad issues, and more important, they indicated a pattern of disclosure.

The mere threat of a suit, in some cases, influenced the government agencies to take a second look at their information practices, and the second look often resulted in disclosure. A similar pattern is apparent in the administrative decisions made in the first few months of the new law's life.

By granting any person the right of access to government records and by permitting court enforcement of that right, the law removed decisions on disclosure of public information from the lower levels of bureaucracy. The top officials who now make the decisions are much more responsive to the democratic pressures implicit in the people's right to know. Arbitrary refusals to disclose information—the hallmark of the petty bureaucrat— are becoming fewer and fewer.

During the first months the new law was in operation, the Freedom of Information Center of The University of Missouri studied the instances in which the law was used to force administrative decisions on public access to government records. In the great majority of cases, the study showed, the decision was on the side of disclosure. Some of these cases follow.

· A news magazine was given the amount bid by unsuccessful competitors on contracts to supply drugs to the military.

· A newspaper was given the report by federal investigators on racial discrimination in the Mississippi welfare program.

· A manufacturer was given details of medical examinations of miners suffering from uranium poisoning.

· A trade association was given the backup details for the Surgeon General's report on the dangers of smoking.

· Social security applicants were permitted to study the manual followed by claims adjusters in making decisions.

· Retired servicemen were granted access to their military effectiveness reports.

The federal public records law did not, of course, open all government information to public view. For instance:

· The Defense Department refused to give an insurance company the names and addresses of discharged servicemen.

· The Civil Rights Commission refused to disclose the names of witnesses appearing before a state advisory committee.

The value of the law depends not only upon court enforcement but, even more important, upon intelligent administration and continued public pressure. Some of the regulations issued by federal agencies to administer the law are good. Others show that some federal officials still have a minimum regard for the people's right to know the facts of government.

On the positive side is the Health, Education, and Welfare Department, which used the new law to set up information centers at its offices throughout the nation. The Department's regulations grant authority to deny information only to the top public information officer in each agency—an official who, by virtue of his experience, has a built-in prejudice in favor of the people's right to know. Appeals against a denial must be handled by the head of the agency—an official like the Surgeon General in the Public Health Service or the Commissioner of Education or the Commissioner of the Social Security Administration.

On the opposite side of this attempt to disseminate more public information and to place responsibility for refusals at a high level are some of the military agencies. Four months after the new federal public records law became effective, the U.S. Navy still had not issued regulations spelling out its new procedures for handling public information. No one could find out how to appeal against Navy refusals to honor the public's right to know. The U.S. Army tried to add a new dimension to the nine categories of restricted government records, claiming that details of an attempt to pressure liquor lobbyists to donate their wares for an Army party need not be made public because disclosure would "serve no useful purpose."

The smaller government agencies also vary greatly in their administration of the federal public records law. Many of them took a careful look at their old regulations and adopted new ones to spell out the spirit of the law. Others did little more than nod toward the ideal of the people's right to know, and some used the law as an excuse for new restrictions. The Civil Service Commission, for instance, contended that the bulk of the government's personnel procedures could be withheld under a provision of the law governing *internal* personnel rules. And the Selective Service System, in spite of the law, permitted withholding of the names of local selective service board members who make life and death decisions on draft deferment.

Inadequacies in the government's administration of the federal public records law were to be expected—after all, it was violently opposed by *every* executive branch witness testifying before Congress. Not one official of the executive branch testified in favor of the bill. On the other hand, not one single representative of the nation's press—newspapers, broadcasters, or magazines—opposed the legislation. Press organizations, editors, and reporters unanimously urged approval of the federal public records law as a necessary tool to implement the ideal of freedom of the press. Yet the law is little used by the press.

While newspaper editors, magazine publishers, and broadcasters whose testimony helped Congress pass the new law might not be expected to rush to court to enforce the people's right to know, they would be expected to push the government agencies as hard as possible. Yet very, very few of the appeals against administrative secrecy have been filed by the press. Every agency has set up a system to handle appeals against initial decisions on the side of secrecy; very few reporters have used the appeal procedure.

In the first six months the federal public records law was in operation, only 26 percent of the government information problems handled by the Government Information Subcommittee of the House of Representatives were brought to its attention by newspapers, magazines, or broadcasters. Lawyers, businessmen, and other citizens with a special interest in particular government records accounted for 64 percent of the Subcommittee's information work. Members of Congress accounted for the other 10 percent.

The same pattern is apparent in appeals filed directly with federal agencies. A spot check of major agencies by the Washington office of the University of Missouri Freedom of Information Center indicates that fewer than 25 percent of the appeals against initial refusals of public records were filed by the press. And the FoI Center reported that the major enforcement provision of the new law is even less used by the press. Of the dozen court cases filed in the first six months of the law's operation, not a single one was based on press attempts to enforce the people's right to know.

These figures not only indict the press for failure to carry out a responsibility as champion of the democratic right of access to government information, they also help prove what some editors and Washington correspondents have been arguing for many years: the competent reporter backed up by a responsible newspaper can dig out the facts of government without help from Congressional committees, new laws, or the FoI unit of a newspaper fraternity. The failure of the press to use fully the new federal public records law and the appeal procedures resulting from it shows that the press needs little help ferreting out facts which secrecy-minded bureaucrats want to hide. If a government document is not put on the public record, the substance of the document can almost always be uncovered by the inquiring reporter.

There is another excuse for the newspaperman's non-use of the new law. Busy reporters working on a deadline are trying to dig out the news of the moment. Too few of them have the time to use the appeal procedure under the new law to dig deeper for the government records which may—or may not—make a future story. This helps explain the failure of the general press to use the freedom of information law as a weapon to guard the public's right to know. But it does not *justify* that failure.

The federal public records law was not designed to provide easier access by the press to government information. Neither its Congressional authors nor its press supporters ever argued that the law was for the benefit of the press. The idea of freedom of information, and the federal law which translated the idea into actuality, is based on the public's, not the press's, right to know. The press serves as a channel for transmission of government information. But the press must do more than repeat the platitudes fed to it by government agencies. And the press must do more than use the routine techniques for digging out the truth about government plans and policies. It must stand up for the public's right to know by enforcing that right—in the name of the public, not the press. The press must lead the way through the paper jungle of government, following the path laid out by the federal public records law. If complaints about withholding from the public, as distinct from the press, are not prosecuted to the fullest extent by the press, reporters and editors of today are wasting the freedom of information heritage passed on to them by John Peter Zenger, by Thomas Jefferson, by Harold L. Cross, and by those other idealists of yesterday who won the initial battles in the FoI fight.

3. Special Areas of Government Communiation

SOME aspects of government are of special concern to the people and pose special problems to information officers. These "Special Areas of Government Communication" are the subject of this section.

Providing information from the White House and "Speaking for the President" are jobs of particular concern and significance. *George E. Reedy* outlines the reasons why the White House press secretary's position is one of the most important and least understood in all government.

Mr. Reedy was himself press secretary to President Lyndon Johnson during the early years of the Johnson administration. He had served on Johnson's staff during the President's years as Senate minority and majority leader. A graduate of the University of Chicago, he worked for newspapers and for United Press before joining Johnson in the Senate. He is now President of Struthers Research and Development Corporation in Washington but continues to serve as a close confidant and advisor to the President.

People are increasingly concerned with information about international relations, including military as well as diplomatic affairs, but this has always been a particularly sensitive and secretive area of government. In "Opening the Door on Foreign Affairs," *Andrew Berding* shows how the government is giving new voice to international matters.

No man is in a better position to do so. Mr. Berding has been Assistant Secretary of State for Public Affairs (1957-1961); Deputy Director of the U.S. Information Agency (1953-1957); Director of Information, Office of Defense Mobilization, Mutual Security Agency, and the Department of Defense (1951-1953); Deputy Director of Information for ECA (now AID) in Washington (1950-1951); and Chief of Information for the Economic Cooperation Mission to Italy (1948-1950).

Mr. Berding, a native of Cincinnati, graduated from Xavier University and holds a BA and MA from Oxford. He worked for newspapers in Cincinnati and Buffalo, and served as bureau chief for Associated Press in Rome and AP's chief State Department correspondent in Washington. He was Executive Director of the Washington International Center, and is the author of a number of books, the chapter here having first been published in a slightly modified form in his book *Foreign Affairs and You* (Doubleday, 1962).

A third special area of communication is Congress. In a system where members of Congress must go to the people every two or six years for re-election, public information is perhaps the most vital task.

Sherwood L. Boehlert is well-qualified to discuss "Telling the Congressman's Story." He is executive assistant, staff director, and campaign coordinator for Representative Alexander Pirnie (Republican from New York), a position he has held since 1964. Prior to assuming his present post, he was manager of public relations for Wyandotte Chemicals Corporation. He holds a bachelor's degree in public relations from Utica College of Syracuse University.

THE WHITE HOUSE . . .

Speaking for the President

GEORGE E. REEDY, PRESIDENT
STRUTHERS RESEARCH AND DEVELOPMENT
CORPORATION
FORMER PRESS SECRETARY TO THE PRESIDENT

THE problems of the White House press secretary flow directly from the peculiarly personal nature of the institution which he serves.

Other government information officers speak for organizations which may be altered, over a period of time, by the plans and the personality of the man in charge. But no matter how successful the plans or how strong the personality, the man in charge of an agency is essentially a manager and is treated by the press and the public as such. He does not "own" his position in the special sense that a President "owns" the presidency for a four-year period with one possible option for renewal.

It is impossible to think of the presidency without thinking of the President—by name. This is the one position in the United States government where the mere existence of the man occupying the post is fully as significant as his official acts and his official thoughts. In his role as Chief of Government, he is, of course, a manager—but a manager with ultimate powers of decision on a broad front. He plays another role, however. He is also Chief of State and, as such, bears the responsibility of assuring the legitimacy and the continuity of the government. The role of the Chief of State does not increase the work load tremendously, despite the complaints of many Presidents over the necessity of attending rituals and ceremonies. But it does lead to the factor which places upon the White House press office perplexing problems that have never satisfactorily been solved.

The problem is simply that the press seeks continuous access to the President on a 24-hour-a-day, 7-day-a-week basis. The clamor is constant and demanding. If this were merely a matter of overweening curiosity, it could be handled by the abrupt slamming of doors and a few tart reminders of the elementary requirements of good manners. Unfortunately, it is not mere idle curiosity. It is a reflection of the President's relationship to the American people themselves.

This demand for access extends to the President's family as well. It is not satisfied by a few "personality" pieces on the First Lady and the children. As long as they occupy the White House, they are a *reigning* family and the one privilege that is denied to royal personages is the privilege of privacy—except for that form of privacy which can be enforced by walls and guarded doors.

Members of the First Family need not "make news" in order to attract the attention of the press. A casual shopping trip; an evening at the theater; a teen-age coke and hamburger date are sufficient grist for the journalistic mill. Any innocent foray outside of the White House (which is usually regarded by family members as a sanctuary) becomes an experience in running a gauntlet of prying eyes. And every move (this even applies to the teen-age date) must be made under the watchful eyes of a tactful, but still vigilant, armed guard.

There is no similar demand for continuous access to any other official of the government or his family. A cabinet secretary, a member of congress, or a justice can look forward most days to slipping away from his office for a quiet, relaxed evening (depending upon his social schedule) to the total indifference of the press. Newspapermen care only about their official acts and their official thoughts. Their private lives become interesting only in the event that they become unusual and fall into patterns that would qualify any prominent citizen for public attention.

Not so the President. His mere existence is significant and the objective of press coverage is to learn what he *is* as well as what he *does*. He is the symbol of the State, and the people whom he serves are anxious for every tiny detail—not just those which are dramatic but those which in any other person would be considered routine and perhaps even banal.

It is significant that the President both lives and works in the same building—the White House. It is significant because it reveals a basic factor of the conditions under which he must work. There is no way of separating his private life from his public life as the two are inextricably intertwined and what would be a private act in the case of another man (such as a quiet dinner with a friend) can have public consequences for the nation.

These circumstances alone would be sufficient to explain the long-standing antagonisms between Presidents and the press. It is difficult for any man—no matter how much he revels in publicity—to live in the realization that any and all of his acts may be subjected to public examination. But there is another factor which tends to compound the difficulties of the White House press office and that is the uniquely political character of the presidency.

Other officials of the executive branch may be politicians by background, inclination, and ambition. But their *offices* are administrative. They are not political in the sense that they are held by election or possessed of powers of ultimate decision. Only the presidency meets these two qualifications.

Political offices are usually held by politicians and there have been very few Presidents who did not fall into this category. A politician is, by definition, an advocate. And nothing can be more diametrically opposed than the temperament of the advocate and the temperament of the journalist.

The politician is a man who seeks to change things because he is dissatisfied with the conditions as they are. He tends first to fix his mind upon certain goals and then come to regard those goals as reality because they are so much more attractive (and usually so much more logical) than the world that surrounds him. He also instinctively assesses the forces of society (including the press) in terms of help or hindrance in attaining objectives. A newspaper story is "good" if it advances a cause; "bad" if it throws up a roadblock. And, as he is an activist, he is impatient—sometimes explosively so—with roadblocks that impede what he regards as progress.

The newspaperman, on the other hand, earns his salary by recording, or at least trying to record, conditions as they are. His experience tells him that no objective is ever fully attained and that reality always falls short of human desire. He tends to be impatient with "goals" and cynical about those who prefer them. And while he finds advocates entertaining, he also regards them as part of the classification known as the "blue sky" set.

This dichotomy (which, of course, does not characterize *every* politician and *every* newspaperman) is healthy for a democratic society. The optimistic goal-seeking of the politician does lead to some progress. And the "who, where, what and when" approach of the newspaperman helps keep his feet on the ground. But it does not make for a happy relationship and it does add to the tribulations of the press officer who must interpret each to the other.

Under these circumstances, the White House press secretary must fill a role which is played by no other public information officer. It is his responsibility somehow to disentangle the intricate skein of daily activities and determine what should be made available and what can legitimately be withheld. Furthermore, he has the responsibility of administering the rules and procedures under which access to the President by the press is possible at all. It is impossible to grant everyone access and therefore the access that can be granted must be carefully and painstakingly determined.

An information officer who is serving a multiperson institution can do so in an atmosphere of impersonality conducive to orderly procedures. But there can be no such thing as orderly procedures where one man—and one man only—is involved. The press secretary can administer the rules of the White House and he can even advise as to what those rules should be. But he cannot make them, and those that are made can be quickly unmade by the only man in the building whose opinion really counts. It is possible to lose sight of these elementary facts because of the glamor that attaches to the position of press secretary. But no real understanding of the position is possible unless the realities are borne clearly in mind. And failure to keep them in mind has led to the nonsensical portrayal of the press secretary as a superpublicity agent.

In reality, the press secretary has three functions. He serves as a spokesman for the President. He handles the logistical problems that are involved in adequate news coverage of the President. He serves as a point of contact for the press so that newspapermen will have a recognized source from which they can get responses to queries.

The press secretary is best known to the public for his role as a spokesman. This is the aspect which gives him "public exposure." But from the standpoint of the technical demands upon his office, it is probably the simplest task that he performs. The other two are far more complicated and far more demanding.

The logistical problems can at times assume staggering proportions. They include the chartering of modern jet aircraft, arranging for hotel rooms, securing official permits for the placement of television cameras, shepherding large groups of newsmen through police lines and classified installations where the authorities do not wish them to be. The work is unglamorous but without it adequate coverage of the President would be impossible.

The problem of serving as a point of contact is less demanding physically but frequently more complex in character. The queries of the press are constant and newspapermen cannot enter the presidential chamber at any hour of the day or night and put their questions directly to the President. White House assistants who are not authorized to answer questions are likely to be uncooperative. Nevertheless, the queries must be answered as failure to do so might, under some circumstances, touch off a flood of rumors that could have an impact upon the conduct of the affairs of the nation. Consequently, the press secretary and his assistants must be on call 24 hours a day. And they are under the constant strain that attends the process of answering questions for another man. Their mistakes are the President's mistakes even when he is unaware of their activities.

Beyond and above these tasks, of course, a press secretary may or may not be a trusted advisor to the President. In this respect he has no official status other than that accorded to other special assistants to the President. There is nothing in the title itself which determines his closeness to the Chief. And everyone who has ever worked in the White House will remain skeptical forever after over the constant speculation as to which assistant is really close and which is not.

The myth of the press secretary as a public relations specialist is one that persists throughout every administration. The word "myth" is used advisedly (although a press secretary can, under some circumstances, be a press agent for himself). In terms of public relations, every President is his own specialist and his assistants merely carry out what he himself determines is the best course of action. This is as it should be. A President willing to abdicate to a "specialist" his relations with the public would be willing to abdicate the presidency itself and men of such temperament rarely reach the White House. Furthermore, the art of "public relations" in a conventional sense holds forth few opportunities to him.

A President is on such constant display that promotional public relations are more likely to hinder than to help "the image." There is an old saying, "What you do speaks so loudly that I can't hear what you say." There is no other living person to whom this epigram can be applied with greater validity. What a President does every day of his life affects so many millions of people, immediately and directly, that what he says about it becomes secondary. Promotional public relations are effective only for people who can appear and disappear at will. This is a luxury which is denied the President of the United States.

Basically, the most useful function that can be fulfilled by the press secretary of the White House is to conduct himself in such a way that the statements and pronouncements of the institution remain believable. And if this function is fulfilled, he has discharged his obligations.

DEPARTMENTS OF STATE AND DEFENSE . . . .

Opening the Door on Foreign Affairs

ANDREW H. BERDING
FORMER ASSISTANT SECRETARY OF STATE
FOR PUBLIC AFFAIRS AND FORMER DIRECTOR OF
INFORMATION, DEPARTMENT OF DEFENSE

Nothing is clearer today than that the support of the American people is required for the effective conduct of foreign relations. Virtually every major foreign policy needs the physical and financial as well as the moral backing of the American people. A foreign policy that attracts only lukewarm support or arouses opposition is impaired in its application. For example, the success of this nation's armed intervention in support of the independence of the Republic of South Vietnam was impeded by the fact that the American public was less than wholeheartedly behind the action because of the existence of what some have called a "credibility gap."

The support of the American people for foreign relations policy can be obtained only if they are kept adequately informed of foreign policy thinking and developments. If they understand what foreign policy makers have in mind, they are far more likely to give their approval. The American people would have given more support to the Vietnam policy, I believe, if they had been provided more information, sooner and more clearly, on their country's stake in South Vietnam and what the loss of the new nation to Communist China would mean to all of Southeast Asia. The people need to know this, to understand it.

We have given to our citizens enormous power to influence foreign policy. It is therefore wise to consider George Washington's remark in his Farewell Address:

"In proportion as the structure of a government gives force to public opinion, it is essential that public opinion should be enlightened."

And Lord Macaulay's caution that "nothing could be more irrational than to give to the people power and to withhold from them the knowledge without which power may be abused."

Realization of the need to inform the public of major policies in order to obtain their support goes back several centuries, however much it may have been abused in the meantime. Cardinal Richelieu, Louis XIII's premier, maintained that the success of a policy depended upon the support of national opinion. Furthermore, he took steps to inform and instruct those who today would be characterized as "opinion-molders." He was the first to initiate a system of domestic propaganda. He ordered what he called "my

111

little leaflets" written and circulated to develop an informed public opinion in line with his policies.

The requirement of public support, however, does not mean that foreign policy should be created by public opinion. Former Secretary of State John Foster Dulles, in discussing American public opinion with me, made this point categorically on several occasions. He believed that the President and the Secretary of State had the duty to take the leadership in foreign affairs. They could not simply accept a majority public view as the one to follow. They had access to fuller and faster information than the public; they were expected to be in close contact with other interested nations on a given policy; and the initiative lay with them. A Secretary of State who waited for public opinion of the right kind to develop before taking action was derelict in his duty. However, Mr. Dulles made two important qualifications: the Administration could not be too far ahead of public opinion, and the Administration had a responsibility to inform the people adequately and bring public opinion along with it.

There are many methods of conveying adequate information on foreign affairs to the American public. In my four years as Assistant Secretary of State for Public Affairs I saw them all employed.

The voice of the President is, of course, the most important in the land. He needs to feel it his obligation to speak to the American people from time to time on foreign affairs. This cannot be done simply through a press conference, where the questions may be of such sequence, grouping, and phraseology as to hinder full and orderly exposition. A useful device for the press conference, however, is for the President to lead off with a prepared statement on a foreign policy matter of importance and then subordinate to the statement his answers to questions on the same subject. Occasionally he may have to refuse to provide further comment for fear of diluting or obscuring the substance of his statement. An additional method, however, needs to be employed—speeches or, better still, TV and radio addresses to the nation. Presidents Roosevelt, Truman, Eisenhower, Kennedy, and Johnson made good use of this method.

The next most important voice is that of the Secretary of State, and it should be heard in the same way. Some Secretaries of State take easily to press conferences and speeches, others dread them. Secretary Dulles used to say to me that every time he went down in the elevator with me and one of my most valued associates, Lincoln White, chief of the News Division, to the auditorium for his press conference, his knees knocked together.

Nevertheless, he regarded press conferences as an opportunity to put some of his thinking across to our own and other peoples. He felt that a press conference, because of its informality and because what he was saying was in response to questions, gave him an opportunity to speak out and say certain things it would be difficult to say in formal communications. Certainly when he stood up before 150 to 175 correspondents and fielded their barrage of questions he gave not the slightest sign that his "knees knocked together."

His press conferences were interesting and helpful because he not only was informative but also described his process of thinking and the background of a given event or policy. Several times he complained to me about the length of a conference. I had to reply that frankly it was his own fault because his answers to questions toward the end of the session had been so interesting that the correspondents wanted to pursue them still further. Mr. Dulles realized the value of speeches as a vehicle for conveying ideas, as indicated by the fact that he dictated the final versions himself so that they expressed in his own words exactly what he had in mind.

Secretary Herter felt that press conferences for a Secretary of State were dangerous. He eschewed them as much as possible. When the press room in the new State Department building was opened in 1960, Mr. Herter was asked to speak at a reception given by the press corps accredited to the Department. I had written out some suggestions for him. To my dismay, however, he told the newsmen in all honesty he did not like press conferences, and why. But in background conferences, where what he said was not for attribution, he was at his ease and superb. He was also most cooperative with regard to speeches.

Secretary Rusk has been sparing of press conferences, the correspondents have been somewhat disappointed at the amount of usable material, and, perhaps in consequence, the press has given them inadequate play. My opinion, from reading the transcripts, is that Mr. Rusk has handled the answers well and has gone as far as he reasonably could.

Secretary Dulles said to me that the most important feature of his press conferences was the transcript as published the following morning textually by *The New York Times*. This, he believed, was read word for word by every embassy in Washington and many foreign offices overseas and by thousands of influential people in the United States and abroad. Whatever might have been the flash news stories that followed the conference, readers could exactly perceive his thinking by reading the full text. I am sure he was right.

Therefore the transcript of a press conference by the President or the Secretary of State needs to be gone over with great care to make sure that it reflects exactly what the principal had in mind. The system I followed with Secretaries Dulles and Herter was, I believe, effective. The Secretary, Link White, and I would each go over a copy of the transcript immediately after the press conference. (Three or four State stenotypists rotated in taking the verbatim, so that by the time we returned to our offices after the conference, copies were already coming to us.) We then met in the Secretary's office to compare notes. Here and there stenographic errors had to be corrected, punctuation altered, a word changed, or long sentences broken up, rearranged, or otherwise straightened out. If any change of substance had to be made it was inserted in parentheses. This was infrequent. The correspondents could not use direct quotes until the verbatim was mimeographed and distributed. That then became the record of the press conference on which the Secretary of State was willing to stand before history.

At the White House the system was different. There the staff permitted the private court-reporting company to distribute the verbatim directly to anyone who wanted to pay the subscription price. There was no effort to straighten out President Eisenhower's phraseology. The result was that Mr. Eisenhower, with sentences lopped off, with dangling, unfinished phrases drooping here and there, tangential clauses striking out in all directions, and punctuation misplaced, was often made to appear almost illiterate. Worse still, some of what he said was open to unfortunate misinterpretation.

I likened President Eisenhower's press conferences to a nineteenth-century French impressionistic painting. If one looked at the painting close up, it was awful; but if one saw it across the room, it was wonderful. If one scrutinized the President's verbatim close up, it too was awful; but if one was present at the conference and caught his words and also his gestures, facial expressions, vitality, and honesty it was generally wonderful.

The White House staff felt it was keeping faith with the correspondents to give them the verbatim exactly as the stenotypists turned it out. But what stenotypist can say he has heard perfectly everything a President says, that he knows where every sentence starts and ends, that he can punctuate with complete accuracy—and we know that the placing or misplacing of a comma can radically alter the sense of words? I believe the correspondents would have been satisfied with an edited verbatim if they knew that the President himself had gone over and approved it as his final word. I know that many officials of our own and other governments would have been happier with a fully understandable text that had the President's stamp of approval.

This would also have been fairer to the President himself. Any average person knows that, if a stenographic record were to be made of his off-the-cuff remarks, it would read very curiously in parts, and he would relish the opportunity to smooth it out before it was published. No eyebrow is raised at the daily custom of Senators and Congressmen asking for and automatically receiving leave to amend their remarks before they appear in the Congressional Record. Congressional committees also give the executive departments the courtesy of amending, within reason, the transcript of their testimony before it is published in committee reports.

President Kennedy and Secretary Rusk continued unchanged the respective practices of their predecessors. In the White House the transcript was not edited, in the State Department it was. Mr. Kennedy's answers at press conferences were more cohesive in language than were President Eisenhower's, but I came across some of his answers that made the transcript look like a map of bypasses, road blocks, and repair signs so that the traveler in foreign policy easily got lost. That traveler has a hard enough time as it is; he needs every little added help.

Fortunately, President Johnson altered this practice and permitted his press secretary to go over the transcript before it was released to the press. The press secretary was to make sure the stenotypist caught the exact words used by the President, checking back to the recording tape if necessary. He was to tighten up sentences, breaking up long ones where required, to make the meaning clearer. This I considered an important improvement.

In directing the public relations of State I sought to carry out certain principles which I believe are valid and should be generally followed in making our foreign relations understandable to the public.

The first was to rely in major part on the private mass media of communication—newspapers, news agencies such as the United Press International and the Associated Press, news magazines, magazines, radio, TV, and newsreels—to carry the message of our foreign affairs, as contrasted with government created and financed dissemination of information. I was confident that these public media could do the job far better than government distribution, and at comparatively very little expense to the government, and that the government could not and should not try to compete with them. The government should try only to supplement this effort with its own publications which would go into greater detail than current articles but would also form the basis for such articles.

The second principle, in line with the preceding, was to try to make the maximum amount of information available to the press. This was a constant struggle. I found myself always in the middle between the press, which wanted everything (for instance, what were we going to say in reply to a Soviet note when we had not yet made up our minds), and many State Department officers, who wanted to give nothing (they might not even admit we were going to reply).

In carrying out this principle I tried to have as many press conferences as possible by the Secretary of State and background conferences by other top Department officials. I met daily with various correspondents, American and foreign; I sought to keep the department spokesman, Lincoln White, and his assistants widely informed and to get usable information into their hands; and I endeavored to induce department officers to get over their fears of the press and to see reporters as frequently as they could.

At summit and foreign ministers conferences, I spent literally thousands of hours briefing the press myself.

The scheduling of press conferences for the Secretary of State was a constant trial. My own desire was to have them frequently. On the other hand, the Secretary of State is one of the busiest men in the world and always has important obligations which conflict with press conferences and seem essential to meet at their expense. Another obstacle was the feeling of some of the Assistant Secretaries that if there were a crisis in their areas the Secretary should not meet with the press. One week it would be in Europe, the next week in the Far East, the next in the Near East, and so on. "He can't meet the press now, they will crucify him," "It will be disastrous," "Our relations with country X will go down the drain," or "Why can't you wait a few weeks?" were typical.

I argued that crises were always occurring, and if the Secretary of State avoided a press conference when a crisis was prevailing he would never meet with the press. Furthermore, a Secretary of State is not obliged to answer every question with something substantive; he has the right to refuse to comment; and the press, even though they would have preferred a headline, would understand his reasons. Also these objections seemed to me to indicate a lack of confidence in the Secretary, as if he were not wise and strong-minded enough to handle a delicate situation. Finally, the fact of canceling a press conference when a crisis develops might well create the impression that the crisis was more serious than it was. My own hope, never fully realized, was that the Secretary of State would hold news conferences on a regular basis, on a given day each week or every other week. With periodicity established, no individual press conference would assume undue importance.

While striving to get into the hands of the press the largest amount of information, I rigidly eschewed "leaks" and trial balloons.

I do not believe in leaks. Official news is the property of no one official to give as largesse. It is the property of the government as a whole to be given to the press as a whole.

The third principle was to try to simplify and clarify the information made available both through the public media and through department releases and publications.

Foreign affairs are exceedingly complicated and get more so as each passing year brings more nations into being. They are not easy to understand. This is particularly true of the economic side of international relations. People generally seem to be interested first in the military side of foreign affairs, second in the political, and third in the economic. With less interest goes less understanding. And, admittedly, international economic relations can be exceedingly abstruse.

Simply putting out a long press release with governmental gobbledygook and terminology comprehensible only to experts, if to them, is therefore almost criminal negligence. A release should not be issued unless an American with a high school education can understand it. And it needs to be rounded out with adequate and simple explanation, whether written or oral, of the background and purpose of the action. As often as possible we induced one of the substantive officers who had been handling the matter to appear with Mr. White when he issued the release, so as to answer questions that inevitably came from the press. Not infrequently these questions were useful in revealing points that had been overlooked.

I am convinced we have lost much in world public opinion by our inability to state Western disarmament proposals simply and clearly. Disarmament is no simple matter, but we have unduly complicated it by the semi-intelligible way we have formulated and stated our positions.

I have been grimly amused at reading activity reports of some departments which give the total of press releases issued in a given period. The number matters little, the quality much. The very fact of numerous press releases may indicate that not enough attention has been devoted to making each one clear.

One type of press statement, whether written or oral, I should like to see less rather than more of is the castigation of another government, generally the Soviet Union or Communist China or Castro's Cuba. Often we react too quickly and sharply to Soviet bloc actions or statements. The tone of many of our utterances has become in recent years undignified for a nation with the traditions and standing of the United States. We have fallen at times into the bad diplomatic habits of the Soviet Union. Virulent and tropically colored adjectives have appeared in our statements that could have been omitted with increased effect. Such statements run greater risk of being dismissed as propa-

ganda. The explanation given me by top State Department officers is that most of our relations with the Soviet Union are conducted through public statements. This is unfortunately true, but
one can still use a gentleman's language in replying to a blas-
phemer.

During my years at State the department was singularly successful in requiring officials of other departments to submit for
clearance speeches and statements dealing wholly or partly with
foreign affairs. President Eisenhower issued an Executive Order
governing this submission and, with very few exceptions, it was
observed after an initial period of education. President Kennedy
renewed this Executive Order and President Johnson permitted
it to continue unchanged. The Bureau of Public Affairs, which
I headed, was the channel for clearance. By far the largest number of papers submitted from any one department came from
Defense, which was natural in view of Defense's military commitments around the world and their importance in our foreign
relations. Initial resistance from some high officers was overcome
when we were able to point out convincingly why certain utterances would harm our foreign relations and to offer alternatives
that left the speech or statement as good, if not better, than
before.

The Department of State conducts one effort which is especially beneficial—periodical briefings for representatives of national nongovernmental organizations and of the public media
of communication, not only those in Washington but anywhere
in the United States. The briefings may last from half a day to
two days. The President, the Secretary of State, and top officers
of State and other departments and agencies talk to the participants and remain to answer questions. This initiative brings to
Washington people like editorial writers who otherwise might
have mused in their ivory towers a thousand miles away from
the capital, partly unaware of the problems we face and the
efforts made to solve them. Similar briefings have been held in
other major American cities.

Overseas our ambassadors can be of real help in conveying
foreign policy information to permanent or visiting American
correspondents. Although an ambassador naturally has to exercise great care in his contacts with the local press he has more
assurance in periodically meeting with American correspondents

on a background basis. Some of our ambassadors do this effectively on a regular schedule, others on an ad hoc basis, and others avoid it like all ten plagues.

I deem it essential that American correspondents filing from overseas have a good current comprehension of American foreign policy objectives and developments. Otherwise they tend to reflect solely the views of the local foreign office, which may be at variance with American policy, without any attempt to interpret them in the light of United States thinking. During one of his trips to Europe President Eisenhower expressed his dismay that American correspondents stationed in European capitals were sending many dispatches adverse to United States interests. This situation can be improved as American ambassadors make it their function to meet with American correspondents and to the extent of their ability give them our "slant" on current foreign affairs developments.

In general, the staffs of the White House and the State Department still need to take the public affairs factor more into consideration—first of all in making their decisions, and second in the manner of announcing them. Many officers think they have taken public opinion fully into account in reaching decisions, but it is surprising how often they have overlooked vital points of presentation. Or they have thought only of the public opinion in another country concerned in the decision and not of that in the United States.

What a difference would exist in our standing in the world had both the Truman and Eisenhower Administrations fully realized the public relations importance of being the first nation to put a satellite into orbit around the earth! Our decisions in developing the satellite were purely scientific and military, connected in part with the International Geophysical Year. We therefore proceeded scientifically with measured steps, avoiding a crash program and undue expense. Little if any thought was given to the psychological implications of the project except on the negative side of being prepared if other nations around the world became worried or objected when our satellite passed over their air space. In consequence, the Soviets scored with the first Sputnik and secured not only a scientific but also a psychological triumph which has colored their conduct ever since. I vividly remember taking a prominent American newspaper publisher in to see one of the highest officials in the Department of State on the afternoon when the Soviets announced their initial Sputnik and hearing the official say, while my heart sank, that the feat was a stunt of slight importance that would soon be forgotten.

As to the manner of announcing a foreign policy decision, an officer should realize that, without changing the substance of this idea one iota, he can gain added impact by the way he states it.

The press handling of the U-2 incident in 1960 was a disaster, partly because the Public Affairs Bureau of State was not consulted. I was with Secretary Herter at the NATO Foreign Ministers conference in Istanbul when the reconnaissance plane went down. Neither my deputy, Edwin M. J. Kretzmann, nor the chief of the news office, Lincoln White, was consulted, however, before the initial unfortunate press statements, which were shortly to make State look ridiculous, were prepared and released. Later, after my return to Washington, came the meetings in the State Department at which the statement was drafted admitting the United States' connection with four years of U-2 flights, and, two days later, the statement in which the President accepted responsibility. I was not present at either of these meetings. I gave Secretary Herter a memo protesting this fact and calling attention to the tremendous public relations connotations of the case. Wonderful gentleman that he is, Mr. Herter immediately called me to his office and expressed his regret. He said only a very few persons had been cleared for knowledge of the U-2 flights and I, not being one of them, had not been requested to attend the meetings. Whether I would have taken a substantially different position if I had attended I cannot say. I am convinced I would have argued against the President's acceptance of personal responsibility. And I believe I could have improved the statements that were made.

A few times—fortunately only a few—I have encountered among top officials what I consider a strange point of view toward public affairs officers. It was expressed in most memorable form by the late Secretary of Defense Charles E. Wilson in his early days in office, when I was Director of Information of the Department of Defense. Not having been informed of an important development in Defense, I protested to Mr. Wilson. He in turn expressed genuine surprise that I should have wanted to be informed. He said, in essence, "Why should we have said anything to you about this, in view of the fact you are meeting with the press all the time? Because you are seeing the press every day I shouldn't think you'd want to know about an important classified matter like this." A public affairs officer, however, must be fully informed if he is to carry out his duties effectively. The public affairs officer is the least likely of all government officials to "spill" something to a reporter. The "spilling" is more likely to come from officers unaccustomed to meeting with the press, who are alternately timorous and indiscreet. Furthermore, a public affairs officer must have adequate information so that he will know not only what to say to the press but also what not to say.

I long maintained in the Department of State that insufficient attention is given to the form and method of stating our foreign policies. Many solid hours of thinking by many solid citizens, from the President down to a humble junior officer in State, may have gone into the formulation of a foreign policy. But all too little thought is given to its public presentation. The result is often confusion as to what the policy actually means. Also, other countries and our own citizens give only partial acceptance to an idea that should have been warmly welcomed. Some makers of foreign policy are like some parents who throw their child into the water to make him swim; this is rather hard on the child.

A number of elements enter into effective public presentation. First, the policy should be clearly and convincingly written. A mass of bureaucratic verbiage—perhaps arrived at through many compromises with competing bureaus in the State Department or with other departments or with our allies—puts hobbles on a policy before it has begun to walk. At the same time, sufficient background material should be prepared so that through the press our own people and those of other nations are given an understanding of the policy.

Our formal note to the Soviets on Berlin, in July 1961, warrants reading solely as an example of lame-and-halt language. Highly important because it was the answer to a memorandum from Premier Khrushchev to President Kennedy, it threw away much of its effect on the public by its clumsy phraseology, awkward sentences, and poor construction. Six weeks had been required for the completion of the note and admittedly every sentence was the result of compromise. But, without changing the substance or even the tone in the slightest, a far better job of writing could have been achieved. When it reached the White House much dismay was voiced; but rather than do a rewrite job President Kennedy decided to open his press conference the following day with a statement on Berlin emphasizing more cogently the points in the note.

Second, the staging of the presentation needs to be carefully worked out. Should it be in the setting of the White House or the Congress or the State Department? What sort of ceremony, if any, should be connected with the announcement and who should preside? How about the timing of the announcement? Does it conflict with another event that would overshadow it? Is the date chosen unfortunate because of previous events on that date and could unpleasant implications be read into this choice?

Third, have the other nations and persons concerned been prepared for the announcement of the new policy? Foreign nations affected might react unfavorably simply because they should have been consulted and were not. This is also true of congressional leaders. Other government departments and concerned foreign governments might be informed so they could provide support instead of expressing surprise. The United States Information Agency should always be brought in in advance so that it can be ready to transmit to other countries full information and background on the new policy. One would think all this should be axiomatic, but it is baffling how often it has been disregarded.

The White House announcement of July 1960 on the policy of extending government economic aid to Latin America to produce social development is a good example of the nonobservance of several of these points. Here was a brand-new policy which later, with more sophisticated presentation, became President Kennedy's Alianza para el Progreso. It reversed the government's former conviction that government economic assistance should not be extended to Latin America, which should be made to rely on private investment. And it embraced a new concept, that of assisting in the promotion of social gains. Instead of concentrating on economic projects like industrial plants, harbors, and transportation systems, as under the past approach in other areas, the new program would promote agricultural reform, better housing conditions, and the like.

But how was this dramatic policy handled? The announcement itself was a vaguely worded, rambling statement that left everyone in doubt as to what it meant. It conveyed no impression even remotely of its great importance. The program involved half-a-billion dollars as just the first step of assistance, but no figure was even mentioned, and one could not tell from the release whether the program was paltry or substantial. The announcement was handed to the press at the summer White House at Newport, Rhode Island, and no one there was in a position to give the correspondents the essential background required.

As to timing, it was put out in the midst of a bitter quarrel with Fidel Castro, so that the press and public naturally conjectured it was a reaction to Castro and not an affirmative action genuinely designed to help Latin America.

No advance consultation had been held with Latin American countries, with the result that it burst upon them in a vacuum. This fact, plus the cloudy wording of the announcement, might partly justify the statement President Juscelino Kubitschek of Brazil issued immediately thereafter, glossing over what was actually a development of great importance to his country.

Few foreign policy innovations have been introduced under less happy auspices. Following the initial announcement, I organized background conferences for Washington correspondents with several State Department officials; Latin American Ambassadors were briefed; and a better understanding of the policy soon became evident. President Kubitschek reversed his original statement. But epilogue efforts seldom make up for prologue neglect. A true opportunity had been frittered away.

President Kennedy took over the same program less than two months after his inauguration and launched it with appropriate eclat. First, he gave it an attractive title, "Alliance for Progress," which translated well into Spanish, "Alianza para el Progreso." Second, he stated it dramatically at a White House reception for Latin American diplomats, members of Congress, and their wives. Third, he rounded it out with additional proposals, such as working with Latin American governments to end violent price changes in their export commodities. And he sent Adlai Stevenson on an exploratory tour of Latin American countries as his representative to demonstrate the United States' increased interest in them. Already, I am sure, as a result of his contrast in presentation, most Americans believe that President Kennedy, not President Eisenhower, launched the new program to help our hemisphere neighbors.

A good example of the opposite effect was President Eisenhower's Atoms-for-Peace policy. This was carefully worked out in Washington well in advance. Meetings were held with interested departments of the government to plan adequate presentation. These were chaired by imaginative C. D. Jackson of the White House staff; I attended as Assistant Director of the U. S. Information Agency. President Eisenhower took the policy with him to the Bermuda Conference with Prime Minister Winston Churchill and Premier Joseph Laniel and discussed it there. It was launched in a great forum, the General Assembly of the United Nations, by the President in person. It had enough information built into it so that all could understand it. The U.S. Information Agency was ready with a worldwide information campaign to make the policy known quickly to all peoples. This policy was eminently successful, for it led to the creation of the International Atomic Energy Agency under the United Nations.

Summing up, I believe that United States foreign policy, to be truly effective, has to have the support of the distinct majority of the American people; that the people need to be kept fully informed of foreign affairs developments; and that the public affairs aspect needs to be taken into complete account as foreign policy is created, stated, and carried out.

THE LEGISLATIVE BRANCH . . .

Telling the Congressman's Story

SHERWOOD L. BOEHLERT
EXECUTIVE ASSISTANT TO
CONGRESSMAN ALEXANDER PIRNIE

"Your Representative owes you, not his industry only, but his judgment; and he betrays, instead of serving you, if he sacrifices it to your opinion."
Edmund Burke

CONSENSUS is a word that has probably caused more problems for the elected representatives, at all levels of government, than any other in common usage. This is especially true with members of the Senate and House of Representatives of the United States, for the activities of the Congress are daily chronicled by the news media and followed with interest by the most potent force in our Republic—the people.

Somehow, over the years, there has developed in the minds of many Americans a picture of a legislator in Washington dutifully studying constituent mail, carefully keeping a scorecard of the numbers for and against a given bill, and then, upon examining the totals, solemnly and irrevocably pledging his support to the view of the majority. Fortunately, it doesn't work that way and because it doesn't the importance of telling the Congressman's story is difficult to overstate. The effectiveness with which the assignment is handled is measured at the polls. Political survival often hangs in the balance.

There are, barring vacancies, 535 members of the Senate and the House and probably an equal number of approaches to the task. However, certain fundamentals apply in like manner to all.

No story is any better than its principal character. What a person is and does, not what he says he is and claims he does, will eventually come to the surface and prove to be the factors by which he is judged. Therefore the only way to tell the Congressman's story is to be honest.

Since the House of Representatives is my base of experience, illustrations will be drawn from this background.

Basically, there are three main objectives to be accomplished by a public information program for a member of Congress: to educate the people on the issues of the day, thereby presenting them with the facts needed to make intelligent judgments; to set the stage for acceptance of a future action by the Congressman; and to promote a favorable attitude toward the Congressman by relating his accomplishments and establishing his identity as an individual knowledgeable about and working toward the solution of the problems in his district, the nation, and beyond.

129

Of course, there are ancillary objectives such as demonstrating that the Congressman is able to work with his colleagues "on the other side of the aisle" (especially important if the legislator is a member of the minority party) and providing evidence that he has access to the key officials in the executive branch who, in addition to their decision-making roles in charting the future course of all governmental activity, domestic and foreign, also administer the myriad federal grant and loan programs.

Talking about objectives is one thing, accomplishing them quite another. To achieve a measure of success with the previously listed objectives and those of lesser importance, a total communications program, involving all the news media and every phase of office activity, should be used to the maximum advantage. Greater emphasis should be given to some, frequency variation to others, but none should be ignored. And all are interrelated.

A prerequisite for any possibility of success with such an undertaking is a sincere, relatively consistent, hard-working member of Congress whose aspirations to serve are accompanied by the ability to do so effectively.

A review of the activities of one such member of Congress, Representative Alexander Pirnie of New York, illustrates the varied communications techniques used to accomplish the objectives of a comprehensive public information program.

In addition to answering *every* letter received from his constituents, the New Yorker, like many of his colleagues, also sends to all the news media in his district an average of two prepared statements per week outlining an activity or anticipated action; writes a bimonthly column for the weekly newspapers in his district; has a monthly radio-television program covering a major issue before the Congress and featuring a guest expert on the subject discussed (the program is distributed to and used by two television and eleven radio stations in his district); twice per session of Congress sends to every household in his district a "Special Legislative Report" outlining his voting record on the 20 or 25 measures of special importance that have come before the House and his reasons for supporting or opposing each bill; and answers *every* media query received.

Also, Congressman Pirnie accepts some 100 speaking engagements per year, mainly in his district, and endeavors to be available in his home office whenever Congress is not in session and on the Saturday mornings of the average of 30 weeks in each session he makes the round trip from Washington to central New York.

When in the district, the Congressman visits area factories, inspects programs operating with federal funds, and meets with local officials as time permits.

Why all this activity? The answer is very simple. The Congressman realizes that he is public property and, as such, will be scrutinized, analyzed, and publicized at will. He knows that the inquisitive voter, inquiring reporter, and probing camera are omnipresent. He also knows that one way or the other, his story will be told and, as in so many areas of activity, there is a direct correlation between input and outcome. In short, the Congressman is always mindful of the value of a sound public information program and never loses sight of the objectives he hopes to achieve with his.

A transition from the general to the specific gives a better glimpse of the "how."

Unquestionably the best opportunity a Congressman has to communicate with and have a direct impact on a large part of his constituency is through the U.S. mail. According to a popular Capitol Hill story, a veteran lawmaker once counseled a freshman colleague "there are three secrets to success if you want to stay here—use your frank, use your frank, use your frank."

The frank is the privilege accorded members of Congress to use the mail, free of charge, for all official correspondence and special mailings pertaining to official business, simply by affixing the member's signature to the envelope in the space usually reserved for a stamp.

There is wide flexibility in the interpretation of what qualifies as official business and is thereby frankable. In general, the Post Office Department has ruled that the frank may be used by a member of Congress (it is not transferable or cannot be used by an organization in his behalf) if the contents of the mailing piece pertain to "matters or issues which reasonably can be considered as arising from a member's work in the Congress." Thus all replies to constituent mail about legislation and activities involving federal agencies are frankable. So, too, are special reports, or newsletters, covering the Congressman's voting record, work in Washington, and views on the issues of the day.

Strictly personal correspondence and campaign literature, such as an outright appeal for votes, are obviously not within the realm of official business and therefore, under normal circumstances, not frankable. (One Congressman, who sent, in the form of a newsletter, Christmas greetings to all of his constituents, learned the lesson the hard way when the Post Office Department presented him with a bill for several thousand dollars to cover the postage on an item not deemed frankable.) However, no matter how personal, partisan, or political the material may be, it is, by law, frankable if it appeared in the *Congressional Record.*

Discretion is the better part of valor when using the frank and by sticking to the spirit of the law, that is, using it only for official business, such as forwarding to constituents reports and replies to their letters, the Congressman can reap great dividends without subjecting himself to criticism or heavy expense. He is expected to answer his mail and it is one of his major responsibilities to keep his people informed.

For most Congressmen, there is one hard and fast rule for all constituent mail. It must be answered. Whether a letter contains an expression of opinion, seeks a position statement, or requests assistance, it presents a golden opportunity for the Congressman to win friends and influence people.

Simple arithmetic produces some startling figures to place in perspective the importance of an exchange of correspondence between a Congressman and his constituents.

Of the approximately 450,000 people in the typical Congressional district, 160,000 register and vote. If a Representative receives and replies to an average of 100 unsolicited constituent communications per day, which is not unusual and, in fact, would be termed light by some, he will send out 26,000 letters per year and 52,000 per term. Allowing 12,000, or just over 22 percent, for duplication, still leaves the impressive total of 40,000 direct, personal contacts with the people who, by their ballots, will help determine the political fate of the Congressman.

In most cases, the individual who takes the time to write his Congressman makes the effort to go to the polls. By replying, the lawmaker has a chance to contact and impress 25 percent of the probable voters in the next election.

No other single phase of a Congressman's communications program can compete with replying to constituent mail for the top of the priority list. The news releases, the radio and television programs, and the unexpected visits to the district may be delayed temporarily, sometimes for long periods, without creating any significant notice. The declination of speaking invitations because of other commitments is understood. Visitors to Washington who find their Congressman elsewhere on business seldom give the matter a second thought. But the constituent whose letter is unanswered does not forget the failure of *his* Representative to respond. The hope of retaining or eventually earning his support is automatically diminished, sometimes permanently lost.

Letter-writing is, or should be, a staff function. Although there undoubtedly is a sizable segment of the population which still harbors the thought that a Congressman personally replies to every one of the thousands of communications that annually flood his office, in most cases the system does not work that way.

Usually the legislator reads incoming mail, notes the type of answers he desires, and then turns the correspondence over to staff specialists for the preparation of definitive replies and any follow-through required. The finished product is almost always signed by House members, but in the Senate, where mail volume is higher, this responsibility is sometimes delegated to staff members or an automatic pen, an amazing—and expensive—mechanical device that can duplicate any signature for which it is programmed.

It is easy to understand why a member of Congress cannot get involved in the mechanics of most letter-writing. If he takes three minutes to read and three minutes to respond to each one of the hundred or so letters that flow into the typical office each day, he would be spending ten hours a day on this alone, leaving him little or no time to attend committee meetings, listen to and participate in floor debate, explore problem areas, draft proposals, and study legislation.

The staff member handling constituent mail must regard himself first as an extension of the Congressman and therefore must reflect his employer's thinking and basic style in his writing, always remembering that the lawmaker is the one who must sign the mail.

Actually there is not as much delegation of authority as might appear on the surface. Obviously, the individual entrusted with this assignment must have more to go on than his imagination. If he is not a partner in the policy-making process—in most offices at least one staff member is—he should at least have frequent policy reviews with the top man to make certain the Congressman's thoughts are accurately communicated. Complications and questions are also avoided when the member personally responds to the first few letters on an involved issue, his replies serving as guides for future correspondence.

The reply to the constituent letter is the most effective communications tool used in telling the Congressman's story. There are a few basics worthy of special mention. The reply should be prompt and to the point. It should definitely refer to the subject mentioned in the constituent letter and not be the general "thank you for writing" type of response. (The sender's letter need not have been read to elicit this, and the constituent knows it.)

The letter expressing a viewpoint contrary to that of the Congressman should be recognized for what it is, an opportunity to bring to the constituent's attention some factual material that he may not have been exposed to which, if it does not convince him to change his position, at least should serve to develop in him an appreciation that the matter is not just one-sided. Even the letter to the most avowed critic should not be argumentative, but rather instructive. If the Congressman's position on an issue is requested, and he has one, the position should be stated clearly and supported. There should be no reluctance, however, to be noncommittal if the Congressman's position is not yet formulated. This type of reply should bring out some of the pros and cons of the issue. The letter asking for assistance not only should receive a reply that demonstrates the Congressman's understanding of the problem but also a report on the steps he is taking in an effort to produce a solution.

Examples from Representative Pirnie's files illustrate the relationship of this focal point of the New Yorker's public information program to his other communications activities. How the objectives mentioned earlier were and are being achieved will be highlighted.

One of the most controversial and complex issues debated in the House in recent years involved the disposition of Section 14(b) of the Taft-Hartley Act. The question was: "Should Congress retain or repeal this provision of law permitting the individual states to pass legislation prohibiting labor-management contracts requiring union membership as a condition of employment?"

At the peak of debate, in the summer of 1965, there was a lot of "heat" on Capitol Hill. It had nothing to do with the weather. Tons of mail advocating or opposing repeal of the mislabeled "right-to-work" law crowded Congressional offices. Lobbying on both sides of the question was intense. Emotional outbursts were frequent and there were charges and countercharges about denying rights, anti-unionism, and political arm-twisting. The setting was anything but calm and conducive to straight, logical thinking. It was clearly one of those no-win, damned-if-you-do, damned-if-you-don't issues. Congressmen had their work cut out for them in trying to bring order from chaos.

Representative Pirnie studied dozens of special reports on the subject, reviewed hundreds of written opinions from constituents and engaged in lengthy conferences with business, labor, and government officials before deciding to support repeal of 14(b).

The Congressman sent at least three communications to everyone who contacted him on 14(b). Responses to constituent mail were noncommittal prior to the House vote (the repeal legislation was approved, 221-203, on July 28, 1965 but was not acted upon by the Senate and subsequently died). Recognition of the seriousness of the issue was evidenced and a pledge made to retain an open mind until the full debate was aired. Also, to give constituents an idea of the many factors that had to be considered, arguments for and against repeal were mentioned and special emphasis was given to the effect repeal of 14(b) would have in New York state.

Following his vote, the Congressman issued to the news media a statement outlining his reasons for supporting the repeal move.

A second letter, with a copy of his statement, was sent to everyone who had written him on the subject, even the most adamant critics of his position.

While this second communication may have been deemed unnecessary and viewed by some less concerned with public relations as inviting unfavorable reaction, especially since it was sent also to those with whom there was disagreement, the Congressman felt that everyone who had taken the trouble to write him on the legislation was entitled to know how he voted and why. In reply, he received several "I still think you are wrong, but respect your honesty" letters.

When legislation to launch a concerted Federal war against poverty was first enacted in 1964, it did not have the Congressman's endorsement. He was not opposed to the concept embodied in the measure, but strongly believed too much was requested too soon and that the effort lacked direction. Congressman Pirnie preferred "seed money" to underwrite pilot antipoverty programs; those successful would be given added attention and funding, the failures scrapped.

Several programs for Representative Pirnie's district were approved by the Office of Economic Opportunity during its first two years, however, and the Congressman followed their progress with great interest. On visits home, he would talk with program leaders and enrollees, visit classes and neighborhood centers, all the time asking questions and noting responses. He liked what he saw. And yet, from all over the country came criticism of the antipoverty effort and many persons associated with it. The Congressman wanted fuller answers before making a decision on the pending legislation.

After a thorough study of the war against poverty, including a long, probing session with its director, Sargent Shriver, and a careful review of the alternatives proposed by its opponents, the Congressman concluded that the legislation to continue and expand the operation deserved support. In his view, some battles were lost, but the total war was progressing satisfactorily and could be improved.

The Congressman's job became one of preparing his constituency for his "new thinking" on the antipoverty effort. A significant change in position on a major issue without forewarning can be like a bolt of lightning: very visible and often damaging.

Through a series of actions, Representative Pirnie simultaneously accomplished several objectives. Mr. Shriver was guest on his monthly radio-television program and the OEO director was asked difficult questions that were on the minds of those in Central New York and elsewhere who were critical of and opposed to the programs under his jurisdiction: "Are antipoverty workers contributing to the riots in our cities, as some charge? Isn't the overhead for OEO too high? Is the money really reaching the poor? Is the Administration playing politics with the grants, aiding only those districts where the Representative is a member of the majority party?"

Mr. Shriver was articulate and factual in refuting the charges. A transcript of the exchange between the two men was released to the newspapers when the program was given to the area stations. Extensive coverage resulted.

In addition, a comprehensive "guide letter" was prepared for responding to constituent correspondence and all future letters followed the same pattern: acknowledge the past mistakes, express the feeling that the biggest obstacles have been overcome, pinpoint the major objections remaining and the proposed changes to eliminate them, and, finally, highlight the success of the local programs. A transcript of the radio-TV program was enclosed.

As the House began consideration of the Economic Opportunity Amendments of 1967, interest in the issue was at its high point. It was decided that conditions were ripe for an expression of the Congressman's views to have the maximum impact and, accordingly, early in the debate Representative Pirnie delivered a major address that had been several weeks in preparation. A press packet, including the full text of his remarks, cover release, and assorted photographs taken during the Pirnie-Shriver conference, was released to the news media. The pickup was especially gratifying, with the two daily newspapers having the largest circulation in his district carrying favorable editorials hailing the Congressman's "progressive thinking" on the issue.

By the time the House voted on the antipoverty legislation, the

Congressman had already achieved the principal, and some secondary, objectives of his information program. By his responses to constituent mail, his radio-television program with Mr. Shriver, his floor speech during debate and his news releases, Representative Pirnie had helped to educate the voters at home, set the stage for acceptance of his ultimate decision on the legislation, and established his identity as an individual knowledgeable about and working toward the solution of the poverty problem. The photographs of Mr. Pirnie with Mr. Shriver that appeared in the hometown papers provided evidence of his personal dialogue with key officials in the executive branch.

Few were surprised, therefore, to receive reports of the Congressman's votes in favor of continuing and expanding the program without any drastic change in direction.

Once again, everyone who had written Representative Pirnie —and there were several hundred—received a second mailing. This extra communication contained a letter explaining how he voted and a *Congressional Record* reprint of his remarks during the House debate. And, once again, the Congressman received in response numerous letters, telegrams, and telephone calls praising him for his forthright manner in keeping the public informed. It was especially interesting to note that the Congressman did not receive one letter of criticism from what at one time was a sizable and vociferous number of war-against-poverty critics in his district, although one individual who had long made a habit of being against everything, never for anything, wrote a letter to the editor of a local newspaper intimating that Mr. Shriver "had gotten to Pirnie" by promising more grants for his district. The reaction to such sad letters is usually directly opposite to that hoped for by the writer; several people, with tongue in cheek, told the Congressman he was a "good horse trader."

Before attempting to tell the Congressman's story, there has to be developed something worthy of relating. One of the most important behind-the-scenes activities on Capitol Hill involves the liaison between a member of Congress and officials of the executive branch.

Contrary to popular belief, experience indicates that one's manner of conduct, rather than party affiliation, will determine the type of rapport established and the results that will derive therefrom. The partisan with vision so narrow he can only see one side of the picture is usually either taken for granted or ignored. It is the member of Congress who establishes a reputation for being receptive to proposals and objective in his analysis, willing to adjust his thinking to meet the challenges of these rapidly changing times, who receives the most attention and, not surprisingly, the most cooperation.

A case in point is the interesting history of Representative Pirnie's productive association with the Economic Development Administration.

The Public Works and Economic Development Act of 1965 is the vehicle that carried the Economic Development Administration into existence. Although the 89th Congress passed one major new program after another, for this measure the road was rocky with many detours along the way. Several legislative battles had to be fought before the favorable outcome was assured and it is only because Representative Pirnie had done his homework and had friends "on the other side of the aisle" that he was able to play a role in helping to obtain passage of an amendment that was to prove vital to his District's long-range economic development.

Primarily, the Act was designed to help depressed areas of the country by funding planning activities and a host of public works projects, such as sewer lines and access roads for industrial parks, that would help provide new industry and permanent jobs in areas where they were most needed.

To the Congressman, the proposal appeared basically sound in theory. Despite some drawbacks and unhappy memories of its predecessor, the Accelerated Public Works Act, he split with his party and supported the measure. However, the support came only after the legislation was amended to correct what he considered deficiencies in the original bill. One such deficiency dealt with a lack of eligibility for aid for those areas, like Central New York, which had been depressed but were on the way up. The Congressman was in favor of limited aid to permit these areas to continue making progress necessary for the establishment of a solid economic base. "Don't abandon them now," he argued.

The importance of developing and maintaining good relations with an executive agency is documented by what followed passage of the legislation creating EDA. Immediate contact was made by the Congressman with the agency's director, Eugene P. Foley, and a pledge of cooperation given. In the following months, Representative Pirnie continually checked on EDA's progress and displayed a special interest in its operation, twice appearing before the Public Works Committee to express personal satisfaction with the job the infant agency was doing. Frequent conferences were arranged to discuss projects important to Central New York and letters of praise were sent by the Congressman to those officials who were especially helpful.

The upshot of it all? The Utica-Rome labor market area, encompassing Oneida and Herkimer Counties (which, with Madison County, comprise Representative Pirnie's district) received more EDA public works assistance grants than any other area in the country of comparable size and not designated "depressed." To be sure, the grant applications were meritorious in their own right, but a convincing case can be made for the fact that the Utica-Rome-EDA success story was made possible, in large measure, because of the relationship existing between the agency and the area's Congressman.

A Congressman, to be effective, must remain in office. He can never afford to lose sight of this elementary fact. There are no guarantees in politics, no warranties that can be secured on a seat. But there are steps that can be taken to eliminate some of the chance involved. One of the most important steps involves the telling of the Congressman's story. The effectiveness with which the assignment is handled is measured at the polls.

4. Special Audiences of Public Information

T HE "publics" of public information are varied. In addition to the general public, there are specialized groups and audiences that must be reached, both to send and to receive communication. Four such "Special Audiences of Public Information" are described in Part IV.

Local communities constitute one of the most important audiences, especially when they come into direct contact with federal government projects and installations. *William G. McNamara* examines what he calls the "informal channels of public communication" for a community relations program.

Mr. McNamara is intimately involved in one of government's most extensive community relations programs, the Directorate for Community Relations of the U.S. Department of Defense. In this field, his own specialty in informal communication techniques is sports. In addition to being special assistant to the Assistant Secretary of Defense for Public Affairs, he is advisor to the President's Council on Physical Fitness, advisor to the U.S. Olympic Committee, consultant to the Amateur Athletic Union, advisor to the National Collegiate Athletic Association, and Chief of Information for the worldwide Conseil Internationale du Sport Militaire. Mr. McNamara holds a master's degree in public relations from the American University.

Congress is also an important audience for government information, since the lawmakers establish federal programs and provide the funds for their operations. *Ralph K. Huitt* discusses the myths as well as the realities of "Informing the Lawmakers."

141

Mr. Huitt is Assistant Secretary of Health, Education, and Welfare for Legislation. He was formerly professor of political science at the University of Wisconsin. He has worked on both sides of Congressional communications, having served on the staffs of Senator Lyndon B. Johnson, Senator William Proxmire, and Representative Jack Brooks. He was a Johnson speechwriter during the 1960 presidential campaign. A graduate of the University of Texas (Ph.D. in 1950), he has directed research on Congress and legislative processes and is the author of many journal articles.

The business community is another special audience for the government voice. Business relations in the federal government have often been strained, but *James G. Morton* describes the increasing partnership between business and government and the growing lines of communication.

Mr. Morton was formerly special assistant to the Secretary of Commerce for Public Affairs, serving under Luther Hodges, John T. Connor, and Alexander Trowbridge. Prior to entering the government, he was a writer and editorial executive with the *New York Journal American* and an executive of the Hearst Publishing Company, serving as vice president of the American Weekly division.

Mr. Morton is currently director of government relations for the Manufacturing Chemists Association.

One of the most crucial special publics of public information is the taxpaying public. *Joseph S. Rosapepe* examines the manner in which the Internal Revenue Service keeps the taxpayer informed so that the United States government may efficiently collect more than $155 billion a year.

Mr. Rosapepe came to his position as Director of Information for IRS in 1961, after extensive experience as a writer and editor in financial and business news as well as in corporate and government public information. He has been a reporter in Ohio, New York, and Europe, and served as a financial and business editor of the Associated Press in New York. During World War II he served with the Office of War Information and was an account executive for two New York public relations firms for ten years before joining the government in his present position.

COMMUNITY RELATIONS . . .

Communicating at the Grassroots

WILLIAM G. MC NAMARA, SPECIAL ASSISTANT
DIRECTORATE FOR COMMUNITY RELATIONS
U. S. DEPARTMENT OF DEFENSE

THE Department of Defense currently has nearly 3½ million men in uniform and 1½ million civilian employees, concentrated at 483 major military installations throughout the United States and at installations in 54 foreign countries. Each of these installations poses potential community relations problems and offers challenges to military community relations officers.

But community relations problems are not peculiar to the military. Large corporations and other government agencies experience many similar problems in the communities surrounding their domestic and overseas plants and installations. Consequently, the primary effort of many industrial public relations departments is today in the relatively new field of community relations. And skills, techniques, and principles for effective community action are beginning to emerge.

The basic purpose of industrial community relations programs is to effect constructive changes in the attitudinal, legal, and physical environment of the community in which a business operates so as to safeguard and advance the interests of that business in ways which are compatible with the best interests of the community as a whole. In contrast, the basic purposes of the Department of Defense's public information and community relations programs, stated simply, are to bring about the broadest possible public understanding and support of the objectives, accomplishments, problems, and activities of the Department, both at home and abroad.

Their mission is to develop and maintain full understanding by the American people and our overseas allies of our national policy to defend the United States and assist the free world and to demonstrate United States partnership with our allies, not only in matters of collective security but also in matters of mutual interest to the United States and the host nation where our armed forces might be assigned and where United States military facilities are maintained.

The overseas public information and community relations programs of our armed forces have therefore become major segments of the United States effort to promote friendship and communicate the facts about our American way of life. Overall responsibility for these worldwide programs is vested in the Assistant Secretary of Defense for Public Affairs. The incumbent Secretary, the Honorable Phil G. Goulding, is involved in myriad activities, with his charter charging him with responsibility for three broad areas:

1. Provide the American people with maximum information about the Department of Defense, consistent with national security.

2. Initiate and support activities contributing to good relations between the Department of Defense and all segments of the public at home and abroad.

3. Plan for Department of Defense national public media censorship activities during a declared national emergency.

It is the second of these responsibilities that will be explained in this paper. But first we must define community relations and community relations programs. The Department of Defense defines community relations as: "The relationship between military and civilian communities."

Community relations programs may be described as: "That command function which evaluates public attitudes, identifies the mission of a military organization with the public interest, and executes a program of action to earn public understanding and acceptance. Community relations programs include, but are not limited to, such activities as cooperation with government officials and community leaders; encouragement of personnel and their dependents to participate in activities of local schools, churches, fraternal, social and civic organizations, sports and recreation programs, and other aspects of community life; installation open houses and orientation tours; liaison and cooperation with national associations and organizations at all levels; participation in public events; and people-to-people and humanitarian acts."

In light of the current world situation, two primary tasks of the armed forces must be to deter aggression and to maintain the respect and confidence of our friends and allies.

In discharging the latter responsibility, the services utilize two means of communicating with its publics. The first is through the highly organized mass media, and the second is based on direct personal face-to-face contact.

The first might be called a formal means and the latter an informal communication channel. It is with the informal channel that community relations is concerned.

The primary activities in a typical military information office might be informally classified under the two systems as shown in Figure 1.

Persons employing the informal communication channels engage in face-to-face communication with opinion leaders and ascertain what the public does not know about the Department of

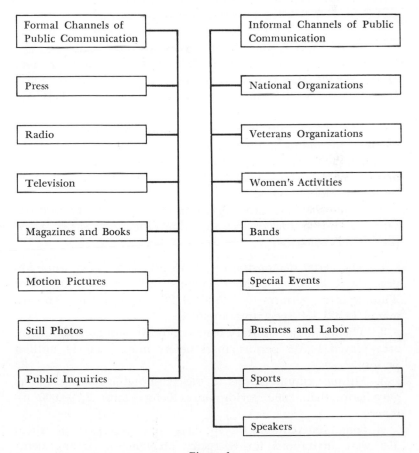

Formal Channels of Public Communication	Informal Channels of Public Communication
Press	National Organizations
Radio	Veterans Organizations
Television	Women's Activities
Magazines and Books	Bands
Motion Pictures	Special Events
Still Photos	Business and Labor
Public Inquiries	Sports
	Speakers

Figure 1

Defense, what it wants to know, and in what areas it is the prey to ignorance, distortion, or misconception.

In summary, the informal communication channel provides the "feedback" which a modern communication system requires to be effective. The two systems are interrelated, with each supporting the other.

Although the organization of community relations offices at all levels is quite similar, their responsibilities vary widely. Consequently, responsibilities and functions at four different command levels will be described—Department of Defense, Military Department, U.S. base, and overseas levels.

As the chart at Figure 2 indicates, the Directorate for Community Relations is organized into divisions and branches. The Director serves as principal staff advisor to the Assistant Secretary of Defense (Public Affairs) in the area of community relations. It is the responsibility of this Directorate to develop plans and formulate policy governing the worldwide program, to provide guidance, and to assure that these programs are properly implemented. In addition, this office becomes directly involved in events of national or international significance and monitors major events at the seat of government involving participation by two or more Services.

The following statistics concerning some community relations activities during 1967 reflect the wide range and varied activities of this office.

1. The aerial demonstration teams, the U.S. Navy Blue Angels, the U.S. Army Golden Knights and the U.S. Air Force Thunderbirds performed a total of 287 engagements. An estimated 14,321,439 spectators attended.

2. The five major military bands in the Washington-Baltimore area played 14,835 performances before more than 11 million persons.

3. Military choral groups in the Washington-Baltimore area gave more than 2000 performances before some 2,700,000 listeners.

4. Some 750 requests for speakers were processed, of which 550 were invitations for Secretary McNamara. Arrangements were completed for more than 300 speakers, including 3 speeches

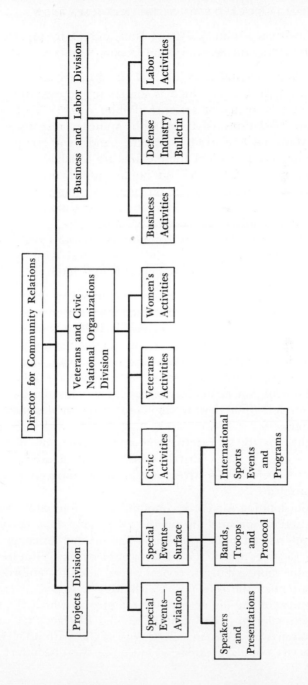

Figure 2

149

by the Chairman, Joint Chiefs of Staff and 44 by top Defense officials, including the Secretary and Deputy Secretary of Defense.

At the Departmental level, each of the military services has a public information office which is similar to the organization of the Assistant Secretary of Defense (Public Affairs). Each has a Community Relations Division with branches responsible for special events, civil relations, speakers, bands, and troops.

The primary functions of these offices are to advise the service secretaries and chiefs of staff on public information and community relations matters. They provide programming and guidance and support to field installations in the United States and overseas, and handle single service programs.

The following extracts from community relations 1967 reports will serve to illustrate the type and variety of activities planned and conducted or supervised at departmental level.

· All four of the military services cooperated in the planning and support of Armed Forces Day activities nationwide.

· From August 1, 1967, to February 1, 1968, a total of 15,312 speeches dealing totally or in part with Vietnam were presented before U. S. audiences. The breakdown by Service was: Marine Corps 5500; Air Force 3812; Army 4800; and Navy 1200.

· Millions of Americans learned about various aspects of the military services from viewing their professionally designed touring exhibits.

· Thanks partly to careful community relations planning, actions to close military installations, in accordance with Department of Defense directives, continued to progress with few serious problems.

· An outstanding Air Force community relations effort was the series of nationwide briefings on the SR-71 aircraft cross-country flights and related noise problems. Twenty-one briefings were given in 15 states which the SR-71 would overfly. Hundreds of news media representatives, civic leaders, and law enforcement officials attended the briefings, which were designed to explain the necessity for the flights and the manner in which the flight routes were selected. The briefings stressed the fact that careful consideration was given to selecting a flight path that would avoid heavily populated areas to minimize the discomfort from possible sonic boom disturbance. As a result, few sonic boom complaints were received.

· The hundredth anniversary of the Navy's Civil Engineer Corps and the twenty-fifth anniversary of the Seabees in 1967 required careful planning and resulted in a number of celebrations across the nation which included participation in the ceremonies by high-ranking state and city officials.

· Under its Command Visit Program, the Marine Corps hosted hundreds of civilian opinion leaders and acquainted them with its activities through direct observation of Marines at work.

· All four services placed increasingly heavier emphasis upon youth activities. Last summer the military services participated in the President's Youth Opportunity Program, providing summer employment for thousands of youngsters. In fact, the military services employed more youths than any other branch of the federal government. Also, many military bases were opened up to underprivileged boys and girls for sports, camping, and other activities.

· Under the guidance of the military services, reserve forces throughout the land are becoming increasingly aware of their community relations role. The young men who have completed active duty and are returning to their reserve units as "veterans" take pride in their past and present contribution to the welfare of this nation and they are now acting as spokesmen for their respective services in the cities and towns where they reside. With the encouragement of their respective services, they are participating more in local and civic events.

A compilation of the most successful community relations projects of the military services would require volumes. Unfortunately, space permits only a sketchy outline of their functions and activities. In summary, they plan single service programs of national interest and provide guidance and direction to their field installations, reservists, and retired personnel.

The base information relations officer must assess the situation in his community relations area (generally a 50-mile radius), develop a plan, and commit all of his resources into the implementation of the plan.

His first function is to evaluate public attitudes for his commander and to correlate the mission of the military organization with public interest. Some information officers conduct their own informal opinion polls to determine what civilians in a given area think about a military base and its personnel. However, one of the most effective methods is the formation of a base-community council. Most bases of any size have such a council.

A typical council would include the mayor, his chief of police, the head of the chamber of commerce and other civilian leaders. Representing the military would be the base commander, his information officer, chaplain, provost marshal, special service officer, housing officer, and others as appropriate.

These councils, which are formed both at home and abroad, provide a vehicle for spotting potential trouble spots in military-civilian relations and for planning effective action to either head them off or minimize their effect.

Next, the base information officer develops a comprehensive community relations plan, generally including the following features:

1. Extending the maximum cooperation and assistance possible to all eligible groups.

2. Encouraging official and unofficial membership of base personnel in community organizations.

3. Including information annexes dealing with community relations aspects to all local plans, whatever their nature.

4. Insuring that local media representatives are given full cooperation, including periodic briefings, access to the highest authority when justified by events, and informal access in addition to officially requested interviews and assignments.

5. Instituting a community relations portion of the local internal information program to inform personnel, both uniformed and civilian, about the community relations program and their part in it. (This generally includes a continuing orientation on local history, customs, and socio-economic factors important to integrating the installation into the community.)

All base resources are then committed to the program. Open houses are held to provide the civilian community with an opportunity to learn about the mission of the base, see some of the military hardware, and ask questions. Bands and troops participate in local events and observances. Military personnel participate in local charity drives. Chaplains, medical officers, judge advocates, and other military professionals are encouraged to participate in the activities and programs of their local civilian counterparts. Military sports teams compete against civilian teams. Military personnel living off base are encouraged to become active in local civilian church affairs and civic activities. An effort is made to get the military and civilians to know each other and to promote mutual understanding and respect.

Overseas bases occasionally encounter community relations problems. A typical case was that of the Strategic Air Command's Moron Air Base, located 40 miles south of Seville, Spain.

The problems Moron faced in the establishment of its program were the religious and cultural differences, and the obvious language barriers. A completely new approach was necessary. An area had to be found where mutual understanding could exist, one which could lead the Americans into a position of respect in the community.

Needed was a common meeting-ground for the jet-age professional SAC-man and the ancient donkey driver and Andalusian shepherd who know animals, the soil, and the weather—and, of course, the church.

The conclusion was that since one novice bullfighter is to be found in any group of ten Andalusians, there would be at least one cowboy in a group of ten of those tall "Norte Americanos."

The Andalusian, who was reared in an agrarian land, and spends his entire life within sight of the bull ring, must have something in common with the American cowboy—the animals and the soil.

It was obvious that this offered a way to bridge the gap. The Americans and the Spanish had found a meeting place where both could use a common language without benefit of formal schooling.

On Sunday, February 21, 1960, more than 10,800 Spaniards were in the stands to see the first of ten full-fledged American rodeos.

Complete coverage was given to the event in the four Seville newspapers and on the radio, but most publicity came from the tradition-bound "Carteles" (Handbills) used to advertise Spanish bullfights.

Close to $3000 was left after bills had been paid and this money was quietly donated to a children's hospital. Nothing but word-of-mouth or newspaper accounts placed by the agencies receiving the charity were ever used to advertise the gifts.

In the Republic of Germany the common meeting ground was found to be music. During the first six months of 1967, command bands played more than 900 engagements to live audiences containing in excess of 4,250,000 people. The Seventh Army Soldiers Chorus toured the Ruhr Valley, performing before enthusiastic audiences at each stop.

In Ethiopia the common meeting ground was found to be wild-life conservation. American members of the Ethiopian Rod and Gun Club inaugurated a program to transplant fresh water trout and bass to streams and lakes near Addis Ababa.

In Libya it was sports. The government appealed for coaching assistance to help prepare its national weightlifting team for the Pan Arab Games. An American private first class, who had been 1964 U.S. national and North American weightlifting champion in his weight class, was assigned to 90 days temporary duty in Tripoli. Under his tutelage, every man on the Libyan team lifted more weight than ever before. In the course of his daily coaching duties this young American private first class was working with the Minister of Youth and Sport, the President of the Libyan Olympic Committee, and the President of the Weightlifting Federation. Needless to say, he won the enduring gratitude of all three.

Carnivals are *the* thing in Latin America. The U.S. military has helped support them and assure their success. For example, in addition to broad participation by military personnel and their dependents in the 1967 carnival celebration in Panama, U.S. military bands were committed during the week of February 18, and 27 trucks of various sizes were provided, 500 folding chairs were loaned, and sundry other items of equipment with operating personnel were loaned. U.S. military participation in the carnival received wide favorable publicity in the Panamanian press and on both Panamanian TV networks.

Support of youth organizations proved another common meeting ground in Latin America. The U.S. Army won widespread gratitude for providing messing and billeting facilities for the Second Inter-American Rural Youth Congress in which representatives of 19 Latin American countries participated.

In far off, war-ravaged Korea, where 50 percent of the entire population is under age 15, the emphasis has been on community improvement and youth activities.

The 314th Air Division assisted in the completion of seven school construction projects, one medical/health center, and one flood drainage project during fiscal year 1967. Thirty-four additional construction projects are currently underway.

Fifty thousand residents of Pyongtaek Eup benefited from a street paving project completed by personnel from Osan Air Base. Asphalt for the project was donated by the base as a part of the excess property disposal plan.

One hundred sixty-eight U.S. military units were sponsoring a total of 134 Korean orphanages by June 1967. Their voluntary contributions provided children's homes throughout the republic with supplies, clothing, money, and various services such as transportation and use of construction equipment.

The Eighth U.S. Army even furnished refrigerated transportation for polio vaccine from the Port of Inchon to the National Institute of Health, at the request of the American-Korean Foundation. The Foundation had received a million dollar shipment of the vaccine from the United States. Later similar arrangements were made for the transport of 130 cartons of diphtheria serum and tetanus-toxoid vaccine donated through the American-Korean Foundation by American sources.

In the Ryukyu Islands 27 emergency medical airlifts of residents of the off-shore islands were provided by the helicopters and aircraft belonging to U.S. military forces in Okinawa.

In the Philippines the U.S. Navy, at the request of local authorities, launched a program to upgrade the caliber of police protection provided for the city of Zambales. Marksmanship training courses were held for 120 officers. Considerable publicity appeared in local newspapers on the program. Because of its popularity, additional courses were conducted with volunteer Marines as instructors.

A four-nation naval task force, on a training exercise, arrived in Buenos Aires in November 1967. The U.S. Navy show band went ashore to make two live appearances on a Buenos Aires TV station and reached an estimated 12 million people. Then the show band played two radio shows, reaching another estimated 12 million listeners. In addition, the band played at four official functions. A great deal of favorable publicity resulted.

In Thailand the Air Force established a tour program for Thai village chiefs. These important leaders from all areas of the country were shown our base and its assigned aircraft. Crews from B-52's and KC-135's briefed the visitors and answered questions. Photographs of the aircraft and a certificate, in Thai, naming each visitor an honorary member of the U.S. Air Force, were given to each chief.

All four of the services are doing a similar job in South Vietnam. The men are contributing their own funds to adopt orphanages and build schools. They are digging wells and teaching farmers new agricultural techniques. In their spare time many are volunteering to do road and bridge repair work. And their role in alleviating the suffering of the refugees is immeasurable. A number of private civilian relief agencies say quite frankly that it would be virtually impossible for them to operate in Vietnam without the assistance of the U.S. armed forces. State Department, USIA, and AID officials also praise the military cooperation they receive in carrying out their programs.

And in far away Alaska many of our citizens would find it difficult to survive without the U.S. armed forces. Almost daily Alaskans read newspaper accounts of daring rescues made in the desolate interior by men of the 21st Composite Wing. As part of the overall search and rescue effort for inland Alaska, these men respond to both civilian and military emergencies. When earthquakes or other natural disasters strike, the armed forces are there caring for the injured, providing shelter, feeding the survivors, guarding against looters and later helping the people get re-established.

Although the foregoing is only a partial list of the thousands of community relations activities carried on by the armed forces, day-in and day-out, throughout the world, it is illustrative of the variety and scope of programs conducted in an effort to win the respect, confidence, and support of both U.S. and foreign nationals.

The effectiveness of overseas military community relations activities was recognized in the final report of the House Committee on Government Operations' findings on overseas military information programs. The Committee found:

"The enormous material and personnel resources represented by American Armed Forces are a major positive factor in the overall effort of the U. S. Government to develop and reserve good relations with the people of the world."*

The overseas community relations program has been described in some detail simply because the average American is frequently unaware of the magnitude of this effort. He reads of isolated incidents and erroneously concludes that troop-community relations in that particular country must be at a low ebb. The hundreds of offsetting good deeds and the thousands of dollars poured into this effort from nonappropriated funds and out of the pockets of individual servicemen go unreported.

It is obvious that the military encounters varied community relations problems throughout the world and that individual community relations officers display skill, ingenuity, and imagination in solving them. Although these officers do have considerable latitude in advising and developing programs for their commanding officers, they are not free-lancing on their own.

The Assistant Secretary of Defense (Public Affairs) is charged with initiating and supporting activities contributing to good relations between the Department of Defense and all segments of the public at home and abroad and he has a military chain of command for implementing this responsibility. He issues guidance and direction to the entire defense establishment. To assist in taking inventory of community relations activities of the armed forces, the Assistant Secretary of Defense for Public Affairs requires a semi-annual report from subordinate echelons of the Department of Defense.

The reader may judge for himself just how effectively the As-

* U.S. Congress, *House Report No. 1549*, 87th Congress, 2d Session, p. 7.

sistant Secretary of Defense for Public Affairs is discharging his community relations responsibilities after considering the following:

· The armed forces sponsor more boy scout and girl scout troops than any other single organization in America. They sponsor more little league teams than any other single organization in the country. More than one million high school students participated last year in the U.S. Marine Corps high school physical fitness program. In fact, the military is active in nearly every aspect of youth work.

· Who has not heard at least one military band during the past year? The hundreds of post, camp, and station bands are constantly playing in the civilian domain. The big Washington-based Army, Navy, Air Force, and Marine Corps bands go on annual tours, and make dozens of radio and TV appearances.

· The aerial demonstration teams perform before live audiences numbering in the millions and additional millions see them on TV.

· Exhibits and static displays of military hardware are placed in hundreds of major air shows. Additional hundreds of military exhibits are seen at state and county fairs, at trade shows, at conventions and even in local shopping centers.

· Millions of people attend open houses at military installations throughout the world and have the opportunity to inspect the latest military hardware and view demonstrations of the combat readiness of our troops.

· Speakers bureaus at our military installations provide thousands of speakers for interested civilian groups. And the Department of Defense speakers bureau in the Pentagon handled hundreds of additional requests for appearances or talks by our "top" military leaders.

· Pentagon tours and briefings are given to thousands of visitors. Full cooperation is given in the planning and execution of dozens of multi-agency federal programs.

In summary, the main objective of the Department of Defense is obtaining and operating the required level of military power at the lowest possible cost. That goal is sensible in a department that is spending over $70 billion per year, 10 percent of the nation's wealth. It is the public's business to know what we are doing in the armed services because we belong to the public.

But we cannot let them know what we are doing if we simply stay at our stations. We have to mix with them, let them know what we are like, what we are thinking about, that we are humans just as they are, and that we are only citizens wearing uniforms. Consequently, at all of our installations throughout the world our officers and men are urged to join in the community life of the cities and towns nearby. They are asked to get out and mix and talk and associate with the leaders of the communities, and make clear to them that our mission is to defend America and assist our free-world allies. This, in sum and substance, is why the Department of Defense has community relations programs.

CONGRESSIONAL RELATIONS . . .

Informing the Lawmakers

RALPH K. HUITT
ASSISTANT SECRETARY FOR LEGISLATION
U.S. DEPARTMENT OF HEALTH,
EDUCATION, AND WELFARE

WHEN I talk to old friends about my new life in Washington sooner or later the question comes: How much time do you spend on the cocktail circuit? This notion that public policy is made at parties is a durable myth. There are even old Washington hands who insist that they read the society page each day to know what policy is being decided. There is just enough truth in this old canard to keep it alive—and that is very little truth indeed.

Many times I have had a warm, friendly conversation at a party with a member of Congress who a week later did not recognize me in the House Office Building. But that has not happened after I have done an honest piece of mutually productive work with a member in his office.

There are other myths about working with Congress.

One is that the really big issues are won by "arm-twisting"— that is, by pressure of some sort. Again, it would be foolish to deny that this has ever happened. But not many public officials or private interest groups can muster enough leverage to influence a member of Congress against his will. And when it *is* done successfully the price is high. No one likes to be pushed around and most people will "pay it back" if they can. The number and variety of ways a congressman can pay back make "arm-twisting" a technique to shun.

Another myth is that votes can be bought by favors from executive officials, by votes in elections, by campaign contributions, or by just plain cash from interest groups.

It certainly is true that powerful congressmen are likely to get more for their districts than freshmen do. But laws on grants and contracts are strict and no favor makes a permanent friend, so this is a limited game at best. Members of Congress indubitably must raise campaign money, but they get it from many sources; no one contributor is likely to be indispensable. Moreover, people tend to give money to politicians whose views they share; the oldest rule in politics is to support one's friends.

The simple fact is that the conditions of modern politics make corruption an extremely high-risk enterprise with no insurance against failure available at any price. Private associations invest large sums over long periods of time to create a favorable "image" and advance their interests with the public. A whiff of scandal

163

may spoil it all. Who will forget the expensive but legitimate campaign of natural gas interests to pass a bill (favored by President Eisenhower) which was wrecked overnight by a few injudicious "campaign contributions" offered by an eager amateur?

The situation of a member of Congress is much the same. His career is the major investment of his life. It would be hard to offer him enough to justify his putting it in jeopardy.

If these popular conceptions of ways to move members of Congress are largely myths, how then may one go about it with a chance of success?

A good way to answer this question about any man is to pay attention to how he gets and keeps his job and how he goes about making good at it.

A member of Congress gets his job by persuading enough people in his district or state to vote for him. He keeps it the same way. And most of the time his success at the polls depends on what he is able to do for himself.

Political parties are important in American life but they are seldom decisive in congressional elections. It is true that in a bad year for their party many marginal members will lose, and in a very bad year even established politicians can be defeated—just as a presidential landslide may carry with it many temporary seats in Congress. But these tides are too large for the individual member to do anything about.

Moreover, he knows the crucial importance of his personal relationship with his constituency. He knows that President Roosevelt at the height of his popularity could not purge dissident Democratic congressmen. He knows that party leaders in Congress (Lucas of Illinois, McFarland of Arizona, Ferguson of Michigan, to name a few) were retired irrevocably from national politics by their own states.

It is understandable, therefore, that his ear is attuned to the voices back home, however contradictory and ill-informed they may seem to be. That is why he spends so much time on airplanes that connect him with his constituents. That is why the Washington representatives of private associations try to reach him through their members in his constituency. And that is why Washington officials work closely with private associations who share their point of view.

Broadly speaking, there are two ways to see to it that the voices from home tell the congressman what one wants him to hear.

One was demonstrated most effectively in the 1920s by the electric light and power industry. Finding that most expressions of public opinion showed a clear majority favoring public ownership of utilities, the industry launched a massive public relations campaign to create a favorable climate of opinion for private ownership. All the techniques of persuasion known and available in that day were employed—and within a decade were highly successful.

Obviously, no agency of government can proceed in quite the same way; indeed, Congress has attempted in numerous statutes to keep it from trying. Paradoxically, the agency *must* make an effort. The law requires it to promote public acceptance of its programs and to report on them to Congress and the public. Not surprisingly, the agency will try to put its best foot forward.

The rules for success are roughly the same for both public and private information programs. The information officers must participate in policy councils; they do not make policy but they assess probable public reaction to it and they must know it to explain it. Needless to say, the explanation must be honest. Nothing else will stand up long.

The second way was developed even earlier by the Anti-Saloon League. Their strength came from organizing at every level of government so that pressure could be applied to most any public official by the people who could make it hurt. They set out frankly to reward their friends and punish their enemies. The test was a single issue: How does he stand on prohibition? Not many private associations have proceeded with such brutal directness, but the basic formula has not changed. On national issues the Washington office supplies intelligence and calls signals; the local membership communicates with congressmen. This technique is *not* available to public agencies but it will be freely employed by friends and opponents alike in the private sphere.

So it is not liquor or pressure or favors that most influence a congressman but support from his friends at home. This is what secures his political base and makes it possible for him to be an effective member of Congress.

This makes it possible, but does not assure it. For this he must make good in his own house. Which means preeminently that he must participate successfully in the work of its committees.

Woodrow Wilson recognized this long ago in his classic work, *Congressional Committees,* where he wrote that "Congressional government is Committee government" and that "it is not far from the truth to say that Congress in session is Congress on public exhibition, whilst Congress in its committee-rooms is Congress at work."

That is as close to the truth today as it was in 1884. Because Congress and the executive branch are separated by the Constitution, the bridge between legislature and executive which is provided in parliamentary systems by the ministers (who are leaders of *both* branches of government) must be made some other way. For the same reason the houses of Congress cannot look to their own leaders to vouch for the information provided by the bureaucracy; they must establish some independent agencies of their own to sift and test it. The agencies they have provided are the standing committees with their respective specialized jurisdictions.

The committees have come to be legislative subsystems (or "little legislatures" as they are often called) with usually decisive influence on legislation. The bills considered by the parent bodies are the bills their committees report. When there are differences in bills passed by the two houses, the bill sent to the President is the one agreed upon in conference between the leaders of the respective committees.

Needless to say, the chairmen and the ranking minority members of the committees are important legislative leaders; if they are weak, their lack of effectiveness is a vital factor in the output of their committees. When they are effective, they are prime forces in the policy they consider and in the life of their house. The committees make up among them more than a system of information; they are also a system of power. The committee chairmen are chieftains with whom the party leaders in both branches must deal or contend. When chairmen must divide up the work among subcommittees they also share power, however grudgingly, with subcommittee chairmen.

For the individual member the road is clear: the respect of his peers and influence on policy come from hard and competent work on his committee (for a member of the Senate, who belongs to two or more committees and several subcommittees, the opportunities are more varied, but the development of expertise is correspondingly more difficult). This is the way the junior member can separate himself from his peers in the eyes of senior members. And this is the way he can assure that if he should ever become chairman he can maximize the power and prestige that are potentially his.

The person outside Congress who would influence legislation, for a governmental agency or a private group, must do what the member must do: go to the committee. He must know the leaders of the full committee and the relevant subcommittees and he must know the staff who serve them. He must know the individual member whose interest and expertise in a particular aspect of the committee's subject may make him the vital spur to action.

His task is complicated by the dual character of congressional action: authorization and appropriation. Very little moves in the federal establishment without money; the legislative committees authorize spending but the appropriations committees provide or deny funds. Needless to say, a dramatic legislative victory turns to dust when no money is allowed. The potential power of subcommittees is strikingly realized in the appropriation process because of the complexity of the task of passing on thousands of expenditure items. It is common for our appropriations subcommittee in the House of Representatives to spend several months on a bill which moves through full committee and House in a matter of hours.

Influence with a committee often turns therefore on detailed mastery of the subject matter of the committee. It has a job to do; its members and staff work with those who can help them. That is why anonymous experts in the bureaucracy are so important to federal-agency relations with Congress, and why private associations maintain research divisions. This is not to say that facts speak for themselves, that there are objective data which obviate subjective choices—far from it. Most members of Congress are men with values; they are for or against, they want more or less. But there are better ways to do what one wants to do and there must be persuasive support for one's position. The expert is indispensable.

But beyond that, the position must be dramatized. The committee hearing provides a forum and a stage. Issues are argued and needs dramatized. In this phase, too, resources must be spent wisely; economy may be as imprudent as prodigality. A bureau chief should not be sent to do a secretary's work (nor a private association's executive secretary for its president), nor the reverse. And there are times when a parade of nearly inarticulate beneficiaries of an established program (or people who purportedly need a proposed new one) may be made to tell an eloquent story. The stage manager also has a crucial job to do.

After that, the legislative liaison person follows the general rules of good personal relationships. The policy interests and positions of the committee members are his basic data. He treats his avowed opponents with respect but he does not try to change their minds. He does the best he can to influence the decisions of the uncommitted. But the members who share his values, and are in this sense his friends, are his basic resources, and those among this group who are industrious, intelligent, and deeply committed are his jewels beyond price. To win and keep their allegiance he must work honestly and faithfully with them on mutual concerns; he must give them the best and most reliable information he can; he must keep his word and honor his obligations.

And he must never, never lie—not to them nor to any other member. The legislative lobbyist who is not trusted by friend and enemy alike should read the obituaries: his name is there.

BUSINESS RELATIONS . . .

Dealing with the Industrial World

JAMES G. MORTON
DIRECTOR OF GOVERNMENT RELATIONS
MANUFACTURING CHEMISTS ASSOCIATION
FORMER SPECIAL ASSISTANT TO THE SECRETARY
OF COMMERCE FOR PUBLIC AFFAIRS

WHEN President Kennedy called a White House Conference for Business Editors and Publishers in September 1962, the declared purpose was "to continue and enhance the dialogue between business and government."

This glossy facade failed to obscure the more pressing motive. Washington watchers sized up the conference as a high-powered public relations effort to help heal the deep wounds in the Administration's relations with business. The agenda supported that conclusion with practically the entire Cabinet in the batting order.

The need for ameliorating the government's relationship with business was clear and urgent. Both sides were arrayed in a cold war, and it was imposing serious penalties on an Administration which had gained office by the narrowest margin.

In April, five months earlier, President Kennedy had castigated the steel companies for "wholly unjustifiable and irresponsible defiance of the public interest" when they attempted to raise prices in the wake of a wage settlement. The President angrily denounced industry leaders as "a tiny handful of steel executives whose pursuit of private power and profits exceeds their sense of public responsibility."

As the steel industry succumbed under intolerable pressure from the White House, a shudder went through a business community outraged and frightened by police state methods allegedly employed during the fiasco and resentful of federal dictation over private decision-making.

The steel industry, business writer Joseph R. Slevin later noted, "does not have the same freedom of decision it had before President Kennedy forced it to rescind the price boost. It has permanently changed the relationship between the Federal Government and the steel companies."

In that time frame at least it changed the relationship between the federal government and business as a whole. Apprehension over the infringement of private rights and federal interference in the free market system produced a serious breach in business confidence. The confrontation left livid and lasting scars.

President Kennedy, with his gift for understatement, acknowledged in his meeting with business editors that "there seems to be, on occasion, some question among businessmen as to the views of those of us in Washington" on the competitive market system.

"Our experience during the present expansion," he said, "has demonstrated our ability to achieve impressive economic gains without shrinking the area of market freedom. I regard the preservation and strengthening of the free market as a cardinal objective of this or any other administration's policies."

Kennedy made repeated and earnest efforts to gain the confidence and understanding of businessmen. Although he never succeeded in winning enthusiastic business support, he planted the seeds of thoughtful examination of the relationship between the business community and the government. Those seeds were later to flower and bear fruit.

Following President Kennedy's assassination, Lyndon B. Johnson moved quickly to establish effective channels of communication with business leaders and build trust and confidence and comity between business and the White House.

At a meeting in the East Room on January 22, 1964, he told businessmen participating in the Plans for Progress program: "I think that when the final gong is sounded the thing that is going to determine whether we survive or not is our free enterprise system."

"I believe," President Johnson said, "that the capitalist who sends his dollar out with the hope of getting a return on it, the manager who gets up at daylight and works to midnight and develops stomach ulcers handling the men and the money, and the worker who takes the sweat of his brow and hits the production lines at a trot, taking pride in what comes off the assembly line—the combination of those three, all of whom get a slice of the pie, along with a Government that is friendly and helpful and encouraging, and providing incentive, making the fourth partner—I believe they can outdo and outproduce and outwork any collective system in the world."

President Johnson opened the door of the White House and extended his hand to businessmen. The word went through the business community: we have in the White House a Chief Executive who discerns and understands the needs and problems of business.

This general feeling and the sense of change permeated the massive honeycomb of the Commerce Department. The cold war was over. The President had ushered in an era of good feeling that was to withstand many trials and tests.

Before the National Industrial Conference Board in February 1965 President Johnson enunciated as a central theme of his philosophy and his administration the "partnership for progress." Calling for a joint endeavor by business, labor, and government, Johnson said, "I ask you as enlightened men of our times to join as a full partner in all the problems of the nation, the social problems as well as the economic problems. For we shall be judged not by what we take with us but the society we leave behind us."

The President habitually mixed biblical canons with earthy pragmatism in advancing his ideas. In business thinking there was growing recognition that the conditions that are good for a community cannot be disassociated from the conditions that are good for business. The President knew that enlightened self-interest was an essential motivation in gaining business support of his social objectives.

Johnson took prompt and vigorous action to translate the blueprint for his partnership into brick and mortar. The Treasury liberalized its depreciation guidelines to encourage and facilitate the modernization and expansion of industry.

The Administration pushed for a seven percent investment tax credit, a major piece of legislation that set the country on a new course of growth and prosperity.

Corporate income taxes, along with individual income taxes, which had been maintained at excessive levels established in time of emergency, were reduced to stimulate the economy and produce a new surge of business gains.

The relations between business and government buoy and ebb according to the flow of events. The relationship warms as the economy prospers, and a cooling trend sets in as problems emerge. In this respect the problems of prosperity tend to produce strains more difficult than a period of economic stagnation.

The President's efforts to apply the brakes to an overheated economy led to serious difficulties with the business community and differences within his inner circle of advisers.

The wage-price guideposts, with their built-in inequities, uneven application, and heavy-handed administration, proved a constant irritant between business and the White House.

Ignored in large part by labor, the wage-price policy was a seedbed of discontent that at times threatened the whole structure of business-government cooperation to which the President devoted so much of his energies and hopes.

The most severe buffeting was occasioned by the use of stockpiles and other devices to enforce guideposts. The President's relations with business sank to a low ebb when government stockpiles were employed to force a price rollback by the aluminum industry.

While President Johnson had his ups and downs with industry, there was never truly any general feeling that the government was hostile to business nor were businessmen in general torn by anxiety and apprehension over infringement of their rights.

Johnson's "partnership for progress" was a rational and positive approach to the problems of the country and the economy. The practical wisdom of it appealed to most businessmen, although on occasion some took issue with certain ways the partnership worked.

The joining of business and government in a common effort to solve the nation's problems was, indeed, an inevitability in the kind of world we live in today.

This is a time of transition for America. It is also, as the President observed, "a time of testing." Dynamic forces of growth and change pose challenges of great magnitude and complexity that test the resilience and viability of our system.

The problems of the day are, in fact, so complicated that the joint participation and best efforts of our public and private institutions are in most cases essential to satisfactory resolution. And partial solutions sometimes are the best that can be expected for the present.

In looking down the road it was clear to the President that the federal government could not by itself produce all the answers. He summoned many hundreds, indeed thousands, of businessmen to help formulate policy and devise programs in a broad range of national endeavors.

He also appealed to business leaders to act on their own initiative in attacking hard-core unemployment, poverty in the ghettos, and a host of other emerging problems of a highly industrialized society.

The estimates vary but certainly the number of businessmen working with federal agencies is the equivalent of several Army divisions and the number cooperating in priority efforts by the government runs to a very high count.

In the Department of Commerce alone the scope of voluntary participation is impressive. More than a thousand business executives are actively engaged in a nationwide drive to increase U.S. exports.

The persistent deficit in the balance of payments and the drain on the nation's gold reserves make it crucially important to build the U.S. trade surplus. The voluntary effort was headed by Carl Gerstacker, chairman of the Dow Chemical Company, as the Vietnam war worsened the dollar outflow.

The Commerce Technical Advisory Board was established to bring business minds and experience to bear on the fuller utilization of technology. A highly prestigious group of industry chieftains headed by Albert Nickerson, chairman, Socony Mobil Corporation, and Carter Burgess, chairman, American Machine and Foundry, guided the voluntary program instituted in February 1965 to redress the balance of payments deficit.

One could go on with a voluminous catalogue of business leaders serving in advisory roles in the Cabinet agencies, the independent federal agencies, on presidential commissions and committees, and in other capacities to aid the government.

President Johnson's approach to business government relations was direct and personal. He maintained a continuing dialogue with numerous leaders of industry and finance, discussing problems and issues with them regularly by telephone and in person.

It was not unusual for a cabinet officer, in discussing a problem with a banker or industrialist, to be told: "The President talked to me about that last evening."

During the Johnson administration the voice of government to business was first and foremost the voice of LBJ. The President shrewdly utilized involvement to gain the support of businessmen and their active participation in the pursuit of his social and economic objectives.

Businessmen are helping to widen employment opportunities, support better education, retrain workers whose skills have been outmoded by change, and end second-class citizenship, which denies many of our people a chance in life.

They are working to ease racial tensions, eradicate the ghettos, curb air and water pollution, combat juvenile delinquency, and make our cities more liveable.

Tens of thousands of employers answered the government's plea to provide a million summer jobs for teenagers under the Youth Opportunity program.

Retired executives were recruited to render technical assistance to small businesses. Others were enlisted in programs to help developing countries acquire American management know-how and efficiency.

Although businessmen frequently complain that "the government asks our advice but doesn't follow it," the fact remains that the ideas and the influence of businessmen are being felt in more places and more levels in government than ever before.

A continuation of this broad participation of businessmen in public affairs will have a profound effect in shaping governmental policies in the future.

The growing rapport has, in fact, elicited concern in liberal quarters. Recently an economist of national stature expressed apprehension that the convergence of public and private establishments threatens the pluralism in our society and the healthy balance that has sustained our freedom and progress.

Executives of large corporations have come to realize that it benefits business to operate in a healthy political and social environment and that it is essential to work for stability and development of the system as a whole.

Beyond this inescapable reality of modern-day America, advancing technology dictates that government and business cooperate in an increasing range of joint endeavors. It was not feasible, and probably not possible, for industry to develop a nuclear ship, a communications satellite, a supersonic transport, or atomic power without government participation. Joint participation was no less essential in manpower training, the development of more modern transportation systems, the expansion of trade, and the development and use of technology. The widening plain of common ground has become so great that the practical realities offer little choice but continuation and extension of business-government cooperation in the future.

There will always be areas of conflict and disagreement, of course. These can be minimized by improved communication. Communication is the precursor of understanding. And understanding—a mutual appreciation of each other's responsibilities and objectives—is the larger part of resolving differences that are more often reconcilable than fundamental.

Hard experience has taught that communication of purpose is unfailingly difficult, however. That is why harmony and cooperation are of such tenuous fiber. In nearly every failure there is somewhere a communication failure.

Communication is especially difficult in a political environment where the interpretation of policies and actions so frequently depends on one's doctrine and one's vantage point.

On the government side, the inhibitions and limitations impeding the communications function far exceed those in any other sphere of activity.

Communication is clearly the lifeline of business-government cooperation. It follows that a breakdown in communications could lead to a breakup in the partnership that is working so well in attacking the complex and demanding problems of a densely urbanized society. Thus it goes without saying that on the part of both business and government maintaining effective communication is a vital and never-ending task.

In this light it is relevant to examine some of the policies and practices the federal government follows in communicating with business and the inhibiting factors that impede the process.

The flow of information from Washington is impressive in the sheer weight and volume of paper. A vast stream of news releases, studies, surveys, technical data, statistics, reports, and other information pours from the federal agencies by the millions.

The Commerce Department alone issues more than 5 million copies of news releases, technical reports, business statistics, economic data, commercial intelligence, and other information each year. A hundred information specialists produce and process this output. The payroll exceeds $1,000,000 a year.

Numerous other agencies contribute to the massive outpouring

of facts and figures and other information of interest to business
—the Securities and Exchange Commission, the Treasury, Small
Business Administration, the State Department, Federal Trade
Commission, the Defense Department, the Post Office, the Tariff
Commission, the Bureau of Labor Statistics, the Department of
Transportation, Federal Communications Commission, the In-
terior Department, Food and Drug Administration, and the list
goes on to a very considerable length.

In 1966 the Government Printing Office supervised the printing of 1.17 billion copies of government releases and documents
for which the executive branch and legislative branch were billed
$167.2 million. Federal spending for informational activities
ranged from $375 to $400 million, apart from printing costs.

Not an inconsiderable part of this substantial outlay is ex-
pended for communication with business. In turn, business makes
huge expenditures for its communication with government.

The tide of information flowing from Washington to the business community is beamed at a broad and varied array of constituents. There is no central focus. Indeed, there is no central
focal point through which the government deals with business or
business with the government.

The businessman calls at one time on the Federal Trade Com-
mission; another time he calls at the Treasury; or at the Defense
Department, the Small Business Administration, the Agency for
International Development, the Export-Import Bank.

Unlike the farmer, who looks to the Department of Agriculture,
or organized labor, which looks to the Department of Labor,
business pursues its interests across the broad range of the federal
establishment, the point of contact depending on the nature of
the problem.

This has tended to deprive the Commerce Department of an
identifiable and substantial constituency and thus weaken its
voice in policy determination.

The varied agencies and strata through which business works
greatly compounds the problem of communication on both sides.
There are many voices of government and very often those voices
reflect differing positions within the government. Industry, too,
has many and diverse voices with the result that the channels of
communication between business and government are neither
clear nor consonant.

Beyond the problem of achieving a good communications focus, the government is burdened with inhibitions and limitations in communicating with business.

The American public is historically suspicious of Big Government, and especially of informational activities, which it is prone to regard as propaganda.

The United States Chamber of Commerce magazine, *Nation's Business,* conducts a running battle against government information practices. In an article titled "Uncle Sam's Brainwashing Machine" it blasted the government for "resorting in a greater and greater degree to propaganda in its rising zeal for promotion and publicity."

The Congress also keeps a vigilant and skeptical eye on government information practices, as it of course should. This is not only healthy but essential under the democratic system where government actions must be regularly examined and called to account.

But it is a fact that the party out of power unfailingly accuses the party in power of employing federal personnel and funds for propaganda. So the government information officer is caught in a political crossfire in which ducking for cover is for many the better part of valor.

On one hand, there are charges that extravagant funds are being spent to publicize federal programs and activities; on the other are accusations of covering up and denying information to the public. The net of it is the information officer is damned if he doesn't and damned if he does.

In my years as a Commerce official the press was by and large fair and objective. More than fair, it often rendered invaluable support to truly important government programs.

The cooperation we received in carrying out the difficult and complex balance of payments program was in the finest tradition of public service.

The four Commerce chiefs who have guided the department through the 1960s—Luther Hodges, John T. Connor, Alexander Trowbridge, and C. R. Smith—all considered the working press an indispensable partner in the pursuit of our missions.

Without the business press especially it would not be possible for the Commerce Department to achieve its objectives. It was our credo in the Commerce Department that the public has a right to know and the federal government a duty to inform. Carrying out this policy was inexpressively more difficult than describing it. A number of times we were under editorial attack for performing functions that were considered the province of private media. Admittedly, it is difficult to draw a definitive boundary and in the case of doubt the decision should benefit the private sector.

A New York magazine publisher once protested that *International Commerce,* the department's weekly digest of worldwide commercial intelligence on investment and market opportunities abroad, was in competition with his own periodical on foreign trade. We indicated our willingness to consider suspending the publication providing he would guarantee to publish the information in full in his magazine. He frankly acknowledged it would be neither feasible nor profitable to do that and the matter was dropped. The magazine in question cost the government more than $250,000 a year over its subscription revenue. But it was a vitally important tool in fulfilling the statutory responsibilities of the agency and achieving U.S. trade objectives.

A major Southern daily was highly critical of a Sunday feature service we initiated in the Commerce Department. Yet in the same issue it devoted a full page to one of the features. Overlooked in the editorial was that a substantial part of our output was devoted to public safety—warnings on hurricanes, tornadoes, earthquakes, tidal waves, floods, and rip currents that claim hundreds of lives and wreak millions of dollars in property losses each year.

On Palm Sunday—April 11, 1965—a rampage of devastating tornadoes killed 272 persons, injured hundreds more, and inflicted $250 million in property damage in the Midwest. Newspapers demanded an improved warning system and better public education on safety measures. Not many weeks before, one of those newspapers had attacked our information output as a waste of public funds. Unused had been an article called "Killer in the Clouds"—a warning on tornadoes.

During John T. Connor's term in the Cabinet the Charleston, W. Va., *Gazette-Mail* launched an attack on my activities that impugned my motives and conjured up a bogeyman to scare the public. In an editorial titled *Could the CIA Be Behind This*

Baffling Procedure? the writer saw sinister implications in my sending to businessmen and certain news executives a State Department report on President Johnson's historic journey to seven nations in the Pacific.

In studying the document we were convinced it would be very useful to businessmen planning to expand their markets or investments in the Far East. The document spelled out the Manila Declaration and provided an illuminating insight into the concerns and aspirations of the Asian peoples. The main obstacle that many American businessmen encountered in the Far East was the lingering suspicion of colonial exploitation. The Communists shrewdly characterized American enterprise in that region as economic colonialism.

It stood to reason that businessmen could achieve their objectives far more effectively if they could identify their activities with the objectives and aspirations of the Asian peoples. The document was an effective guide for such an approach. For that reason it was mailed to hundreds of businessmen active in international trade and investment and those who were primary prospects for overseas ventures. Scores of appreciative responses were received and a substantial number of additional copies was requested.

One might ask why the document was also sent to news media. It was a courtesy we always practiced. I thought that if businessmen were to discuss in local circles any of the informational matter we distributed, an editor or publisher would want to be familiar with it.

From the U.S. commercial listening posts all over the world a steady stream of trade leads and investment opportunities flows into Washington regularly. To bring the American businessman together with opportunities abroad was a constant challenge to the Commerce Department. As Secretary, Luther Hodges devoted much attention to improving the flow and widening the use of commercial intelligence.

One of the problems was how to win the interest of those who were not aware of profit opportunities in export trade. We created a weekly news service called *Trade Tips* for Monday business pages when the normal news flow was slack. Through this device we succeeded in reaching 4 million business readers. Large dailies like the *Philadelphia Bulletin,* the *Cleveland Plain Dealer,* the *Pittsburgh Post Gazette,* and the *Newark News* instituted the new feature on a regular basis.

But a respected editor in one of the nation's major gateways blasted us with both barrels for wasting money and duplicating a service performed by trade organizations. He was wrong on one score—the project was handled by existing staff. He missed the point on the other—we were endeavoring to reach the man who had not taken the plunge in foreign trade, not those already engaged.

These examples are cited to indicate the kind of obstacles a federal agency encounters in endeavoring to communicate with business and the public.

Federal agencies are exceedingly sensitive, as they should be, to public criticism, especially in the press. More often than not a critical editorial back home prompts an inquiry from a Congressman or Senator. There often follows an investigation.

A certain defensiveness and timidity inhibit government information practice as a result of long exposure to the slings and arrows which come from many directions.

Caution and hesitance tend to suffocate initiative and innovation and dynamic ideas. And the process of communication suffers. Federal employees often are blamed for the frequently dull and lackluster character of government information; but it is the circumstances under which they must work that are mainly at fault.

As the official chiefly responsible for the public affairs of the Commerce Department I discovered a high level of competence in the career ranks. Writers like Horace Knowles, Ann Cook, Paul Walsh, Fred Philips, Barbara Boardman, Ray Wilcove, Irma White, Jim Southerland, Miles Waggoner, Gene Fleming, J. F. Reilly, and numerous others had the imagination and intellectual gifts to succeed anywhere. Despite the inhibitions and limitations, they turned out inspired work in communicating with the business and technical communities.

Communication is fundamental to a functioning partnership between business and government. If these two creative forces are to succeed in the great tasks of America, there must be a clear and constant dialogue. We must strive for excellence in communications; and, perhaps even more important, we must set the conditions that produce excellence.

TO COLLECT $155 BILLION . . .

Keeping the Taxpayers Informed

JOSEPH S. ROSAPEPE
DIRECTOR OF INFORMATION
U. S. INTERNAL REVENUE SERVICE

No one likes to pay taxes. Overcoming the obstacles to understanding created by this negative emotional attitude about taxes is a public relations challenge.

On a strictly intellectual level nearly everyone recognizes that taxes are necessary. "Taxes are the price we pay for civilization," said Oliver Wendell Holmes. National defense, roads, schools, welfare and health services, interest on the public debt, and subsidies to various industries are all reasons for taxes. Unfortunately, the correlation between wanting certain services from organized government and actually paying the taxes that make them possible often gets lost.

From a public relations standpoint, the problem of raising the level of understanding about taxes is not a simple one, mainly because it is difficult to find even one segment of the public that has a favorable or receptive attitude toward taxes.

The public relations program of the Internal Revenue Service is a broadly based consumer effort to help 100,000,000 individuals file some 80,000,000 accurate federal returns—and to help some 5,000,000 business organizations ranging from two-man partnerships to the nation's largest corporations. In addition, there is an effort to reach two specialized publics—the 200,000 accountants and lawyers who service taxpayers and the 30,000,000 high school students who, if not paying taxes already, will become taxpayers when they complete their education.

To achieve the goal of informing this vast group of individual taxpayers and other special segments of the public, the IRS uses most of the standard methods and techniques developed over the years in professional public relations practice.

From a professional standpoint, evaluation of the IRS public information activities is helped by the relatively measurable elements of money collected, money refunded, and percentage of correct or incorrect returns.

The IRS was established by Abraham Lincoln in 1862, to collect a wartime income tax that lasted a decade. Legislative and judicial skirmishes from 1894 to 1913 ended in passage of the Sixteenth Amendment setting up the income tax. In 1938, the government had collected $5.6 billion from about 8,000,000 taxpayers. Since most of these taxpayers were in the high-income brackets and had tax accountants, there was almost no public information need or problem.

185

By 1945, paying for World War II had broadened the base of taxpayers to 45,000,000. Under the withholding system devised by Beardsley Ruml of Macy's, collections had soared to nearly $44 billion. With this mass operation, the need for informing the newly taxed public became apparent.

Today the need is greater than ever. With almost 80,000,000 individual returns expected this year, with a total collection of more than $155 billion, there is an absolute necessity for having well-informed taxpayers. Moreover, the tax collecting machinery is complicated by the technological impact of computer systems and their effect on tax administration.

Until 1961, the IRS had been using almost every kind of business machine available on the market, but the avalanche of paper was threatening to inundate it. Nearly half a billion pieces of paper were expected by the mid-'60's; some 100,000,000 individual and business returns and 400,000,000 information returns (W-2's from employers and 1099's from banks and corporations) could have overwhelmed the system completely.

Now, computers at the national center in Martinsburg, West Virginia, and at regional centers in seven other locations have made it possible to check every tax return.

More errors are detected by the computers, and more people are being contacted by letters, bills, and notices as errors are found. There are, however, two sides to this coin. First, the negative one, which is inherent in the cyclical nature of the IRS computer system. For example, if a taxpayer sends in an explanation of an error or a payment that has been requested, the transaction may not be recorded on the magnetic tape until the next weekly cycle of the tightly scheduled 24-hour a day three-shift operation. Meanwhile, the taxpayer may get another computer-generated bill. This frustrates him and he writes another letter. To make matters worse, he may get still another bill before the master file account is reconciled.

This is obviously a major public relations problem and there are no easy solutions. Any effort to take a return out of the computer processing system—to answer an inquiry by manual means—would take it out of the cycle and delay any refund a taxpayer might have coming.

Persons who have encountered difficulties with banks or department stores embarking on computer systems know how frustrating the situation can get before it is smoothed out.

To cope with the situation, IRS has embarked on a concentrated program of simplifying the computer-generated letters. With the participation of interdivisional committees and the aid of an experienced management consultant, IRS has attempted to take the legal jargon out of the letters and make them understandable to the ordinary taxpayer.

The whole public information program has been designed to prevent errors which inconvenience the taxpayer by delaying his refund, requiring time-consuming correspondence, or necessitating an audit. For the government, errors mean increased costs of operation, which, in the final analysis, mean more expense to the public.

Costs of operation are important to IRS, because its reputation for being one of the best-managed government agencies rests not only on its efforts to deal fairly with taxpayers, but also on its efficiency in collecting the revenue. Everyone who has been involved in any fund-raising activity recognizes the difficulty of keeping costs down. For the past decade it has cost IRS less than half a cent to collect each dollar. This is a far cry from the highest figure recorded—5.8 cents in 1871.

For the IRS, the computers point the way to the public information objectives of error prevention. In 1967, some 3,900,000 taxpayers made mathematical errors of addition or subtraction. These were caught by the computers in the seven regional centers and resulted in additional taxes of $207,000,000 and refunds of $94,000,000 (nearly a third of these mistakes resulted in overpayments).

A second type of error is the "processing" error. This is where errors foul up the processing of returns and delay some of the 50,000,000 refunds of nearly $10 billion that taxpayers will receive. In 1967 these errors included nearly 2,300,000 omitted or erroneous Social Security numbers, 903,000 uses of wrong tables or columns, 466,000 returns without W-2's or schedules and 309,000 without signatures.

News releases based on these statistics of errors by taxpayers are issued to the news media and are heavily used during the filing period between January 1 and April 15. Positive information that can help prevent inconvenience or delays to taxpayers is also the theme of radio announcements and television spots that are used as a public service.

The theme is basically "Read the Instructions." This message was emblazoned on 50,000 Post Office trucks throughout March and was the basic story in IRS' 30-minute film, "Paying for the U.S.A.," starring E. G. Marshall, which is being telecast by many commercial and educational stations.

The wire services, feature syndicates, individual columnists, and some legal and accounting societies prepare columns of tax tips for newspapers and magazines. The IRS supplements these efforts with a weekly question and answer column based on inquiries made each week to the IRS offices throughout the nation.

This emphasis on dialogue is carried out in many of the IRS offices where experienced and articulate personnel—from IRS district directors to revenue agents and revenue officers—participate in TV and radio audience "Q&A" programs. Officers also appear before professional, business and civic clubs in their local areas.

The public information program goes beyond attempting to reduce the incidence of math errors or processing shortcomings. It also focuses on substantive errors in interpretation of the law. Of the 70,000,000 tax returns filed each year, about 3,000,000, or 4 percent, are selected for audit examination because of the likelihood of error.

In 1967, of the 3,100,000 examined, 52 percent were found to have misinterpreted the law and were required to pay an addition $3.3 billion in tax. But of the total examined, 40 percent were able to substantiate all entries and were notified of "no change." Another 7.6 percent or 200,000 were found to have overpaid and were refunded $362,000,000—which they had neither expected nor requested.

In 1968, for the first time, IRS focused on these substantive errors. Audit research studies showed the following breakdown by type of error: dependency exemption, 27 percent; interest income and interest payments, 17 percent; contributions, 16 percent; and medical expense, 13 percent.

The effectiveness of this program in cost reduction and the improved services to taxpayers has been widely recognized by IRS top management in Washington and officials in the regional and district offices who are in close contact with the problems of the individual taxpayer.

Commissioner of Internal Revenue Sheldon S. Cohen offered this philosophy:

"We have first of all recognized that taxpayers cannot comply with the law if they don't know what their responsibilities are. This may surprise you, but 40,000,000 taxpayers have no contact of any kind with the Revenue Service except for receipt of the tax package every year. These people can only learn about their tax responsibilities through the educational process and through the mass media.

"We have in recent years, therefore, given increased stature and modest staff increases to our public information activity as our liaison with the mass media and our vehicle for reaching this great taxpayer audience. We have stepped up our production of television and radio spots, films, news releases, and pamphlets and booklets as part of this expanded information program."

These communications efforts involve many divisions and offices in the 50 states beyond Washington, where Public Information is one of the management and administrative activities. Among the many offices and units of IRS directly involved in some phase of communications with taxpayers are:

· Top management including the Commissioner, other national officials, the seven Regional Commissioners and the 58 District Directors, who make scores of speeches annually, write articles and are readily accessible to news media, including press, radio, and TV.

· Lawyers, accountants, and writers in Technical Publications Branch, who, in cooperation with the Facilities Management Division, annually issue the 160-page "Your Federal Income Tax" —one of the government's "best sellers,"—some 70 individual pamphlets, and hundreds of forms and letters that go to taxpayers.

· Taxpayer Assistance in the Collection Division, which provides phone and counter assistance to some 25 million taxpayers who annually call or visit one of the 900 IRS offices located in the 50 states.

· Taxpayer education, furnished by the Training Division, in the form of supplementary course material, to 85 percent of the nation's high schools, and annual Tax Institutes for lawyers, accountants, employment officers of industrial plants, and education officers of military bases.

· The IRS Forms Committee, which, in cooperation with Printing and Publications Branch, each year conducts the largest mail-order operation in the world, by mailing out more than 100 million special packages of forms and instructions to individuals, businesses, farmers, fiduciaries, and many others.

· Audit and Collection Divisions with 14,000 Revenue Agents and 6000 Tax Technicians who patiently explain the tax laws to some 3 million taxpayers who possibly have made mistakes, and 6000 Revenue Officers dealing with the 2 million who are behind in their payments.

In all states, the IRS District Director is "Mr. Internal Revenue" and is responsible for providing necessary services to taxpayers and serving as spokesman to news media in reaching the 45 million taxpayers who rely on mass media to keep them informed.

And in the 900 local offices, representatives of the District Director try to implement the President's injunction that "every taxpayer is entitled to fair and courteous treatment."

It is becoming evident that public relations is not solely the responsibility of public information officers, but of every official and employee. This position can be summarized in a statement given in testimony before a subcommittee of the Senate Judiciary Committee:

"We recognize that without the good will, cooperation and assistance of the public and news media, effective administration of the Federal Tax Laws would not be possible.

"We know that public attitudes are created by the manner in which IRS operates—how responsive, helpful and fair it is to taxpayers; how efficiently it conducts its activities—and not through the issuance of press releases or other publicity efforts. We know that it is what we do—rather than what we say we do —that determines the attitude of the public."

A self-assessment system of tax collection, where the taxpayer fills out his own return by reporting his annual income, taking the deductions to which he is entitled, and either requesting a refund or sending a check for the balance owed, surely depends heavily on communications.

5. Special Sources of Public Information

THE government information officer must pay attention to a variety of "special sources of public information." Since he does not manufacture the facts himself, he must know how to find the material for his communication.

James T. McCrory deals with one of the most important tasks of the information man, "getting information from specialists." He is himself a specialist in public information. Prior to his present position as Director of Information for the U.S. Agency for International Development, he was Deputy Director of Information at HEW, and, from 1962 to 1966, chief of the public affairs division on the information staff at AID.

A graduate of the Marquette University College of Journalism, he worked as a reporter in Wisconsin for five years. He has also had experience as a television producer in St. Louis and was a Ford Foundation Fellow in India.

Much government information is scientific or technical, so the public information officer often must deal with scientists and technicians as sources of data. *Michael Amrine* discusses the problems of "explaining the world of science." A graduate of the Columbia Graduate School of Journalism, he is the Public Information Officer of the American Psychological Association.

Writing on science and public affairs has occupied Mr. Amrine for the past 20 years. Agencies for whom he has written include the National Institutes of Health, the National Academy of Sciences, the Air Research and Development Command, the Office of Intelligence and Research in the State Department, and the Research Analysis Corporation. Before joining APA in 1952, he was public relations advisor to the Federation of Atomic Scientists and has co-authored many articles with leading physicists. He is also author of a number of his own books, including *The Great Decision: The Secret of the Atomic Bomb* and *This Awesome Challenge: The Hundred Days of Lyndon Johnson*.

Another important source is the executive or administrator himself, especially when he must deliver a speech. *Phillip T. Drotning* discusses the problems of information men when they must serve as ghost writers of the boss's speeches. Before taking on his present assignment as Manager of Communication Services for the American Oil Company, he served as Special Assistant to the Administrator of the National Aeronautics and Space Administration from 1962 to 1965, a position where he was directly involved in speech writing.

Mr. Drotning was Vice President for Public Relations for Northwest Orient Airlines from 1956 to 1962, and from 1948 to 1956 he served as Executive Secretary to two Wisconsin governors. A journalism and political science graduate of the University of Wisconsin, he worked for the *Milwaukee Journal* and other Wisconsin newspapers and has written many articles for top magazines.

Cooperation between business and government is another necessary ingredient for the flow of information to the public. *Dan H. Fenn, Jr.,* discusses "getting government to hear business," both in making government sensitive to the voice of business and making business receptive to the voice of government.

Mr. Fenn has had a distinguished career in business-government relations. He is President of the Center for Business-Government Relations, and former Vice Chairman of the U.S. Tariff Commission. He served as a staff assistant to President Kennedy from 1961 to 1963. Before entering government service he was a dean and faculty member at Harvard University. A graduate of Harvard, he was president of the *Harvard Crimson,* the undergraduate daily newspaper.

BREAKING BUREAUCRATIC BARRIERS . . .

Getting Information from Specialists

JAMES T. MC CRORY
DIRECTOR, OFFICE OF PUBLIC INFORMATION
U. S. AGENCY FOR INTERNATIONAL DEVELOPMENT

NEARLY every official in government is a specialist in some sense. Even if the activities over which he presides are patently mundane, the probabilities are that he pursues them through complex and mysterious procedures which only he understands.

This is unavoidable.

Any large bureaucracy, public or private, becomes more complex and specialized as it grows. Moreover, government programs grow by accretion over the years, as the Congress acts. Similar activities in the same Department (and sometimes even in the same division) may operate quite differently because they were set up at different times by legislative interest groups with different bents.

Accountability adds a special layer of complication to government activities. Any program that must answer for the way in which it has regulated some activity, or the way in which it has distributed grants, contracts, or benefits develops elaborate procedures to bring order to its actions—and to defend them later.

The result is a thicket of expectations, abstractions, and complications in which government information officers must work —and in which many expire of frustration.

The varieties of bafflement can seem infinite.

I once asked the operators of an investment insurance program how much additional investment the program had actually encouraged to date. It seemed a reasonable request, since that was the stated purpose of the program. The answer was: "We can give you the total value of insurance in force, but of course we don't know what relation that bears to actual investment."

A request to an office for a brief summary of the exciting new innovations their programs have enabled may well produce this kind of reply:

"The messkit sanitation program has made a substantive and impressive beginning. But it is only the beginning. The task ahead is to bring to fruition a truly unique and promising venture designed to advance the effectiveness and quality of sanitation procedures available to those with dirty messkits. Critical issues remain, and effective local patterns are not yet completely realized. But as we enter the period of full operation, the prospects for success appear highly favorable."

The answer to your question about how many people were retrained by program X turns out to be: "So far, 11,500, but of course our really big program here is Project Outdate which we do on delegation from the Labor Department and their figures are kept on an entirely different basis. . . ."

A direct question like "How many people work here?" may draw the discouraging reply: "What do you want to know that for?"

And so on.

A few passages like this are sufficient to set off the perennial wish-dream of the government information officer: if only he had enough power and rank, he could *force* the bureaucrats to come up with straight answers. This is a nice dream, but it is kin to the colonial conviction that if one just shouted loudly enough at the Asian natives they would *have* to understand English.

The only real way to get information from specialists is to learn enough about what they are doing to begin asking them the right questions—and in language they can understand. This is tedious and hard work, but there is no substitute for it.

A good place to begin is with the question: "What do you want to know that for?" Sometimes a bureaucrat who says that in response to a request for data is being evasive and bureaucratic. Often, however, it is simply the most helpful place to begin.

Information officers normally work under time pressure and it is only human to pass this pressure on to program officers in the form of terse requests for "the number of child health centers opened in fiscal 1967" or "two brief examples of successful technical assistance in rice culture," or whatever the immediate problem is.

The "just give me the facts, Mac," approach may seem the shortest route to hard information. But it is nearly always a waste of time.

Terse, unexplained requests for data are generally answered with unintelligible or clearly irrelevant data or—more likely in government—by delivery of a mass of mimeographed reports in which it is alleged the data you want can be found (it never can). Instead of saving time, you are back where you started.

It is *always* desirable to preface any request to a program office with a brief explanation of the problem you are trying to solve: "Look, I've been asked for illustrations of the increased federal investment in health services, as compared with health research." Then you make your request: "Can you give me the comparative annual figures on the Hill-Burton program for fiscal 1960 and fiscal 1967." Or whatever the question is.

In practice, it is usually wise to put the request in memo form —the "piece of paper" that bureaucrats expect if you are serious. A piece of paper lying on somebody's desk is a more durable reminder than the memory of a verbal request. It also helps to ensure that the request stays the way you intended it if, as often happens, the official you talked with must pass it on to somebody else in his shop.

At the same time, it is seldom wise to rely on a written request alone. A simultaneous telephone call (or a request on your memo for a call on its receipt) prevents any possible misunderstanding over what you want and why you need it.

This approach does several things at once. Immediately it settles one continuing problem in any organization the size of the federal government—it establishes at the outset whether or not you are talking to the right office. It also eliminates any dispute about what data you want: you want the Hill-Burton program figures (grants for hospital construction) that will illustrate an increase in federal support for health services. In stating why you want the data, you have identified it in the most precise way possible, and you have avoided one of the many semantic traps that beset dealings with specialists. Again, this enables you to establish some important facts with your source at the outset, including these possibilities: (a) you are dead wrong and the program has declined; (b) fiscal 1967 was a statistical freak; use fiscal 1966 or 1968 instead; (c) the grant totals include some items you did not even know about, which cannot be counted contributions to health services; and so forth.

By explaining at the outset why you want your information, another set of possibilities is opened: the program office may be able to help in ways you did not anticipate. Staying with the examples, an alert program officer may ask: "What other grant programs are you including in your definition?" and suggest several more that you had not thought of. Or he may tip you off to the fact that another office, for quite different reasons and unknown to you, has just finished a survey of precisely what you are asking.

The "related study" is the will-o'-the-wisp of government. There are lazy program officers who have learned that the way to "get rid of" a request for information is to tout the inquirer off on "a study of just what you're asking that Jack Shortley over in P/SLOP has been working on." Jack Shortley may prove to be on annual leave for three weeks (you need your answer tomorrow) or he may not exist ("perhaps they meant Ben Shockley in Labor") or his study may not even touch on your question. On the other hand, the "related study" does turn out to be exactly what you are seeking just often enough to make it always worth pursuing.

"Why do you want to know?" becomes even more important if the data you are requesting are numbers. Suppose your question is "How many people work here?" The answer may well vary according to why you want to know. Permanent work force may be one figure. But if you wish to know how many people your agency is applying to its problem area, the answer might well be a much larger figure that includes consultants and bureaucrats on detail from other agencies.

Numbers of any kind, whether they involve people or money, are always sensitive subjects to bureaucrats because it is numbers for which they are chiefly held accountable.

The week you ask it, the question "how many people work here?" may be a matter of extreme delicacy in some hot place: in a Congressional subcommittee bent on documenting executive inattention to its area of concern, or perhaps in the Bureau of the Budget, the Civil Service Commission, or the General Accounting Office because of some commitment to peg manpower at a given level at a given date.

If the "wrong" number gets out, both the bureaucrat and his agency can land in hot water. The number may be "wrong" only in some narrow technical sense, and wrong only to a highly specialized audience at that, but this does not diminish the trouble.

To understand this sort of thing, however, is not to forgive and forget. Understanding is useful chiefly because it provides the patience to negotiate an answer that *will* satisfy both public bureaucratic needs. Sometimes the answer to the simplest-appearing questions may have to be literally "bargained out"—but an answer can always be found.

The fragmentation of programs produces its own problems. There may, for example, be no simple answer to the question: "How many crippled children have been rehabilitated by federal programs?" because pieces of the particular job fall within half a dozen agencies or bureaus. Some programs may carry all rehabilitation costs for particular groups (Indians, Eskimos, orphans), another program may underwrite costs for youngsters whose parents are welfare cases, still another may aid youngsters served by urban clinics under a special grant authority, and others may underwrite specialized elements in the rehabilitation process (surgery, prosthesis, physical therapy, counseling) for children among others.

This kind of fragmentation presents obstacles to the information job but not, given time and attention, insurmountable ones. Somewhere in the data compiled in each separate program are figures for children that can be "broken out," and, with the cooperation of program people, added together to provide a composite picture. The "adding" may be tedious, requiring agreements on definitions of what is to be counted in and counted out, and so forth. It will probably demand persistence on the part of information specialists to see that it does get done. But it can be done.

The reason simple questions often seem hard to answer in government is not because bureaucrats are stupid, but because these are not the kinds of questions that bureaucrats are most regularly asked. Government keeps detailed records of its operations, but the things that are recorded most assiduously are those that are demanded most assiduously. These, by and large, are the fiscal and administrative records by which government servants account for their stewardship of public funds.

In every federal agency there are fiscal and administrative divisions whose job it is to see that program offices account for every nickel, dime, and man-hour. They set up statistical systems that operating divisions are required to follow, and they police the record-keeping to see that their instructions are followed.

This continuing attention is the reason why most federal agencies can disgorge, on little notice, detailed data on expenditures, obligations, program administration, and so forth.

Nothing like the same attention has been paid to organizing records for public information needs. The result is predictable: there is no guarantee that the wealth of records available in any agency will reveal the answers to obvious (to the layman) questions such as "How many trainees actually got jobs?" or "How much did the program cut infant mortality?" or "How much new investment did the program actually encourage?"

In part, this inequality exists because public information offices in government are seldom as powerful, bureaucratically, as comptrollers or administrative types. They lack the same authority to compel changes in systems of operating and record-keeping.

But authority is not everything, even in a bureaucracy. There is quite a lot that public information offices can do, without any special authority, to insure that program offices have the data they need when they need them. To do this, however, they must give the problem time and attention and too many public information types tend to be bored by statistics and record systems.

There is an opportunity to change things every time there is an emergency encounter with a program office that discloses records that do not match, or critical gaps in data. Normally, once the emergency is over the public information officer moves on to new problems. But this is precisely the best time to go back to the program office and talk about changing its records systems. The program people have just had an illustration of the need for improvement and are likely to be interested in preventing a recurrence of the confusion. The public information officer has just completed a forced-draft education in the intricacies of that particular specialty and is better-equipped than he will be again to recommend practical improvements in its records. An hour's discussion, right then when memories are green, can produce some changes that count—perhaps an extra question in a form that contractors fill out or the regular tabulation of data already supplied are all that you need to change to see that your questions are answerable the next time around.

Second, most agencies regularly review their records systems for one purpose or another. These reviews are conducted by committees.

The committees that conduct these reviews are usually constituted by the administrative offices of an agency. It seldom occurs to them to ask public information people to serve on the committees—and if asked, public information people often decline on grounds they have more important things to do with their time. Both are wrong. It is a mistake to carry out a serious review of an agency's records and reporting systems without active participation by the public information office.

Third, the PPBS (planning, programming, budgeting system) operations underway government-wide offer public information offices a unique opportunity to get a handle on the perennial problem of evaluating results, and getting some usable data on results from the specialists they work with.

You can normally plunge the most relaxed meeting with program specialists into instant anxiety by asking a mild question about the program's effectiveness: "What percent of your trainees actually get jobs?" or "How many of the aged actually use the center?"

A fascinating (for me) evening at a halfway house for retarded young people became a tense confrontation with its highly trained staff of psychiatrists and social workers when I asked what percent of the youngsters who used the house had "successfully" made the transition from an institution to self-support in the community. There followed 20 minutes of lectures on the complexity of rehabilitation, the difficulty of defining success, and the impossibility of making any judgments after just two years. Only after I had affirmed my loyalty to mental health, confessed publicly to my pitiful understanding of the complexities of rehabilitation, and sworn to distrust the apparent meaning of any facts produced did we get down to counting the numbers of patients who had "made it" on different definitions of what that might mean.

Without going into the reasons (I don't pretend to know them all), this is how it is with specialists. They are uniformly suspicious of any questions that smack of evaluation by an outsider, or any requests for data that an outsider might use to make judgments about program effectiveness. If you need the facts, there is no way to get them without sitting through the lecture, too.

Until recently, public information offices have been the most persistent lobbyists inside government for better information on the concrete results of federal programs. This is because their clients—the media and the public—keep pressing for it. If anything, that interest has increased in recent years.

PPBS is an attempt to quantify as precisely as possible the goals and the actual accomplishments of federal programs. Then, by comparing relative costs it becomes theoretically possible to determine what precise investment of the federal tax dollar will produce the greatest actual return in improved health, transport, and the like.

Quantification is proving more difficult in the non-Defense departments than it apparently did at Defense, but the exercise has already brought fresh resources into an important field. The new troops are economists who sometimes act as if they invented the age of reason—but they *are* good with numbers—understand the difference between a fact and a belief, and are usually helpful if you ask them for help.

It is unlikely that the economists need any help from public information specialists to make PPBS a useful tool for federal managers. And whatever its limitations in the so-called "human development" program areas, PPBS will provide federal managers with much more systematic data on program effectiveness than they have had to date.

So far so good. In government, however, many more people than federal managers participate in making decisions on how federal dollars are spent. The utility of PPBS will be sharply limited if the data it produces are meaningful only to the specialized bureaucrat. Public information specialists might well help to assure that PPBS provides decision-making data that are equally relevant and intelligible to some other key participants in the decision process: the public, the media, and the legislative branch.

Public information officials in government tend to be strewn through the divisions of their agencies like raisins, rather than organized in central working groups. This is because of the sturdy myth that Congress opposes public information and so its practitioners must be hidden. The result is that a lot of relatively minor program officials have somebody else to answer their mail and write their speeches, and agencies end up with sizable public information staffs—but no coherent public information program.

One of the most plausible-sounding defenses for the fragmentation of public information is that this solves the problem of getting information from specialists, because it puts the public information people right there with them.

I believed this myself, before I moved from a federal agency with a central information staff to a department where dispersion was the rule. The result of dispersion is the opposite of what I thought. When they are scattered about as the employees of a department's operating bureaus and divisions, public information people quickly lose their lay or public orientation and take on the coloring and the concerns of the specialists who, in a decentralized system, hire them, fire them, promote or downgrade them, and tell them, by daily behavior, whether they regard them well or poorly.

Neither the public nor the bureaucracy is well served by public information officials who have been "domesticated" and whose first reference is to the specialized needs of some subdivision by which they are employed. The public information people are, if you like, the institutionalized "outsiders" in every bureaucracy, the professional laymen in organizations of specialists. They must face outward not inward, and they cannot retain that orientation if they are dispersed and isolated among masses of specialists in any bureaucracy.

BRIDGING TWO CULTURES . . .

Explaining the World of Science

MICHAEL AMRINE
PUBLIC INFORMATION OFFICER
AMERICAN PSYCHOLOGICAL ASSOCIATION

SCIENCE information is one of the major activities of all government information. Under this heading may be found a thousand different topics and many different kinds of historic events, from the presidential announcement that nuclear energy has been harnessed and the Hiroshima bomb has been dropped to the report that statisticians have found that cigarette smoking is linked with cancer.

These two examples indicate the range of topics covered by government science, and they also illustrate how the public is concerned with major science news and decisions. In both these cases there are elements of fear and controversy and an irreducible core of demonstrable fact. It is to that hard core of demonstrable fact that the scientist and the information man should be dedicated when accounting to the public on new developments in the laboratory.

The size of public information from science can be judged by the billions of dollars spent on research and development directly in large government laboratories such as the U.S. Bureau of Standards, the Atomic Energy Commission, the Office of Naval Research, and the like, and indirectly through thousands of research contracts which are written under the National Institutes of Health, the National Science Foundation, and many other sponsoring agencies—contracts which reach almost every university and private research institution in the country. Approximately one person in ten in government employment (not counting the military services) is a scientist, an engineer, or at work on a technical program. About one dollar in ten of the federal budget goes for science.

The progress of the government and of science have gone hand in hand since Benjamin Franklin tinkered with inventions and did scientific research at the same time he and his colleagues were working on social innovations such as the invention of the United States. Our constitution *in fact wrote in science from the beginning.* It provided for a Patent Office in order to reserve to inventors a proper share in the profits to be made from their contributions to society. Many other links between the federal government and science have been a part of federal assistance to education. The recent narrow definitions of "federal aid to education" should not blur the fact that through the land-grant college system and other methods the federal government has long demonstrated a direct supportive role in education and science.

It was in the time of Abraham Lincoln more than 100 years ago that the President in the middle of civil war was persuaded of the need to get the best technical information into the hands of the military. Accordingly he founded the National Academy of Sciences which continues to this day, although vastly enlarged in scope and somewhat changed in the nature of its functions.

It may also be noted that today the President has not only the National Academy and the National Research Council and the National Science Foundation, but in the White House itself he has the Office of Science and Technology and a personal staff of science advisers under a Chief Science Adviser, head of the President's Science Advisory Committee. Most, if not all, of government agencies have some research agency or agencies reporting to them.

The problems of handling science information are fundamentally the same as handling other kinds of information. But surely today few would think of "science" as an area removed from the interests of everyday life, and almost all would agree that science makes news. But it is harmful to say "Any topnotch reporter can cover a science story just as he can cover any other kind of story." Frequently the information problem is getting a decent job done without Pulitzer prize caliber reporters and editors. And "average" reporters sometimes do great harm by approaching science news as if there were nothing different about it.

Perhaps the first cautionary note then is to be painstakingly accurate; a rule important for all government information. Whether it is the spelling of a man's name or a figure in a budget, the accuracy of the information is always of prime importance. But in science stories it is often more difficult to know when one has a full and accurate story and whether the facts will be conveyed truthfully and accurately by the time they have been rewritten from the original release or digested out of the original report. It is certainly true that in science information one has to be endlessly careful to check facts.

It is sometimes said that the whole problem of teaching freshman physics in this complicated atomic world comes down to the "art of judicious lying." According to this theory it is impossible to tell the beginning freshman physics student the fundamental truth about the atom; he just cannot understand it. In ordinary science writing, one is dealing with simplification, and therefore—perhaps—with half truths and a kind of "deception." In a phrase, the problem is to achieve genuine simplification, and at the same time avoid misleading oversimplification.

The objective is to put something simply enough that the audience can read it and understand something from it. In all science writing, of course, one has to expect to be read by laymen and also by scientists. And there is no more difficult audience, say many science writers, than the latter.

Scientists still sometimes cause delay or other difficulty because "the story should be held up until it appears in a technical journal."

Not so often as in times past but still often enough to be a major problem in science information one finds a roadblock related to publication of information in a technical journal. Sometimes the author of the information or the director of the laboratory refuses to have any article written and refuses any interviews until the data have been analyzed and have been written up in a technical fashion and been sent off to some journal such as the *Physics Review* or the *Psychological Bulletin*. This difficulty can usually be overcome, but the situation requires more understanding than most newsmen or most beginning information persons will give it.

This is all according to the tradition and to the ethical code of scientists as it has been practiced for many decades. From the scientist's point of view, he should not permit public attention nor lend his name to a preliminary report until he has submitted his facts in such form that they can be criticized by fellow scientists. Another factor from the scientist's point of view is that he does not want to discuss what his conclusions may be until he has had time to sift out the data, establish the fine points, and make absolutely certain of the major points. To the outsider the delay may appear ridiculous, but a good scientist places first his facts, and second the respect of his colleagues far above any temporary publicity.

This viewpoint of the scientists is important and not to be lightly brushed aside. It is the open criticism by his colleagues which is at the heart of the validation procedure in the community of science.

Here is an example. When the late Dr. Alfred Kinsey came to the publication of his second major report, he fully realized that it was a story of national and international importance. Accordingly he invited reporters to come to the Kinsey Institute in Bloomington, Indiana, to spend some days reading and preparing for a press conference and seminar. Presumably this was not simply to maximize publicity and attention to the Institute but more important, to maximize accuracy. However, one of the stipulations in the agreement which the reporters signed was a provision that they could not take away any of the galley proofs of the book to show them to any person outside the Institute. This provision was bitterly, and in this author's opinion, justly criticized by science writers (some of whom were also scientists), for this "security" clamp meant that the reporters could not call up a biologist or statistician outside the institute and ask for some opinions from Kinsey's peers in science. This kind of procedure should be avoided, and scientists are justifiably concerned about anything resembling it.

Most information men and most science editors (outside the small band of technical editors) would agree that changing conditions require a greater openness by the scientists. In the laboratory (certainly in government laboratories and agencies) he should speak without waiting until the technical publication is all wrapped up, polished, sent away and printed.

When the public really expects the news and wants it *now*, the public—and the information man—nearly always win. For example, it would not be likely that one would hold back photographs of the moon for six months until after they appeared in a technical publication. As a matter of fact, however, such photographs *may be held back for several hours,* or even for a couple of days, in order that they may be put together with reasonable accuracy. But our times have demanded a different order of communications accessibility and a different time scale.

If the public has put up two million dollars for a cyclotron or 50 million dollars for a nuclear reactor, or half a billion dollars for a space enterprise, even though the basic goal is scientific information, the news factor and the accounting to the taxpayer take precedence.

Where millions of taxpayers' dollars are concerned, or where the public safety is concerned, one has to treat the information differently than one may have treated the solitary researcher of yesterday who was spending very little money, using few assistants, and coming in with results in a time when the public was less interested in scientific and technical achievement than it is today.

In this matter, a key spokesman for the President's Science Advisory Committee, Dr. Ivan Bennett, in a recent speech asked the scientific community itself to be more reasonable about this particular problem. In effect he warned scientists that the old rule of waiting for final results and final publication could no longer hold. It is of course not only the public which needs more information, but the government itself. For example, in the Bureau of the Budget, there is now virtually a science department and a definable science budget each year. Men who are making decisions—including the men who are making budgets—have to be told some of the preliminary results of large-scale experiments and vast research endeavors. They cannot wait until a technical journal appears two years after the fact. The science information man must help interpret new scientific information.

In health research stories and many other technical information stories, one may often find that science stories are related to strong fears—rational or irrational. In such cases one has some responsibility not only to the *facts,* but to take some account of the *fears* which may cause a story to be wrongly perceived. A few years ago it was sometimes said that most science writing, or at least the common and most corny, belonged generally in one of two schools. One was the "Gee Whiz! school," or, "Gee Whiz, ain't science wonderful?" The other was the "scare 'em to death school," which was sometimes in the magazine trade divided into further categories: "There's this terrible new thing, but science says actually it isn't so terrible after all," or "There's this terrible new thing, but our editors have found experts who have a very simple way to prevent it right in your home." It can be seen that articles on air pollution or "staph" infections in hospitals or the evils of being too fat or new discoveries about contraception could be promoted to some magazine under either category.

Today the science writers and science editors who regularly follow medicine and science do a much more careful job. But the science information man who is protecting the original source of the information and who is working for the protection of the ultimate consumer of such information, the taxpayer, has to observe some special care with regard to subjects which may frighten the public. He should have his facts in perfect order before he publishes news of any research affecting human life and safety. This may be as large a topic as atomic fallout or as small an item as the discovery of some new weed which causes "hayfever."

At one government laboratory it was finally decided that no information of any kind relating to cancer was to be published *without the personal approval of the directors of the laboratory.* This ban applied to anything to be written in a press release, published in an annual report, and even to scientific papers that were to be read at meetings. This laboratory was attached to a hospital using radiation to find methods of alleviating or curing cancer. It was found, as it has been found in other places, that almost any mention of progress toward a cure for cancer resulted in sensational stories. Then the information office would receive the most heart-rending letters from the families of persons considered hopelessly condemned to death. This is a most extreme case of information which is so hot that it is entitled to be handled with the utmost prudence and double-checking.

But the same is true of many other stories which relate to health, or to the conservation of natural resources, or even to such items as the strength and durability of certain materials, or the safety of certain equipment. It is the writer's business to understand human hopes and fears, and it is the science information man's business to do all that he can to see that false hopes and fears are not aroused by careless interpretation.

Press conferences are probably less frequently called for in science news than in other areas, and are perhaps a greater risk in terms of distortion of the basic facts. If there is a story of such scope that it might otherwise warrant a press conference, it is usually worthwhile to prepare written background material of depth and detail. If it is an extraordinary story, of national interest, it would be preferable to have the background material, and a careful briefing during the period when the news is being "held for release" under an embargo on advance publication.

Most frequently, except in the case of stories such as space shots, for which reporters have by their training already been prepared, it will be found that science stories are not best handled by live and on-the-spot new conferences. The ultimate decision depends, of course, upon a judgment as to the experience of the scientists and the reporters who will be concerned. But, as every experienced information man knows, press conferences are generally too random to be the preferred means of communication. Every experienced science information man knows that an inexperienced scientist may begin by speaking in restrained terms but as the press conference goes on may slip into a more conversational and speculative vein, and create headlines quite different from those expected or desired.

Frequently the first job in taking over any public information operation is to make a list of "publics," or specific audiences. In the science field it will often be found that the most valuable and influential audience, and the audience where a little effort will bring back the greatest dividends, is the semitechnical or popular science field.

Even within the field of more-or-less popular presentation of science, there is a wide range of approaches. Generally acknowledged to be the leading magazine of science interpretation in today's market is *Scientific American,* but many of its articles are believed too "difficult" for those not trained in science. The weekly magazine of *Science,* published by the American Association for the Advancement of Science, carries quite technical articles and also carries semitechnical survey articles. It now has an extraordinary audience for its ably written and ably edited department of science in public affairs. The syndicated material of Science Service and of other science news services are also basic. Most men will remember when they read *Popular Science* and *Popular Mechanics* but perhaps most of them may not know these magazines have a tremendous adult audience in the hundreds of thousands.

In nearly every field of human endeavor today, such as education, health, and industry, there are semitechnical magazines which help to acquaint the people at work with new developments that are changing their jobs and the world about them.

When there is a new development in the research laboratory or in an area of research, one may assume if it is important that it will receive some attention in the major newspapers but that very likely after momentary notice it will disappear rapidly from the news. One may also assume that it will be published in the appropriate technical journals, although that will take many months. Perhaps it will be two or three years before that development is abstracted and referenced in the basic journals of the field and available in most scientific libraries.

In other words, a big new development will be picked up by the major news services of major newspapers. Also, one may see that the scientists in their own network spread technical information to many places. But there are audiences to be reached between the mass media and the technical journal. In fact the most valuable media, some feel, are precisely those between the general and the truly technical.

There will be a wide variety, for example, in the educational field, or in the health field. Suppose there is a new discovery which helps to prevent infections in hospitals. One may assume that this will go into medical journals and very likely be a news story besides. But it well may be that the greatest service to the public will be to see that the message is published in magazines read by hospital administrators and also in those special journals read by hospital technicians.

In many fields there are journals run by business management or sometimes by labor unions which carry a rather surprising amount of technical information. To take another example, who would be interested in a new development in the use of solar energy to heat a house? There are many markets for this, but one recent publication in which such an article appeared was the union magazine of the plumbers and pipefitters. (Solar heating will still use hot water and hot water will still travel in pipes; this should be of interest to half a million pipefitters.)

The proper semitechnical market for a given topic may be an encyclopedia or it may be a news broadcast, such as those sponsored throughout the country by electronics and aircraft firms. It may be noted that one does not have to find out for himself by roaming through the thousands of publications in a library. There are available excellent directories for public information persons (such as *Bacon's Publicity Checker*), which do pretty well in science fields and many other fields. In the research library of any research agency of any size, there will be a librarian who can guide the information person to the middle-range publications as well as to those which are extremely technical.

The benefits from doing a good job on research findings in some semitechnical source may well include some positive benefits to the public information office. When technicians and scientists find that the information specialist has helped their work to be accurately described in a magazine they respect, even though it is not devoted to "pure" science, they will feel that the information function is really becoming a part of the scientific community.

The public information man and his writers may never become completely accepted as part of the inner scientific community because it is such a very tight little clan. However, the information man may certainly hope to become accepted as a valuable accessory to the business of science.

In fields other than science it is recognized that one cannot expect reporters to submit material for editing by their sources. But in medicine and science one still now and then finds a man who demands to see a reporter's story before it is published. When this concerns daily journalism, however, this request is ordinarily turned down.

But when it is a matter of material being gathered for a television broadcast or a magazine article, a scientist sometimes is able to make this qualification and make it stick: "Tell your reporter that I will see him only on condition that he let me see what he writes for publication or plans to ask me on the air." Here again the science information man needs all the arts of diplomacy.

It is sometimes possible to explain to research people that the reporter—somewhat like the scientist—is a professional who lives by his ability to report accurately and objectively. Therefore, in the case of a good reporter, it is insulting to him to be asked to submit his material to be edited by the interview subject.

There are, of course, many reporters, some of them the best in the science field, who on a very intricate story do not mind and even prefer to submit their stories for what is called "fact checking." In the early days of atomic energy the information offices of the AEC were burdened with the reading of manuscripts because they made a standing offer to give a careful review of any article that was submitted for fact checking. This of course did not give officials of the AEC the right to argue about conclusions drawn from facts, but human nature being what it is, there were more than a few arguments in AEC offices through the nation.

If the public information man has a good grasp of his material, and takes care to build up a good relationship with the researchers as well as with the administrators of the research facility, it is usually possible to negotiate some reasonable understanding even in the case of a stubborn scientist who insists that he should have some guarantee before he speaks. The ultraconservatives are being pushed into public view by changing times and the Freedom of Information Act.

In general it is considered a good idea to offer a "fact check," but seldom a good idea to insist upon it. One should try to avoid ever letting the scientist achieve the position of being editor of both facts *and* the style of presentation.

The following is sometimes taken as a flippant remark, unworthy of the critical responsibilities of a public information officer, but it is quite true that the information man should congratulate himself if he can come to be accepted in science at the same level as the instrument maker or the glass blower who helps the progress of some complicated experiment. The man who makes the instruments or the public information man who in some way actually eases the progress of the arduous and sometimes frustrating task of the researcher may find that he has earned a satisfying place in the world of science.

If he can also be a help in making the work of the research facility more understandable to the top management of a government agency and the public, he will find that he has become a quite influential person. He will be someone who is most likely to know what is going to happen tomorrow, not only to his agency, but to society at large, and he will share in the excitement and contribution of science.

GHOSTS AND OFFICIALS . . .

Making the Most of Speeches

PHILLIP T. DROTNING
MANAGER, COMMUNICATION SERVICES
AMERICAN OIL COMPANY
FORMER SPECIAL ASSISTANT
TO THE ADMINISTRATOR
NATIONAL AERONAUTICS AND
SPACE ADMINISTRATION

E VERY dedicated Rotarian, inured to an endless succession of luncheon speeches as the price of his weekly ration of green peas and fried chicken, knows that the Voice of Government is often literally that. Unfortunately, even the most durable of these faithful auditors must ultimately come to share the view of poet George Meredith that "speech is the small change of silence."

Not that "small change" is an appropriate label for the torrent of words that pours forth each day from luncheon tables and lecture platforms all over the country. Ours is a nation of joiners: Americans have banded together in more than 12,500 national organizations. Of these, a handful of national service clubs have proliferated into more than 48,000 local chapters that demand the talents of a luncheon speaker every week.

A little mental arithmetic will tell you that the service clubs alone require some $2\frac{1}{2}$ million speakers a year. If the needs of other organizations are added, the figure—like many of the speeches and most of the lunches—becomes almost impossible to swallow.

Even more remarkable is the fact that if America's social institutions had kept pace with advances in technology, these events and this essay would be as superfluous as a manual on the care of cavalry harness. The survival of the banquet address as a major weapon in the mass communications arsenal defies all logic. Such speeches, along with luncheon talks, convention addresses, and political barnstorming, are an anachronism in today's world; a vestigial remnant of communications techniques that should have become obsolescent the day that Franklin Delano Roosevelt went on the air with his first "fireside chat," and obsolete with the advent of television.

Nevertheless, the public speech, as a social institution, continues to thrive and can therefore be a formidable communications device. Most government administrators, a majority of businessmen, and all politicians have long since accepted platform duties as a professional hazard and concluded—Meredith notwithstanding—that silence is a luxury they can ill afford.

They have learned, first, that many invitations are virtually impossible to reject. More important, however, is their sensitivity to the notion of most editors that what an official has to say is not news unless he says it outside his office. Unless, of course, his office is in the White House.

221

It is patently ridiculous that a perfectly respectable, neatly multilithed statement, hand-delivered to the media by the information branch, is not an acceptable way for a public official to communicate with his constituency. He knows, however, that his words are likely to be ignored unless he climbs on an airplane, flies a thousand miles, puts on a dinner jacket, ruins his digestion with a third-rate dinner, and delivers precisely the same message at some kind of public meeting.

But for the public information practitioner, this is the point at which a wearisome nuisance often becomes a personal disaster. Having gone to all of this effort to manufacture what Madison Avenue calls a "non-event," the speaker is apt to scan the morning paper and discover that his efforts produced nothing more rewarding than, "Mr. Jones also spoke."

This is the moment that every speech-writer and information officer has come to dread; the moment of truth when the boss asks pointedly, and with some rancor, "What did you guys do wrong?"

There is no environment in which most executives are less at ease than on the speaker's platform. Many seek guidance from the plethora of books offering advice on how to write a speech or how to give one. Others turn to the six-foot shelf of anthologies of jokes, anecdotes, and quotations guaranteed to turn the most inept of orators into another William Jennings Bryan. Ultimately they discover that missing from that shelf is the book they really need: one that offers guidance on how to approach the whole problem of public speaking in an intelligent and effective manner. That is what will be attempted in this chapter.

The development of a productive speaking program is perhaps the most harrowing and difficult responsibility of the public relations practitioner. It is also one of the most critical, and the one in which information programs most often and most conspicuously fail. The reasons for this are not elusive: public speaking is the one communications activity that demands the personal participation of the boss. It is also one in which his individual performance, rather than that of his organization, is subjected to critical appraisal by a jury that confronts him face to face.

Shortcomings in other areas of responsibility are criticized more obliquely and often can be unloaded on subordinates, or at least shared with them. But the boss can scarcely conclude his remarks to an obviously dissatisfied audience by pleading that some minion wrote a lousy speech.

Given this highly subjective reaction, which may well strongly influence the speaker's judgment of performance in other communications areas as well, it is surprising that so few public information programs approach public speaking problems in a professional manner. And, when one considers the amount of policy formation that occurs in the process of preparing an executive for a speaking performance, it is astonishing that so many public information directors tolerate shortcomings in their speaking program that may well invite disaster.

The basic weaknesses in most programs are the result of failure to appreciate the opportunities and hazards presented by a speaking engagement, and neglect of the planning and preparation that are necessary to capitalize fully on these opportunities and skirt disaster. Administrators and communications directors who would not tolerate unplanned activity in any other aspect of their operations too often permit the speech function to develop on the basis of happenstance, and deal with the preparations required as an unwelcome and wearisome chore.

For example, consider the manner in which most speaking engagements are born. The genesis of every speech, of course, is the invitation to give it. In the perceptively managed information operation, a speaking engagement is a planned element of a structured program designed to fulfill specific communications goals. Often a target audience is selected and an invitation arranged. Unsolicited invitations are evaluated thoroughly to determine whether an appearance would contribute to overall goals. The stature of the audience is examined; an analysis is made of potentially competitive events; consideration is given to problems and communications needs that may exist at the time the speaking date arrives and, most important, thoughtful attention is given to the message that the speaker will deliver if the engagement is accepted.

Unfortunately, such foresight is practiced in few organizations. Far more typical is the engagement which is accepted as a favor to an old friend, because of arm-twisting by a political ally, or because the executive is offered an honorary degree by the Alma

Mater that he has not revisited since he was voted least likely to succeed.

In a well conceived speaking program the executive picks his audiences, instead of letting them pick him. Moreover, he does it in consultation with his public information advisors, to insure that the unusual effort required will contribute effectively to overall communications goals.

Haphazard audience selection is only one characteristic of an inadequate speaking program. It is, however, symptomatic of the failure of many organizations to appreciate the opportunities that speaking engagements present, and to develop effective plans that will maximize the benefits obtained from an enormous investment of priceless executive time.

It is impossible to deal with all of the details of a productive speaking program. Information on the arts of preparing and delivering the speeches themselves are available from a number of competent authorities. For the remainder of this chapter I would like to highlight the following typical shortcomings that are not often discussed:

1. The failure of many executives—and the professional experts on whom they rely—to comprehend the potential audience that the executive should be trying to reach.

2. Failure to assign sufficient priority to speech preparation so that it will merit the high level of talent that is required and deserved.

3. Failure to establish an effective relationship between those responsible for speech preparation and the speakers for whom the manuscripts are prepared.

4. Failure to adequately merchandise the results.

Let us consider these elements individually, beginning with the audience itself.

Heads of major government departments frequently travel across the country to address groups of 100 or 200 people. Since their official activities concern some 200 million Americans, to say nothing of citizens in other nations, an appearance before a handful of people is clearly a waste of time, unless the appearance can be used to bag far bigger game.

This is so obvious a truism that, as a concept, it is universally understood. But in practice and performance it rarely serves as the guiding principle in the preparation of the speech. Typically, the discussion of content concerns itself with the makeup of the audience, and consideration of the sort of discussion they would most like to hear. This is not all wrong, for anyone who accepts an invitation to speak has, out of simple courtesy, some obligation to entertain and to relate his remarks to the audience at hand.

But if his investment of time and energy is to make its maximum contribution to the achievement of a communications goal, the immediate audience must be placed in a secondary role. The prime target must be the immeasurably larger audience—available through the newspapers, radio, and TV—whose attention can be captured by what he has to say. The speaker who allows concern for the immediate audience to dominate the preparation of his speech is doomed to waste an unconscionable amount of energy and time.

To achieve success in reaching the broader audience that is at hand it is essential that the second shortcoming be overcome. Talent must be assigned to the speech preparation function that is intellectually capable of doing an effective job. The talent required involves much more than simple literary skill. A good speech-writer must have the intelligence, experience, and above all, curiosity, to master all of the details of the organization he serves. He must be able to read the public mood, and sense the editor's needs. Most important, he must be innovative and eloquent.

If one were to tick off the most effective speech-writers in the federal establishment over the last two decades, he would quickly realize that these men have had an enormous impact on the policies of the agencies and individuals that they served. More than one major government program and agency has been conceived in the course of researching and preparing a speech. And when ideas are conceived in this environment they are almost certain to be implemented, because the man with the authority and influence to put them in practice has been publicly committed in advance.

As a consequence of this phenomenon, the speech-writer wields an enormous amount of power over the course of public events.

Simple caution demands that his intellectual competence and knowledge approach or even exceed that of his boss. Only thus can the executive be assured that what he has to say will attract the attention he desires, that it will achieve the organizational objectives that are most important to him, and that the ideas he exposes and the action he advocates will not prove embarrassing later on.

Few information programs are staffed with this degree of intellectual competence and judgment in the speech-writer's role. How many Ted Sorensons are there in Washington today? And too often, where such competence does exist, the writer is handicapped by the third deficiency on my list—failure to grant him a relationship with the speaker that permits him to do his job.

The most common complaint of government speech-writers is that they are expected to work in a vacuum. The complaint is a valid one, for no writer can produce a truly first-rate speech that will achieve everything that is expected of it unless he is granted frequent and intimate contact with the executive who is to give the speech.

I have suggested that a competent speech writer must have intellectual competence and knowledge of the agency he serves. This knowledge cannot be limited to the documentary material with which he can be provided. He should, rather, have access to all of the information that flows through his principal's telephone, and across his desk. He should, in short, be in a position to put himself inside the speaker's head—to generate ideas and even formulate policies because he knows his boss intimately and has access to the same informational base.

In the ideal arrangement, there should be no intervening layers between the writer and the speaker, where the discussion of speech content is concerned. In the most successful arrangements that I have known, the speech-writer was attached to the principal's personal staff, saw every piece of paper that flowed across his desk, and was privileged to sit in on any meeting, formal or informal, that he felt might contribute information that would help him do a better job.

Obviously, such an arrangement must make provision for coordination of his effort to make certain that the results take into account, and contribute to, overall goals. Certainly, also, there must be some sort of clearance procedure that will forestall error of fact or inadvertent conflict with agency objectives of which even the principal may be unaware.

The first requirement, in the case of an agency head, can be met quite effectively by assigning the speech-writer to the information or public affairs director, but locating him physically in the senior official's suite. This maximizes his access to essential information, and his personal contact with the speaker, but retains a close liaison with those concerned with overall information needs. As for clearances, the ideal time to obtain them is *after* the speaker has approved the speech. This is important for two reasons. First, it disposes of the compulsion that many technical experts have to convert perfectly good English into legal or engineer-ese. More important, it prevents a perfectly good speech —one readily acceptable to the boss—from being converted into garbage by intervening officials before he has a chance to read it himself. More than once I have had a butchered manuscript rejected by a speaker and then, after humbly accepting his critique, satisfied his requirements simply by handing him the original draft.

If the foregoing requirements are fulfilled, where do we stand? We now have a public information operation, and an organizational management that recognizes a speech for what it really should be—an opportunity to say something important to great masses of people across the United States. (Or a state or city if that is the level of official involved.) We also have a planned program that is designed to integrate the speaking effort into the total communications plan, and to use it to achieve overall goals.

Having recognized the significance of the function, we have provided imaginative, intellectually competent, informed, and technically skilled speech-writers to carry out the task of conceiving, researching, and preparing the speech. We have placed them in intimate contact with the individuals they serve, and have given them access to the total flow of information that they need.

The result should be the production of speeches that are more than banalities; that are filled with sound and provocative ideas, related to current problems and opportunities about which the public is concerned, and expressed in language that is stimulating, quotable, and easily understood.

With this basis, a reasonable degree of success in reaching people is virtually assured, simply through use of a duplicating machine and a supply of postage stamps. The wire services and major daily newspapers will see to the rest.

But the information director who is truly conscientious will make certain that no opportunity to reach a secondary audience is overlooked. He will know his media so well that some copies of the talk will go to selected columnists and editorial writers with a hand-written note. They may base a column or an editorial on a particularly incisive quote.

He will excerpt paragraphs that have particular pertinence to magazines and journals serving specialized groups. He will encourage still other specialized publications to use edited versions of the speech for reprinting as articles, almost in full. He will make certain that no speech which contains a fresh idea escapes the attention of the editors of *Vital Speeches,* and magazines such as *Harpers', The Atlantic Monthly,* and *Saturday Review.* It may yield an invitation to expand an idea or proposal into a full-length magazine piece.

Finally, on the day of the speech, he will organize the speaker's schedule to permit coverage of his remarks on radio and television with the greatest of ease. Often this will mean the scheduling of a press conference in advance of the appearance, which all the media can attend. In smaller cities, it may require a studio visit during which brief snatches of the most important points can be recorded on tape.

To the highly professional public information operation, these suggestions may seem as elementary as movable type. Yet most of the failures I have cited here are typical of the vast majority of public agencies and private agencies as well. If the shoe fits at your shop, why not use it to take a giant step toward success at the speaker's rostrum?

COOPERATION FOR COMMUNICATION . . .

Getting Government to Hear Business

DAN H. FENN, JR.
PRESIDENT, CENTER FOR BUSINESS-
GOVERNMENT RELATIONS
FORMER VICE CHAIRMAN
U. S. TARIFF COMMISSION

I HAVE had an unusual opportunity to meet with top corporate executives for extended periods to learn their thoughts and feelings about the government relations of their firms. They are almost universally interested, intrigued, and somewhat concerned about how effective their companies are in their dealing with government; at the same time, many of them are inclined to doubt that they can do much to improve the situation.

Their focus is not so much on the detailed day-to-day discussions which their people are conducting with government types, and they are only peripherally conscious of the growing amount of conversation back and forth between businessmen and government officials at the state, local, and national levels which have such a significant impact on their businesses.

Sometimes these meetings are negotiating sessions; sometimes the manager is seeking a zoning change or a license or a permit from the government agency; sometimes he is utilizing some statute or regulation to restrict his competitor's actions; sometimes he is doing battle with a piece of legislation or an administrative ruling he does not like; sometimes he is looking for information, and sometimes for money.

But the corporate presidents and board chairmen have their eyes on another level of question.

The best statement of this broader concern came from the president of one of the nation's largest, most distinguished companies with far-flung interests. "What keeps you up at night worrying in this field?" I asked him. "What troubles you the most?"

"I'll tell you what it is," he said, without a moment's hesitation. "It is not the more-or-less technical matters which come up all the time. Rather, I'd like to know how I can get Gardner Ackley to *hear* me. We have a serious problem with the wage-price guideline concept which I want to get across to him. I can get an appointment to see him, all right—I get through the guards in the EOB, sit and chat in his high-ceilinged office, and he is very pleasant and cordial. But I just don't think I am really getting through to him. It's not that he actively disbelieves me—I don't think my firm has any particular credibility gap—it's just that our message doesn't have any real impact. He doesn't really *hear* what I am saying to him."

I followed up his comments by asking why he cared. "After

all," I pointed out, "those guidelines never had any legal status anyway."

"That's true enough," he responded, "but I am deeply interested in having men like Ackley understand my position because, in the first place, I have a citizen's sensitivity to public policy and, secondly, my company's interests are spread out all over and I don't want to get cross-wise with those Washington people. If I ever did, they could clobber us in so many ways that I hate even to think about it."

Although this particular president put the issue more candidly and succinctly than most, he was not alone in his awareness of the question. Many managers in many ways are posing the same kind of issue, but they are not actively pursuing answers, partly, I suspect, because they are not at all concerned that there *are* answers. To a degree, they are in the frame of mind that managers with marketing responsibilities must have been in 25 or 30 years ago, before we had accumulated the information, concepts, and tools to break down a marketing question, analyze its components, develop alternatives, collect relevant data, and make rational judgments. Once the business manager felt himself to be totally at the mercy of the market place; now the balance has shifted, and he has learned how to predict and to some extent manipulate the market to his ends. Successful marketing has become the product of more than good instinct and good luck, though they still play a large part; it is susceptible to thoughtful, systematic, businesslike analysis and action.

Government relations, though in a sense a marketing kind of activity, have only begun to be viewed in the same rational fashion—and only by a handful of pioneering companies. Yet managers themselves make the case for approaching it in a managerial way. Brushing aside the all-too-common glib after-dinner speaker who tells them that the government is their "partner," that government officials have a life-or-death hold over their firms; they recognize that most firms will never be as dependent on public policies for their futures as they will on good new product decisions or imaginative merchandising. But clearly government programs and policies are significant now, will be even more so in the future, and dealing with government officials is growing as a part of the manager's daily chores. If we are going to do so much of this, say the wiser corporate managers, we had better do it right.

I want to lay out some general lines of approach to answer my friend's question about Gardner Ackley. Obviously, the precise ways for his company to address the problem are going to depend on the nature of his business, on his current corporate image among Washington types, on how he is presently organized to do the job, on the traditions and attitudes of his company and its executives, on its degree of sophistication, and a number of other factors. One of the great hazards in government relations is the "rainmaker" who is quick to prescribe a cure for a company without the kind of careful diagnosis and custom-designing that is necessary. But one can at least identify some of the questions which my friend should be looking at as he goes about fashioning a program to take care of that troublesome matter which is keeping him up nights.

Roughly speaking, there are two lines of inquiry that should be pursued: the general atmosphere within which the company makes its representations—the climate; and, second, the kind of specific presentations that are made and how they are handled. I will deal with them in that order.

We hear a great deal about the "company image" these days, though there was even more publicity devoted to it a decade or so ago when the terms were new. While managers do tend to get caught up in fads and pursue programs because the company across the street is doing it, the matter of image does have some hard-headed validity, and nowhere more clearly than in dealing with government people. The attitude of the listener, his open-mindedness to what the businessman says, his acceptance of the ideas presented as important and worth considering have much to do with the effectiveness of the businessman's visit; at least he is more likely to gain entree to the government official's already busy and active mind, overstocked as it probably already is with problems and ideas. The company executive wants the government man to react: "Well, if Dick says it, I'd better listen carefully" rather than "I wonder what line this guy is peddling and how quickly I can move him along." Incidentally, it is also true that a businessman is more likely to make an articulate, persuasive presentation if he senses that he has a somewhat receptive audience than if he faces a hostile or disinterested one.

The public relations experts understand a great deal about corporate image-building and some researchers are superbly equipped to identify opinions and the attitudes and values that underlie them as guides and as measures of something constructive about their Washington image.

One of the most dramatic means is to capitalize on some public concern with an aspect of a business to build an image of socially responsible and responsive industry which is anxious to unearth and rectify errors that may inadvertently have been made. Too often businessmen project a defensive, angry and injured attitude when a safety, pollution, or pricing question is raised by a government official. They seem to feel that they have been doing something "bad," when in fact they have simply been overtaken by changing social mores and standards. Not so many years ago dumping junk into the rivers and throwing it into the atmosphere was more or less an accepted part of the manufacturing process; now, the public is reacting differently to the practice. The much maligned "robber barons," whom most businessmen criticize violently today, were similarly caught by changing standards which suddenly made criminal or at least unattractive behavior out of business attitudes and methods that were acceptable or even commendatory in an earlier day.

Failing to discern that changes have passed them by, that they are guilty of a lack of foresight more than of evil intent, they often then seek to prove that they really are good people after all. So they produce reams of figures to show that their bathtubs are *too* safe; that they are spending *millions* to keep the waters clean.

The alternative, adopted by one consumer-goods trade association recently, is joining hands with those who want to accomplish these social ends. Instead of drumming up data on everything noble they were doing, which the listener finds self-serving, this particular group came to Washington as soon as they heard a Congressional investigation was being planned, and asked how they could help and cooperate. Instead of simply meeting the pipeline safety drive head on with scientific reports filled with figures, the leaders of that industry sat down with the Administration to work out a sensible piece of legislation. The point is that by the time that government is attending one of these questions, someone is convinced there is a problem; trying to convince him, at that stage, that there is no problem is like trying to convince some businessmen that government regulators are not socialists. He will just not believe you, that's all.

Thus a firm or an industry, by admitting the existence of a problem even though disagreeing about its dimensions and ways to deal with it, can capitalize on the respect which attitude surveys shows the American public has for business and enhance its own standings as an enterprise which is concerned about the same issues that trouble large segments of its customers and shareholders.

One additional point: a top government regulator said to me recently that the "trouble with businessmen is that they never seriously ask themselves 'why is this government guy trying to do this?' They are too ready to accept the old canards about empire-building or socialism or votes instead of realizing that we see ourselves as professionals with a job to do whose constituency and obligations run differently from their's. They assume we are basically antagonistic to them, whereas the fact is we more often have different sets of objectives from theirs. They would save themselves a lot of grief—and we'd do better regulating—if they sought out the 'why' in an open-minded way."

Of course, businessmen do not have to wait until they are attacked to respond in a wise and cooperative manner to the developing concern with the quality of our national environment, and to create a positive image of their companies. More and more of them are seeking ways in which their companies can make a contribution to the solution of some of our basic social questions, and do it within the accepted commercial requirements of the private enterprise system. In other words, to quote the distinguished Chairman of Corn Products, Alexander MacFarlane, business is finding "great new opportunities in the 'people' market as it always has in the 'thing' market." His own company's subsidiary, MIND, is one of the pioneers with its training operation for government and industry. Like Aerojet's tent factory in Watts or Kodak's sponsorship of inner city companies, MIND is not charity; it is an attempt to turn the resources of the business community to needs which have traditionally been the principal concern of government.

Parenthetically, both businessmen and public officials would do well to be a little more realistic about the possibilities in this growing kind of association. Both tend to be somewhat euphoric about it at the moment, but working out the details of a particular project on the ground is not quite as easy as it looks in the Board Room or the Washington office building. A study of the California experiment in which four major aerospace companies were given funds by the state to work on programs of waste disposal, education, transportation, and welfare indicated that we have some distance to go before the businessman appreciates what the government executive is talking about, and vice versa. It takes some advance planning on both sides; the businessman has to look at accounting procedures and determinations of profitability, at manpower resources, and at ingenious uses of his new expertise. The government official has to turn his back on the attitude which says grudgingly, "I guess we'll have to let them make a profit out of this," and recognize that what the American people want is answers, not ideological maps of who should be doing what and how. If the profit system can make a contribution to rebuilding cities or controlling drug addiction or lowering hospital costs, let's figure out ways to utilize it for those ends.

At any rate, active and effective participation in this new role for business can make a positive contribution to an industry's Washington image, as the insurance companies learned when they announced their $1 billion pledge for investment in construction and job-creating ventures in the cities.

Appropriate and tasteful public relations programs based on such participation seems to work for some firms which advertise their job corps camps or special communications services in underdeveloped areas very widely to the Washington community. One trade association sponsors a classical music program based on the favorite music of learning public officials. Others make certain that their public service projects are passed along to the Washington newspaper fraternity.

All this comes under the heading of creating and maintaining mutually cooperative relationships with government people on endeavors in which such association is appropriate. There are many more opportunities than most businessmen see or seize, unfortunately. How many of them will respond favorably when a Senator or a Congressman asks them to come to Washington to testify at a hearing on some program in which he is interested—even if they have publicly recorded their support for it in other ways? I know more than one firm which turned down specific requests of this kind from Senators or Congressmen who are important to them because they were "too busy" or "didn't know enough about the subject." Why should they not expect the member, when they next seek his assistance, to respond, in the words of the popular song, "Where were you when I needed you; where were you when I wanted you?"—albeit under his breath.

Not enough executives call and say "What can I do to help" when they read that a program they support—foreign aid, poverty, duty reduction—is in trouble on the Hill. Too few, when they are asked to serve on an advisory committee, really tackle the assignment seriously. Nowhere near enough know their own Congressmen and Senators, keep them informed of new company activities, invite them to participate in company meetings and ceremonies.

But the list is endless, and an able businessman can think through a whole series of ways which fit his company's interest and mores, or get some professional guidance in doing so, once he has determined that he does want and need a Washington atmosphere in which the "optics" are good for his firm.

As in marketing, institutional advertising is by no means the whole trick. (I lay aside the matter of product; it goes without saying that Gardner Ackley is never going to hear the business executive if he does not have a good, honest, responsible story to tell in the first place. I simply assume that most companies are wise enough to look at what they are selling and make sure it measures up, or can be reworked to do so, before they even start to sell it.) Another part, as I mentioned, is the kind of presentation that is made and how it is handled. How has the firm organized its distribution system and sales force? What are they saying, and to whom? Who at headquarters is guiding them, listening to their reports on how they are progressing, making sure that the company makes the adjustments necessary to support them? It is to this kind of question in government relations I want now to turn.

I never fail to be surprised at the variety of ways in which companies handle their Washington relations. There seems to be no pattern: large or small, consumer or industrial, product or service, old or new, large government sales or minimal, regulated or unregulated follow Topsy-like approaches which may reflect more the interests of a particular chief executive than any thought-through program. One large consumer goods company has a six-man office for representation duties (not sales); another company in the same field with the same problems has one man, unsupported with office or secretary. One regulated company only recently opened a Washington shop; another has been there for years. One company has only a single man and a secretary, but the chief executive keeps in constant touch with him, would never consider making a Washington call without bringing him along. Another has five people, but "we handle all the really important things from New York."

Too few have ever taken a systematic look at Washington, at their needs now and projected for five years, at the alternative ways which exist for dealing effectively with the federal establishment, at the different approaches Washington representation can take. Too many have drifted into their existing arrangement on an ad hoc basis, perhaps through the government sales route originally, or in response to some particular crisis. A sales and distribution mechanism jerry-built in that fashion would certainly be a candidate for a new look, given the fast-changing times. Should a firm handle Washington through an office of its own, a law firm, a public relations firm, a trade association, a professional Washington representative, or a combination? Should it concentrate on the Hill or the executive branch? Should it have primarily an information post or an active program? Should it call on specialists as it goes along, or expect its Washington man to cover everything? These and hosts of other questions need answers.

Corporate headquarters itself offers another route to more effective government relations. I know one company where the general counsel has extensive Washington experience so he can feed this dimension into the day-to-day policy making that goes on when George pokes his head in Charlie's office and says, "Hey, what do you say we try this?" Further, he can guide the Washington office, understand their reports, ask them the right questions. I know many others where the Washington man is like an ambassador to a foreign country with only limited cable service back home. Corporate headquarters has only the vaguest idea what he is doing, and he is looking on as some type of esoteric specialist, a magician who lives in a mysterious world of his own. It is rather like having a regional sales manager operating virtually independently and out of touch—only at least with the salesman the firm gets some hard monthly figures to inspect.

Unfortunately, too many companies have not equipped themselves with a structure or the personnel necessary to coordinate the government relations activities underway in the firm so the tax man knows that while he is dealing with a state legislature on one issue, the industrial relations man is up there on an equal employment matter. These businesses operate their government relations through a series of independent sovereignties, which may or may not touch base with one another. In many instances, even companies with Washington representation have not tied their federal discussions together. Thus the Washington representative may not know anywhere near all that individual division managers are doing on the federal scene, or why.

There are no set answers; each company should organize itself according to its particular needs, talent, and interests. But someone ought to be generally sensitive to this area, aware of what is going on, and participating in policy decisions in a way that enables him to bring his information and point of view to bear on a continuing basis.

Part of this is the handling of trade associations. When I was still a Tariff Commissioner, I needled a friend of mine who is a company president with some comments about an association presentation to which his firm's name was attached. "Come on now, George," he said. "You don't really believe that nonsense about the desperate need for protection on parts for Product X, do you? You've been buying them from Germany for years; it would cost you money if the tariffs went up on those items." He was somewhat surprised to hear that his organization had been identified with the position, but when he recovered he replied, "Oh well, that's just trade association politics I guess, you know how it is." Some companies are active participants in a few of the associations to which they belong, but unacquainted with stands being taken by others. Some were once active because one or more of their officers were personally involved, but when their terms ran out the company's connection ran out too. Only a few have an actual policy of overseeing, coordinating, and participating in these organizations, using them where they can be helpful and disassociating themselves from positions taken which would be out of step with the firm's interests.

There is a great deal to be said about the actual presentations businessmen make, aside from the organizational aspects of their government relations programs. Unfortunately, they often fail to do their homework and exhibit all too dramatically that they do not know exactly who the man is to whom they are talking, what he does, where his authority reaches, under what regulations he is operating. They ask to see a Cabinet officer to approve a set of plans which are the responsibility of a technician down in his department; they call a Commission a Committee; they have not had themselves briefed sufficiently to know what the conference or hearing is all about and what purpose it serves. They make assumptions about the government man to whom they are talking, usually unflattering, and they have never thought to ask their people to find out a little about him and his background. In a business setting, they would never seek out their supplier's finance vice president to talk about a quality control problem; they would not meet with the purchasing agent without knowing how broad a jurisdiction he has; they would make sure whether Mr. Brown was a vice president or an assistant to the vice president before they sat down with him.

I recall one set of Tariff Commission hearings called to enable the Commission to estimate the economic impact of duty cuts on a range of products. All we wanted to know was what the effect would be on this company's business of tariff reductions. We learned about the financial structure of the UN, the future of American ice hockey, the situation in Appalachia, and hoof and mouth disease. Some of it was fascinating; much of it was irrelevant. Yet the law, the announcement of the hearing, and the

Chairman's opening statement all set forth clearly the purpose of the sessions and the kind of job the Commission was doing.

Carrying my point to extremes, I shall never forget the evening in the White House when the telephone in the office of one of my colleagues began to ring. He was a Special Assistant to the President, concerned, among other things, with Latin American policy and top personnel appointments (Ambassadors, Cabinet, Regulatory Commissioners, and so on). His secretary had left—it was late Saturday—so he picked up the receiver. It was a call from Pittsburgh; the gentleman had a friend who was being evicted from his apartment, and he wanted a statement from the White House that the man's Veteran's check was in the mail to give to the landlord so the eviction could be forestalled. If you are in the government—somewhere, anywhere—you are expected to be involved with everything, everywhere. It is like calling a production engineer in a soap factory to get information about the financial structure of IBM simply because the engineer is "in business."

Most of the weaknesses in business presentations arise from the fundamental misconceptions many of them have about government people. Instead of assuming that the official to whom they are talking is an honest professional trying to do his job in a fair and sensible way, too many of them seem to view him as incompetent, politically motivated, and anti-business. This gives rise to many mistakes which they would never make in a presentation to a fellow businessman: talking down, exaggerating, unsophisticated attempts at deception, unsubtle political pressures, and sometimes direct attacks. A straightforward, candid, and thorough presentation of the facts would be far more effective; even if the businessman has enough evidence to convince himself that the man he is negotiating with is a bureaucratic dullard, if he treats him like one he is going to make the image come true. But if he acts as though the government official is an intelligent citizen trying to do an honest job, he at least creates a more receptive mood for open discussion.

The catalogue of dos and don'ts is long, and I do not want to thumb through it here; suffice to say that the kind of statements businessmen make when they sit down with the government official, and the attitudes they hold as they approach such a conference, have a significant impact on the effectiveness of their efforts. Thoughtful, imaginative preparation here is just as important as it is for a business conference.

One final point in this general area of the actual selling process, as opposed to the setting of the climate: many government executives complain that they do not hear from business interests early enough in the policy-making process so their input will be most effective. By the same token, businessmen wish they had an "early warning system" to alert them to what is coming up. This breakdown of communication, or, better, misfire of timing is worthy of considerable attention on both sides. How can a company position itself to participate in the fashioning of programs before they are formally subjected to the processes of enactment? By the time they hit the floor as a bill or the Federal Register as a proposed set of rules, a great deal of work has gone into them and many positions have been frozen. How can the business cook get into the kitchen when the batter is being mixed? In most cases, he would be welcomed, so it is up to the business manager and the government manager to work out a mechanism for this particular company or industry to let him know when the cake is being made.

Here, then, is an outline of approach to this question of "How do I get the federal government (or the city or state government) to *hear* me?" It is a combination of attention to climate and attention to selling techniques and personnel. Some of the questions or ideas I have raised will be appropriate to a given company; some will not be. But that is unimportant, for, like a marketing policy, each business must formulate it for itself.

The important point is that someone take the lead and sit down to work out such a policy. The real need is for the managers who are beginning to ask that kind of question to seize the initiative and get some satisfactory answers. For business-government relations are manageable, like anything else.

6. Practices of Public Information

"THE Practices of Public Information" in government are as varied as the bureaus, agencies, and departments themselves. However, some basic methods have been developed and are widely employed. This section describes some of them.

How is a public information office organized? *Wayne Phillips* discusses the steps he took in organizing the information function for the new Department of Housing and Urban Development; in the process he learned much about the nature of public information itself.

Mr. Phillips, Director of HUD's Division of Public Affairs, came to that position in 1966 after serving as Director of News and Information for the Democratic National Committee from 1964 to 1966. Prior to that he had been special assistant to Robert C. Weaver, then administrator of the Housing and Home Finance Agency. A graduate of Harvard, he holds two master's degrees from Columbia, in history and journalism. Before entering government service Mr. Phillips worked on a number of newspapers, including the *New York Times* where he was a reporter for ten years.

Perhaps the heart of a public information office is the news room. *Harry Weiss* describes how the Commerce Department news room is organized and explains the myriad details with which the news room officers must deal. He is Chief of the News Division of Commerce's Office of Public Information.

Mr. Weiss holds a degree in science writing from Antioch College and has been with the Commerce Department since 1946.

He also held positions with the Office of War Information, Office of Price Administration, and the War Relocation Authority. He is internationally known for his creative work in origami, the art of paper folding.

The special event is a device to allow the government to focus attention on facts and ideas that the people *need* to know as well as have a *right* to know. *Roy L. Swift,* as the Information Officer for the Social Security Administration, must frequently develop special events to properly disseminate information about his agency's benefits to the American people.

A native of Texas, Mr. Swift taught English and edited country newspapers in Texas before World War II. After military service, he began his career in government information work, first with the Federal Security Agency in Texas. He came to the Social Security Administration's Baltimore headquarters in 1949, and he has been chief of information since 1950.

Sometimes the government must raise its voice to a high decibel to be heard. The technique used most is the promotional campaign, which *Bernard Posner* describes as "government's megaphone." He is responsible for the promotional campaigns of the President's Committee on Employment of the Handicapped, for which he serves as Deputy Executive Secretary.

Mr. Posner graduated from the University of Cincinnati and holds a master's degree in communication from American University, where he also serves as an adjunct professor. He began his career on the staff of an advertising trade journal. After World War II service, he joined the Veterans Administration and rose to Assistant Director of Information before joining the President's Committee in 1960.

FOR EFFECTIVE COMMUNICATION . . .

Organizing an Information Office

WAYNE PHILLIPS
DIRECTOR, DIVISION OF PUBLIC AFFAIRS
U. S. DEPARTMENT OF HOUSING
AND URBAN DEVELOPMENT

No two government public information offices are organized alike. Beyond that, there are no safe generalities on this subject. But, nevertheless, some can be attempted.

Soon after the Department of Housing and Urban Development came into being in late 1965 its first Secretary, Robert C. Weaver, asked me to take on the job of organizing its public information functions. In the course of doing so it was necessary to look at how these functions had been organized in the other federal departments, and to see what this might suggest for HUD.

What was suggested was that HUD had better start from scratch and build an organization based on an analysis of the job the public information office would be asked to perform—rather than to attempt to pattern anything after what had been done by others elsewhere.

The public information function in government is a service function—it came into being as a means of relieving those responsible for operating government programs of a necessary, but necessarily subsidiary, function that was both irksome and distracting.

In this sense it is similar to other service functions which have evolved in government organizations—such as personnel, management, budget, and purchasing. And it is subject to all the problems of organization experienced in administering those functions.

In a new government operation, before there has been any organizational differentiation, one person may have responsibility for what is known as "the program." That one person, in addition to his "program" responsibilities, will have to worry about preparing a budget, ordering supplies, hiring personnel, keeping management records—and answering the questions of the public.

Eventually, if he has sufficient personnel, he will assign these functions to various members of his staff. And there will emerge someone with responsibility for answering the questions of the public. At first that person may have to perform that responsibility together with other related functions—Congressional relations, for example. But nevertheless the organization of a public information office has begun.

Because of this pattern of evolution, most government public information offices have what is known as a "decentralized" pat-

247

tern: they are attached to particular programs or groups of programs and handle all public inquiries relating to those programs.

The larger and more complex these programs become, however, the more complex the public information function becomes. Soon a process of organizational differentiation begins to set in, usually based on the type of information which is required.

Many inquiries from the general public, for example, can be handled in person, or on the telephone, or by letter. But others require more detail than can be conveniently handled in these ways, so various types of written materials may be developed— mimeographed fact sheets, or simple folders, or printed brochures and booklets, depending on the complexity of the material contained.

Other inquiries come from news media, who are in effect representing the public and are entitled to the same service as any citizen. Most of these, too, can be handled in person or by telephone, or by letter, or with duplicated materials. But frequently requests are made for photographs to illustrate articles in printed media, for tape-recorded material for radio, or for motion picture film which can be used on television.

Inquiries also come in from organizations representing public interest groups—groups which frequently are closely related to the operation of government programs, are deeply involved in the success or failure of those programs, and who not only have a citizen's right to be informed, but must be informed if the program is to succeed. These groups often want, in addition to the forms of information already described, speakers for their meetings, information representatives who can answer questions at conferences, motion pictures or slide presentations, exhibits, and posters.

All of these sources of inquiry—the general public, news media, and public interest groups—want more than just answers to their questions, however. They all want a government agency to keep them informed—without waiting to be asked—of significant actions that may affect their interests. This leads to the necessity for announcing these actions publicly, usually in the form of a news release. Or, if the announcement is of sufficient importance, and such that there should be an opportunity for the asking and answering of questions, a news conference may be organized.

Operating program people often want more from a public information function, too, than relief from having to deal with the inquiries of the curious.

They frequently want the help of the public information office in preparing books and pamphlets, motion pictures, slide presentations, or exhibits to assist those who are making use of their programs. Materials of this sort are playing an ever-increasing role in government administration. And this, in turn, is giving both more responsibility and more work to public information offices where the skills can be found to produce them.

Program operators also want to know what the public reaction is to their activities—so an important part of the public information function becomes the collection and analysis of information on this reaction, and making this available to program people. This is valuable in alerting them to areas of public controversy, to mistakes that have been made or might be made, and to enabling them to do better the job that has been assigned to them.

They also want a positive effort to get to the public information which can help them carry out their responsibilities. A key part of an operator's job, for example, is the recruiting of qualified personnel. If he does not have good personnel he cannot carry out the job assigned to him, and the only way he can get this personnel is by a positive recruiting effort. Such an effort can use any and all of the forms of information available—the speech, the news release, duplicated or printed material, audiovisual materials and exhibits, and paid advertising.

Finally program operators frequently want to utilize the skills available in their public information offices for internal information activities. Nearly as important to the operator as his public relations, for example, is his relations with those working for him. In addition to the formal directives and orders he may issue he frequently feels the need for some form of employee publication, training materials including booklets and films, posters and exhibits. While all of these—like recruiting—are an aspect of the personnel function, they require the special skills of the public information office.

As the size and complexity of a government operation grows the number of people involved in the public information function also tends to proliferate.

Public information offices come into being attached to nearly every program function and can vary in size from a single person to several hundreds. The total of their activity can become enormous in terms of the news releases, publications, films, exhibits, and other materials being produced. And there can be a total lack of coordination between these offices.

This is the situation that existed in the Housing and Home Finance Agency prior to the establishment of the Department of Housing and Urban Affairs. And it is the situation that we found in other departments and agencies when we began to study their organization with a view to the organization of HUD's activities.

The Housing and Home Finance Agency, which was the predecessor agency of HUD, had six constituent units—the Office of the Administrator, the Federal Housing Administration, the Public Housing Administration, the Urban Renewal Administration, the Community Facilities Administration, and the Federal National Mortgage Association. Each of them had a separate public information office—as a result of the kind of evolution described above.

Secretary Weaver had decided on the basis of his five years of experience as administrator of the Housing and Home Finance Agency that HUD was going to have a centralized public information operation. The irritations and frustrations that he had experienced as administrator from the lack of coordination between these various public information offices are not to be detailed here. But they can be matched and surpassed by the experiences of every other department in the federal government.

The problem we faced in organizing HUD's information activities, therefore, was how to achieve the direct, centralized control the Secretary wanted and needed for policy purposes, and at the same time maintain a close working relationship with the operating program areas of the department.

The first step toward this was to identify those personnel who were involved in public information activities. This was not easy, because many persons were carrying mixed responsibilities— again because of the evolutionary process described above. There were more than a few instances of persons who were carrying administrative as well as public information responsibilities—and they had to decide which way they wished to go in the future.

There were more than a few instances of competent people who administrators wished to keep close to them, and whose public information involvement was denied or glossed over. There were just as many instances of incompetent employees administrators wished to dispense with who were passed off as public information people.

Eventually 52 persons with public information functions under the old Housing and Home Finance Agency were identified, and they were transferred to a centralized Division of Public Affairs.

At the same time the decision was made that the size of the Public Affairs Division was to remain fixed at this level of 52— so the department could not be accused of creating some enormous new government propaganda operation. No consideration was given to whether or not this was the size of operation that was necessary or desirable to perform the public information function. But that is excusable because no one at that point could forecast what the workloads in public information might be or might become in the new department.

The next step was to establish staff groups within the Division of Public Affairs which could begin to specialize in the various public information functions.

A Radio and Television Services Staff was established to handle relationships with those media and to supervise the production of materials for them.

A Publications Services Staff was established to handle the production of booklets, pamphlets, brochures, and other duplicated materials.

A Consumer Relations Staff was established to handle direct inquiries from the general public and to service public interest groups.

A Press Services Staff was established to handle inquiries from news media, production and processing of press releases, and the screening and analysis of press reports about the department.

Under the Press Services Staff we set up press desks to service each of the assistant secretaries and the programs for which they were responsible.

To minimize the dislocation resulting from the reorganization an effort was made to leave as the chiefs of these press desks the men who had previously headed the public information offices for those program areas. Those who had worked under them were shifted to the new functional staffs depending on their areas of special competence and interest.

The result, in organizational terms, was that we took six virtually independent public information offices and were able to merge them so as to produce five comparatively small "press desks" serving program areas and backed up by four functional staffs serving the department as a whole.

The result, in terms of efficiency, was a degree of specialization that enabled us to take on a greatly enlarged workload without any increase in personnel.

Prior to the organization of the department, for example, the Federal Housing Administration had produced a series of radio and television public service spots. With the new organization this activity was expanded and broadened to provide public service announcements of department-wide interest. (The demand for public service material from radio and television stations, incidentally, is enormous.)

A new service for broadcasters was inaugurated to provide recorded excerpts from news statements by department officials for use on radio and television news broadcasts. Stations are alerted to the availability of these excerpts by notices to the radio wires of the Associated Press and United Press; they can obtain them by telephoning a special number which activates a playback device. The device is standard studio equipment and makes possible recordings of high broadcast fidelity.

A technique of contracting was worked out in connection with motion picture production that has proven extraordinarily successful. Frequently such contracts are let on competitive bid, which results in the lowest price—and the lowest quality. HUD's management people, working with the Radio and Television Services Staff, were able to work out a fixed price competition in which, in effect, we said "This is what this movie is worth; what kind of quality will you give me for it?" More than 30 proposals were received the first time this device was used—and we were able to make the selection from a remarkable array of talent offered by some of the best producers in the country.

Just as the Radio and Television Services Staff functions much as a producer would in relationship to the production of motion pictures, we have tried to reorient the Publications Services Staff to function in the manner of a publishing house.

In other words, we try to develop on our own staff editorial, production, and management talents—and contract for writing services as needed. On this basis we are able to obtain a much higher level of writing talent than we could afford to hire and keep on a staff.

Under the Housing and Home Finance Agency there had been very little competence in motion picture production. We found a half dozen projects in this area had been begun by various operating people, but had soon bogged down for lack of technical competence. Little by little the Radio and Television Services Staff was able to get into these projects and try to sort out what could be salvaged.

In publications the confusion was far worse—in fact, almost beyond comprehension. To begin with no one was very sure what a publication was. We finally worked out the definition that it was duplicated or printed information intended for distribution outside the department. Every publication in existence (and there were hundreds) had been started by some operating person to meet an operating need that had existed at the time—and may long since have been forgotten. None bore any relationship to the overall policies of the department.

We were faced with the agonizing problem of trying to keep up with a skyrocketing demand from the public for information about department programs, pressure from program people to get out new publications on new programs being authorized by Congress, and trying to track down just what publications were in existence and why.

Fortunately the insistence of the Secretary that order be brought out of this chaos as soon as possible, together with the help of the management staff of the department in drafting a Secretary's order for the control of publications, helped us to evolve a publications policy.

Its essence was that a specified amount would be allocated for publications out of the operating funds of the department, and this amount would be broken down for each program area. The assistant secretary responsible for that program area would determine, in consultation with the public information office, how those funds could best be used. The Secretary would approve the overall program, and then it would be up to the public information office to produce.

This was a very significant breakthrough in two respects:

1. It established a precedent from which it is our hope to develop a similar control over the production of motion pictures and exhibits.

2. It established for the first time a budget concept in the administration of public information activities.

In the federal government there are generally three ways of financing public information activities: by appropriation, by allocation, and by revolving fund. Appropriations are rare—very few departmental budgets include funds specifically appropriated for the public information function, and even those that do receive only a small fraction of the funds they use in this fashion. Much more common is an allocation of funds from those appropriated for the administration of government programs. These allocations are usually made on an ad hoc basis by the administrator—so much for a movie, so much for a booklet, as the need develops. There is little if any concept of an overall public information program and how much it should cost in relationship to other demands on administrative funds—let alone any consideration as to how the allocations of numerous administrators may add up for a department as a whole (something that drives Secretaries, budget officers, and appropriations committees wild). The revolving fund is money replenished by some form of user charges—rentals on films or exhibits, for example. These are cumbersome and difficult to manage.

One of the tragedies of government public information activities is that very few (if any) government public information men ever get initiated into the mysteries of budgeting and management. Consequently they are constantly embroiled in controversies over the expenditures of funds and frequently are caught in the crossfire between operating people who want to do one thing and budget people who say it is illegal.

The only honest solution is the establishment of a clearly defined budget for public information activities. But we will never see this day as long as Congress regards public information as synonymous with propaganda—rather than recognizing it as an essential bulwark of a democracy.

The Consumer Relations Staff was, I think, a new concept in the organization of a government public information office and may well prove to be one of the most important innovations we have made at HUD.

It started from a recognition that one of the most difficult areas of public information is the adequate handling of what are sometimes called "little people" queries—the telephone calls, letters, and visits from individuals who want information for their own purposes. They do not represent the press, and they do not represent organizations, and as a result they are often shuffled from pillar to post, getting very little service but a great deal of aggravation.

The principal problem in organizing this service was finding a means of channeling these calls, letters, and visits into this staff. This required a great deal of work with administrative units responsible for screening correspondence and with switchboards on the handling of telephone calls. It required a constant effort to educate operating people that we wanted to help them, not take away their work. And finally it required the opening of a street-level information and visitors reception center in a good downtown location.

This staff was also made responsible for handling relationships with the numerous organizations—more than 200—with a continuing interest in HUD programs. Here, again, the organization job consisted first of identifying these organizations, and then establishing contact with them.

As a part of this function a Conference and Convention Service was established. Each organization's schedule of conferences and meetings was kept in a chronological file; 90 days before the meeting a check would be made to determine what if any information would be needed from HUD: speakers, an information table, literature, exhibits, or motion pictures. Arrangements would then be made to provide the services requested. A booking schedule was maintained for all department exhibits to be sure they were kept up to date and in use. Arrangements were made with a motion picture lending service to handle the mailing, recovery, and cleaning of films sent out to group meetings.

The Department-wide coordination of public appearances also became an important part of this staff's activities.

On the instructions of the Secretary all invitations for public appearances were directed to be sent to the Division of Public Affairs. There a check is made for overlapping and duplication, and replies are prepared in consultation with the officials invited. If the official cannot make the appearance requested, an effort is made to obtain another department speaker, if that is desired. In general we try to restrict Washington officials to national meetings, and to persuade local and regional groups to accept department speakers from local or regional offices. The public appearance schedules for the department are made up at the end of every month for 90 days ahead—at the end of January for February, March, and April; at the end of February for March, April, and May. In this way everyone involved in supporting activities in connection with public appearance knows well in advance everything that is being planned.

The Press Services Staff is the largest of the four organizational units in the HUD Division of Public Affairs and includes nearly half its personnel. This is evidence both of the importance and the complexity of press relationships in a department like HUD.

Newsmen are usually appalled when we tell them that HUD produces more than 6000 press releases a year. But fortunately only the chief of the Press Services Staff and I have to look at them all. Most of them are announcements of local actions of significance in the communities involved, but of little interest beyond them. So only a few copies are produced and they go primarily to the news media serving that community.

Even so, the writing, editing, and production of such a volume of press releases is an enormous task. The only way we have been able to manage it is through automation.

Once again, a study was made of the releases being put out by the Housing and Home Finance Agency. These were broken down to about 50 different types. Standardized formats were devised for each of these 50 so they could be written by filling in blanks on printed forms. Then punched tapes were prepared so the releases could be typed on automatic typewriters at a speed of over 100 words a minute, stopping at the blanks so the typist could manually fill in missing names, figures, and descriptions.

By the use of these procedures we were able to reduce the number of persons necessary to produce press releases from 12 to 6—freeing a half dozen persons for work in other parts of the division.

One result of this saving was being able to spend more time and effort in developing news stories of greater significance about the overall activities of the department and about what those activities meant to individuals. This has meant an important shift away from providing purely statistical news about how much money HUD is spending to news about the people who have benefited from these expenditures. These stories, in turn, have been given a much broader national distribution as picture features.

Every morning in various parts of the old Housing and Home Finance Agency countless people were skimming through newspapers, on government time, trying to find out what had happened that was of importance to them in their administrative responsibilities. How much this time added up to in money, I don't know. But it seemed to be more than was worthwhile.

So one of the first innovations undertaken by the Division of Public Affairs was a daily "clip sheet" produced and distributed to every top administrator's desk before noon. This required a staff member reporting at 7 A.M. each day to screen the local newspapers, clip and paste them. Then it utilized the recently developed Xerox technique to photographically reproduce the pasted clippings for photo-offset printing. With the excellently equipped print shop of the department, and special messengers, what at first seemed like a miracle of production has now become a daily routine in the department. And it was soon followed up with the development of a weekly magazine clip sheet which gives department administrators each Friday (in time for weekend reading) a selection of significant articles from national periodicals.

A final innovation in keeping the department's administrators informed of press opinion was the compilation of a monthly tabulation of editorials listing all those taking positions for or against activities.

Arrangements also were made for an instant reporting from department regional and local offices of the handling of news relating to the department. Thus it is possible for us to collect in three hours, by telephone chain, information from 80 cities on how a news development may have been reported in the local press.

The first year of HUD's public information activities was largely concerned with organizing the operations that have been described here. The second year was devoted increasingly to developing the relationship between the central public information office in Washington and the emerging public information activities in HUD's eight regional offices.

The old Housing and Home Finance Agency had regional public information assistants for both the regional administrators and the regional directors of the Public Housing Administration. In the years just prior to the establishment of the department, however, most of the assistants to the regional administrator's positions had become vacant.

To reorganize the public information function in the regions it was therefore necessary to bring in new assistants to the regional administrators and to integrate their activities with those of the former assistants to the regional directors of the Public Housing Administration. At the same time it was necessary to establish the responsibilities of this new office, and its relationship to the Division of Public Affairs in Washington.

This had to be developed in accordance with the Secretary's general policy, which was:

· All communications to the regions from Washington must flow through the regional administrators.

· So far as possible operations of the department must be decentralized and shifted from Washington to the regions.

Over the past year we have worked to persuade regional administrators that their public affairs assistants should take on responsibilities closely paralleling those of the Division of Public Affairs in the central office.

We have, for example, worked with them to establish Community Development Information Centers similar to the center operated by the Consumer Relations Staff in Washington.

We have gradually shifted to the regions responsibility for drafting the program press releases that comprise the bulk of the department's news announcements, and determining the distribution of those releases.

We have also worked with the special assistants for public affairs to encourage them in seeking out and developing feature stories about department activities for publications in their regions.

We have worked with them, too, in expanding their activities in regard to the provision of speakers and other services for meetings and conventions held in their regions.

Eventually we hope to reach a situation where the bulk of public information contacts with HUD take place through these regional offices. We feel this not only makes more sense administratively, but in the long run it will result in better service to the public by bringing the source of information closer to them.

When we reach that point the Washington Division of Public Affairs should serve primarily as a service organization, preparing materials (publications, exhibits, and films) for use by regional public information offices and working directly only with national media and organizations.

This chapter on the organization of a public information office has been of necessity largely a case study of how such an office has been organized in a major federal department.

As stated at the beginning, no two government public information offices are alike. Nor has anyone, to my knowledge, made a thorough study of the existing organizations. So fragmented is the world in which we live that the public information officers of the twelve federal departments, for example, know each other only casually and have only infrequent contacts in the course of their work. Numerous attempts have been made to bring about more regular communication between them—but the pace of their activity and responsibilities has always precluded any consistent exchange of information and experience.

It may be that there is a science or a profession of public information. But, if so, I am not privy to it. I have operated—and so far as I know all my colleagues have operated—on an ad hoc basis, dealing with problems as they arose and trying to do the best we can with the personnel and resources at our disposal.

INFORMATION'S NETWORK CENTER . . .

Operating a
News Room

HARRY WEISS
CHIEF OF THE NEWS DIVISION
U. S. DEPARTMENT OF COMMERCE

SOMETIMES it seems to me that our news room in the U. S. Department of Commerce is a catch-all for the curious and a turn-to for the frustrated.

When a fire engine races by the building or a 20-gun salute rings out across the street on the White House grounds or a rumor runs rampant through our bureaucratic halls that war has busted out between Amen and So-Be-It, our phones begin to ring.

"What's going on?" "What's it all about?"

And we tell them; for we try to anticipate all questions. "Keep the inmates happy." That's one of our mottos. It relates to keeping good internal relationships.

We have been called upon to lead a kooky messiah out of the inner sanctum of the Secretary of Commerce, to rush out to the street and drop a dime in a parking meter for a reporter while he interviews the boss, and to provide a photogenic newborn baby for a photographer shooting a population recording device.

When major stories break, the news room is an exciting place like the city room of a big metropolitan paper. The buzz and hum are there as the typewriters clatter and the phones ring and the wire service tickers bang out bulletins.

Like most government agencies in Washington, we provide a kind of subsidized service to the news media—free telephones, typewriters in reasonably good working order, a cheap grade of typing paper, and a cozy couch where on occasion a bushed but worthy member of the press corps may konk out. We want to keep the outside boys happy too.

But the news room is not just fun. It's also a place of humdrum toil as day after day we assure ourselves that what passes from our portals is official—hence accurate and factual as we can make it. For that is the public's right.

And the buck stops in the news room.

As we are now organized, no speech or press release or article of any importance may officially be made public without our prior clearance. (Oh yes, there probably is some leakage!)

The Commerce Department has about 25,000 employees with far-flung, dissimilar interests. It promotes foreign trade and measures domestic economics. It determines standards of weights and measures and trys to modify the weather while predicting what it will be by monitoring our nation's own satellites. It sails merchant ships and issues patents and protects trademarks and charts the ocean depths and makes foreign market surveys. It guarantees that critical metals will be available to defense plants. It measures population growth and the production of industrial products. It controls the exports of strategic materials. It shovels out funds to help areas that are economically depressed in the midst of prosperity. It encourages minority groups to get into business. It promotes travel to the United States and it urges big business to apply its talents for profit to some of the urgent social problems of the day.

It is important, then, that public revelations of the Commerce Department's accomplishments at least have some consistency. We in information cannot have one bureau chief supporting an official policy, and another one attacking that same policy. If a bureau chief wants to attack the policy, let him do so privately or join the faculty of some university! A vice president of Bell Telephone does not publicly come out for *reduction* in rates on the heels of the company president's appearance before the public utility commission proving an *increase* is needed.

But we are concerned with more than consistency and conformity with departmental policy. We are interested in clarity and style and honesty in the news room. We are interested in economy. And we are not press agents milking the public payroll to promote the personal ambitions of our officials. We are interested in getting our news used; so timing of releases concerns us, and maintaining good contacts concerns us, and giving expeditious service concerns us.

If we are to understand the operation of the department news room we ought to examine a few of these areas of concern.

Recently a draft release came from one of our bureaus announcing the publication of a "new" booklet containing information for "the first time." It was not new information at all. It had appeared in a much larger book published several months before. The reissuance of the materials in a more convenient form for the use of a specialized segment of the community *was* justified, but the dishonest description was not. We sent the release back for rewriting and passed it for publication later in true perspective.

Not long ago a new bureau information chief, just out of

public relations work with private industry, sent telegrams to a large group of Washington reporters inviting them to a news conference to be held a few days later. There was ample time for ordinary five-cent mail invitations and plenty of time for telephone calls. This waste of public funds was inexcusable, and we said so and inveighed against the use of telegrams again.

Timing of news conferences is important in a town where news flows like "likker" (in Washington that's a deluge) and newsmen on beats are sliced up too thin to give any one bureau the attention it should get. For example, the usual "economic beat" reporter not only covers the Commerce Department but the Treasury Department, Federal Reserve Board, Export-Import Bank, Council of Economic Advisers, Federal Tariff Commission, Federal Trade Commission, World Bank, International Monetary Fund, Small Business Administration, Bureau of the Budget, Securities and Exchange Commission, Federal Deposit Insurance Corporation, and more.

Recently the Commerce Department discovered that a news conference it had scheduled would conflict with the issuance of an important statistic of a sister agency. Reporters could not be in two places at the same time and several indicated their preference for the statistical story since Commerce was under wraps about what its Secretary wanted to talk about.

A call to the information chief of the competing agency led to a decision to have a convenient computer breakdown which would delay the issuance of the statistic for an hour or two. Crisis averted. Wise reporters understood. Problem solved.

We in Commerce are concerned about clarity and style and putting the news in the lead where it belongs. We had a release sent up to us recently which went on for two pages before we could find the news. The writer was so eager to please his boss and various sub-bosses that the names of all the committee members involved in a study preceded what they had labored to produce!

This type of experience proves the importance of having a centralized news set-up in a big agency where the director of news is answerable only to the top of the hierarchy.

About a dozen independent offices and bureaus exist in the Department and each one is rightfully proud of its functions and jealous of its prerogatives. But they cannot push past the central news room where the buck passing stops. Frequently an information officer at the bureau level knows better than to pass along some item of bad judgment or self-serving drivel but he cannot buck a stubborn boss. "Whose bread I eat, his song I sing."

This is where centralized authority comes in and pays off. We are responsive to the wishes of the bureau chiefs—to a point— but can then stand firm in the assurance of topmost support in the interests of the larger institution.

Of course our judgment is occasionally overruled. And of course we are wrong on occasion. But we are there to slow down cases of questionable judgment and reverse them where needed.

Another concern of the news room is to see that unimportant stories are not overplayed or good stories underplayed. Sometimes we will pre-empt a story that an unimaginative bureau chief sees only through narrow eyes. We explore the implications with experts and broaden the meaning judiciously and publish, if so warranted, in the name of the Secretary who thereby makes the program his special program and gives it a worthy launching.

Here is a somewhat fictional example of the judgments we apply. The Department has sent a group of officials into a foreign country to make a study of trade opportunities for American businessmen. They diligently travel the length and breadth of the land and study markets and government attitudes and restrictive business practices and the like. After six months, up comes a report saying opportunities appear to be excellent for U. S. investment there. A release will be written on the report to that effect and it will come to the news room for editing and processing.

In the week before the release arrives, a change in that country's government drastically alters the situation. Everything is in confusion. But the release comes through routinely and still says: "Opportunities for U. S. investment in Boravia, Iturpsk appear to be excellent. . . ."

This is not too much of an exaggeration. The humorless unimaginative specialist, whose report may well have been the quintessence of accuracy when it was written, sometimes cannot see that perhaps things have changed a bit.

I have a sign under my desk blotter which exemplifies the feeling of momentary frustration that overwhelms me when something like that happens. It says in large white letters on a black background:

OH NO! NOT ANOTHER!

But soon the agitation passes and with attempted good grace and humor, we reach for the phone and say to the offender: "Do you suppose things may have changed a bit in Boravia, Iturpsk since you wrote this?"

"Say, I guess you're right. Maybe we ought to hold it up. . . ."

We have mother-henned the releases, gotten the needed clearancs, arranged for the printing and scheduling, and now hold them in our eager fists. How do we get them out to the media and into print or over the air waves where the public may get its just accounting?

A number of ways exist in Washington for getting the releases around to the user. When the news is hot enough, a note on the City News Service wires will bring the reporters running. But we don't leave it to chance. We also get on the telephone and call those we know are interested because they are not always within eye-shot of the tickers.

For $15 to $50 a month, Washington news bureaus support a unique institution known as the "pick-up" service. Depending on the extent of the service requested, these private entrepreneurs go from agency to agency each day or twice a day to pick up news releases and deliver them to their subscribers. We are glad to supply them with bulk copies, for it extends our distribution arm many times over.

Our own messenger services deliver the releases to news racks in the National Press Club, to the Senate and House press galleries, and anywhere else dictated by the nature of the news we are trying to move.

We also maintain mailing lists for pundits who are not in need of daily hot copy but can think through their stories at leisure.

Other ways exist for getting our news to the public. We personally call individual newsmen who may be interested in a particular angle. We also direct inquiries to and arrange interviews with our experts, calling the officials in advance to key them in on anything they ought to know about the reporter (whether his reputation indicates he can be trusted with off-the-record comment, for example).

We arrange news conferences—and are responsible for reserving space, hiring transcription services, distributing pertinent releases, making sure the public address system is working, the air conditioning is not drowning out the speakers, and a carafe of ice water is on hand for thirsty officials (or for those who fumble for time in answering embarrassing questions). And we round up the reporters by calling a checklist of about 50 names and leaving messages.

There is fierce competition in the nation's capital for space in the nation's newspapers, magazines, trade press, and radio and television airwaves. This means that unimportant material should be weeded out before it is ever printed. For example, if a study of multilegged widgets is completed and shows that the widget population is on the increase and the consequently a new market exists for widget feeders, you should not put a national release out on it. But it should be sent to the one magazine that exists for the edification of widgets.

Discrimination needs to be exercised in what a press officer prints, how many he prints, where he sends it after he prints it, when he sends it, how he sends it.

Mailing lists and distribution practices tend to get old and sluggish. And one day a banker in a small town in the west gets a release about the love cycle of the screw tape worm and he blows a gasket about government waste. Now that worm has great economic significance to the cattle grower in Florida. And it's a good study. But it has no direct value to the corn grower or the small town banker in Kansas.

An irate letter goes from banker to congressman; a speech lights up the halls of Congress. An unbusy reporter writes a story about screwballs in government inundating the papers of the west with information about screw worms instead of corn borers. And an investigation is underway that costs a lot more money than the original mailing error ever did.

So mailing programs are re-evaluated. You can't win them all —but you can try.

A news room in a government agency is a nerve center for getting out the message about its activities.

Press officers have an obligation to the public to give an accounting of how the government spends tax dollars. The accounting should be done understandably, expeditiously and objectively.

We in Commerce try to run a news shop reflecting that attitude.

THE NEED TO KNOW . . .

Using Special Events

ROY L. SWIFT
INFORMATION OFFICER
U. S. SOCIAL SECURITY ADMINISTRATION

THE Social Security Administration distributes to every new employee a statement of its objectives. One of these reads:

"Let people know about their rights and responsibilities under the program. People need to be informed before they can act to obtain the program rights to which they are entitled and to discharge their obligations under the law. Moreover, the purpose of the program requires that people know ahead of time what rights they have, for security is not only a matter of getting the money when it is due, but of being conscious ahead of time that the protection is there."

This objective zeroes in on one of two basic informational concepts—the public's "right to know" and its "need to know."

The difference is one of initiative. Under the "right to know" concept, information about the social security program and how it is operating is made available to any citizen who wants it.

But if the citizen *needs* to know something in order to secure his rights or to meet his obligations under the law, the SSA cannot wait for him to ask. The administration must actively seek him out and inform him. This means overcoming apathy, stimulating curiosity, and building motivation.

Herein is the importance of special events as a vehicle for informing the public about social security. Special events, effectively handled, get space and time in the media, gain people's interest, and focus attention on the information that needs to be conveyed.

The initiation of any project to use a special event to inform the public requires, first of all, defining what the public needs to know. The SSA goes about this in a number of ways: it studies the law itself, reviews reports from its district offices, analyzes letters from the public, and evaluates newspaper clippings; it also uses polls and studies.

The basic questions the average citizen needs answers to are, of course, what benefits the social security law provides for him and his family, and what they have to do in order to get them when they are due. These questions raise others, such as: What is the real purpose of social security? What does it cost me to have this protection? Do I get my money's worth for what I pay into the system?

273

Providing meaningful, easily understandable answers to these questions is not always easy. Frequently, the best way is through special events which have drama, action, color, and above all— human interest appeal.

Private industry regularly stages special events as part of its public relations campaigns. It is important, I think, to note some of the differences between government's and industry's versions.

Few people would think it improper for a private business organization to spend a good deal of money simply to tell people that the firm is in business, is staffed by people of good character, and would like to have them as customers.

Little money is spent on such "institutional advertising" in the executive departments of the government. When the SSA spends money to get information to people, it has to be sure that it is for *their* benefit. It hopes people like social security, but whether they do or not depends on the law and the way it is administered, not on persuasion.

A second difference is in the level of financing. The restrictions on the activities of government offices (which are almost total in the area of institutional publicity) are applied even when desirability can be demonstrated with a purely informational rationale.

This chapter is intended to illustrate and discuss the kind of planning that is done after a special event is scheduled. Three areas need careful consideration long before the date is set.

The first consideration is money. Many kinds of special event possibilities present themselves suddenly and evaporate if they are not grasped quickly. If they have to be funded by special request, then the project may have to be planned, explained, justified, and accounted for, only to be abandoned.

If the proper advantage is to be taken of fast-breaking events, the responsible people have to have the money available ahead of time.

The SSA information office, like most of its counterparts in government, must explain and justify its expenditures in terms of the efficient and economical administration of the programs the agency administers or in terms of service to the public. It makes comprehensive annual work plans and establishes a budget based upon its planned activities. The budget requires detailed estimates of the costs of all items—special events as well as public information materials such as publications and motion pictures. Continual control of and financial accounting for expenditures follows the initial budgeting.

The second area that requires long-range planning is a trained, alert field staff, with knowledge and experience in developing special events, and with ever-open channels to the key information people in the central office. In a national program, most of the special event possibilities will present themselves in the field, not to the central office staff.

Social Security is blessed with over 700 district offices, and although these offices do not have any information specialists, each has a manager and field representatives whose duties include some informational responsibilities.

Every national organization has field representatives of some kind, paid or volunteer, and if the organization is really to make effective use of special events, it must look to these people for most of the good ideas. Training them, keeping them informed about objectives and possibilities, and following up on their suggestions are absolutely vital.

The third element in planning is the use of the special event in as many different ways, in as many different media as is advisable.

Occasionally a special event may be worth developing for only one or two media, but usually the time and work that are invested in the project will have been sold short unless there is an effort to reach them all: newspapers, television, radio, and magazines in nearly all events, and often, in addition, motion pictures, posters, exhibits, and talks.

It is difficult really to define a "special event"—and I will defer consideration of this point until later. But it may be useful to put into general categories the kinds of special events the Social Security office of information works with, and give examples of the kinds of planning that go into each general type of event.

The SSA has had experience with three broad types of special events:

1. Those that evolve from legislative changes in the social security programs.
2. Those that are topical, "one-shot" news items.

3. Those that evolve regularly, such as anniversaries and statistical milestones, which often take the form of human interest stories.

These three kinds of events can best be illustrated by the following case histories.

When major changes have been made in the law, it can be assumed that people need to be told what they were, whom they affect, and what needs to be done about them.

This kind of special event is, in some ways, relatively easy to execute. First, the SSA usually knows when congressional action on social security legislation is probable, and roughly what the change is likely to be. Second, because any change in the social security program is of intense interest to the American public, the various media are usually eager to report it.

Perhaps no other event in recent history could so dramatically illustrate this kind of project as the campaign to explain to every older American the facts he needed to decide whether or not he wanted to enroll for the medical insurance part of medicare. This unprecedented effort entailed a multitude of special events. The signing of P.L. 89-97 by President Johnson on July 30, 1965, was in itself a special event, for the ceremony was held in Independence, Missouri, in the company of former President Truman, who a generation before had fought for the health insurance program that had now become a reality for the nation's older citizens.

The program was to go into effect July 1, 1966, which gave us only 11 months to achieve a number of difficult information objectives. The SSA had to reach 19 million Americans over 65 years of age and explain both hospital insurance (which practically all of them would get automatically) and medical insurance (which recipients would get only if they agreed to pay a monthly premium for it).

The medicare enrollment information campaign was only one of many different activities that followed the 1965 amendments to the social security law. At the same time the SSA was explaining medicare, it was carrying out several other major projects and dozens of minor ones. There was a new definition of disability for disability insurance; widows' benefits were made possible at age 60 instead of 62; the earnings of doctors were for the first time covered by the law; children's benefits were extended to age 22 instead of 18; there were important changes in eligibility of blind people for disability benefits; and there were many more changes in the law which had to be explained to various groups. The medicare law itself had dozens of provisions which had to be explained to thousands of groups.

Of all these special projects, however, the campaign to explain the medical insurance part of medicare to some 19 million people 65 or over, so they could decide whether they wanted to "sign up," gives perhaps the best example of the way the SSA handled one very "special event."

The audience was specific: everyone 65 or older, or nearing 65, in the United States; and all citizens of the United States who were outside the country.

All of these people had to be given enough information about the voluntary medical insurance part of the new medicare law to enable them to make an informed decision about whether or not they wanted to make monthly payments for it. Those who wanted it had to be informed how to obtain it, and SSA representatives had to try to get from those who were reluctant to sign up a clear statement of their intent so we could know they had an opportunity to make an informed decision.

There were a number of built-in communications problems. Our audience was aged; some were senile, some had poor vision, and some had poor hearing; a million did not read English, and some could not read at all.

Publications describing medical insurance were first distributed, with the ink still wet, on the press plane accompanying President Johnson to Missouri. The leaflets proved to be of great help to reporters as they wrote their stories about the event. Within hours after the President signed the bill, 4 million copies of the SSA's basic health insurance leaflet were made available to the American people. They had been printed and shipped to social security offices throughout the country in the last days before the signing ceremony.

In addition to the routine television network news coverage, the SSA had films made of the President signing the legislation; the film was developed and edited within four to five hours after the ceremony, copies were made and rushed to every television station in the nation. This served several purposes; it generated immediate public attention and provided film for later use. It made sure that full coverage would be available to the stations even if other breaking news limited or eliminated network coverage. And it gave the local stations film footage for localized news stories in which local social security representatives could participate.

In like manner, the initial news stories from the White House were backed up by stories the SSA moved immediately to the wire services and to social security offices for use by the local press. In these stories, the emphasis rapidly changed from news of the event to information the older person needed in order to make the important decision on enrollment for the medical insurance part of medicare.

The SSA had one of the first exhibits on medicare at the American Hospital Association conference in San Francisco approximately 12 days after the legislation was signed.

A chart devised by the information office while the amendments were still under discussion in Congress helped it to keep things organized during these hectic months. It showed the nature of each project, the planned schedule for completion, the current status, and who was responsible. It saved pages of copy in our reports, and helped to show quickly where reinforcements were needed.

Since the SSA already had the names and addresses of approximately 16½ million social security beneficiaries 65 or over, direct mail was clearly called for. Within two months after medicare became law, the SSA began direct mailings. With the aid of the Civil Service Commission and State public welfare agencies, the Social Security Administration was able to mail information to other large groups of older people.

For about a million and a half elderly people who were not receiving social security benefits, and whose names and addresses we did not have, the SSA had to rely heavily on the mass media and on the cooperation of national and local organizations. Typical of the many groups who helped were the National Council of Senior Citizens, the American Association of Retired Persons, the AFL-CIO and its affiliate unions, Chambers of Commerce, the

Urban League, the National Council of Churches, the Federation of Business and Professional Women's Clubs, and many professional groups in the health field such as the American Hospital Association, the American Medical Association, and the National Association of Retail Druggists. More than 15,000 retail druggists throughout the United States, for instance, distributed more than 8 million copies of a leaflet designed in cooperation with their organization.

Other government agencies helped. The Office of Economic Opportunity, realizing that older people usually listen to other older people, sponsored Operation Medicare Alert. Under this project, for a few weeks in early 1966 older people were hired part-time to go from door to door in their own neighborhood to try to make sure that no other older person would be deprived of medicare because he was too out of touch with the world to hear about it.

Operation Medicare Alert conducted 6000 community meetings, visited 5½ million people, and took 250,000 applications for medicare in neighborhoods where it seemed that this was the only possible way to reach substantial numbers of people before the enrollment deadline.

The U. S. Department of Agriculture cooperated in another special effort to get word to the "hard-to-reach" groups. County-based USDA personnel and volunteers personally visited thousands of rural residents in many isolated areas.

The SSA prepared various leaflets and booklets on medicare for people of different reading habits. Since there are many people in the United States who read Spanish only, most of the publications were printed in Spanish as well as in English. One overall account of all the 1965 amendments was published in 22 different languages.

The SSA expected it would have to print many millions of copies of all these leaflets and reprint them periodically as supplies ran low. Millions were mailed directly to beneficiaries. But the SSA officials did not realize that the public demand would keep the agency going back to the presses time after time, until the total number of medicare publications printed and distributed within a year after the President signed the bill into law was over 200 million copies.

The field force conducted a series of regional meetings with foreign language newspaper editors and foreign language fraternal organization executives. Many of the articles for magazine use were made available in several languages.

Over 50 national press releases were issued during the year between the enactment of medicare and the start of the program. Approximately 85 different releases and articles were prepared for local adaptation and use by social security district managers. But reporters and writers in the various media prepared far more releases and articles than the agency did. To keep them and the entire health community informed of developments, information workers in the SSA began issuing a *Medicare Newsletter*. At the end of its first year, more than 10,000 copies of each issue were being mailed to administrators, writers, and key people in organizations concerned with the health care of older Americans.

A total of 15 posters and flyers on various aspects of the 1965 amendments, including medicare, were produced and put into general use. Special subway posters and car-cards were used in Chicago, New York, and Philadelphia. The Post Office Department agreed to display medicare enrollment posters on every postal truck in the nation for one month.

The Social Security Administration produced many small exhibits on medicare and a few larger ones for use at conventions. But not all of its displays were of conventional types. In Los Angeles, the district office arranged for a blimp to circle overhead with a medicare message without cost to the government. In New York City, an imaginative field representative had the message delivered free to about 4 million people a day on the famous moving sign in Times Square. Not to be outdone, the Chicago district office arranged for the Budweiser sign to flash the same message to passers-by.

Thousands of words appeared in displays across the country, and thousands more were written in direct mail communications, publications, and articles. But the written word was not enough. The spoken word about medicare was also transmitted through speeches at national conventions and local meetings, over radio and television, and in the daily contacts of social security district office people.

Here again, district office ingenuity and initiative was of great importance. In one office, for example, a field representative gave a number of "speeches" to deaf groups, using sign language. Of those who came to see him, 75 enrolled for medical insurance.

Television and radio spot announcements, movies, and film-strips featuring the President, Vice President, former President Truman, and leading Hollywood personalities including Bob Hope and Jimmy Durante, were used throughout the country. About a month before the first medicare deadline, SSA Commissioner Robert Ball made a 15-minute appearance on the NBC "Today" show, explaining to older people their right to decide whether or not they wanted to enroll, outlining the provisions of the law, and telling them how they could enroll if they wished.

Countless special projects were arranged with the medical and health community—the providers of medicare services—and the insurance organizations which serve as fiscal intermediaries.

The launching of medicare was a tremendous, continuing special event, unequaled in social security public information activities.

In this most ambitious single communications effort in the agency's history, the Social Security Administration spent about $4 million on materials and special promotions to introduce medicare to the public and to prepare the elderly enrollees to participate after the law was passed. This sum breaks down to about 23 cents each for the 17.3 million older Americans who signed up for the voluntary medical insurance part of the program.

The topical, "hot" news item, a one-of-a-kind, nonrecurring attraction, is the subject of the following case history. This kind of event may or may not allow time for thorough advance preparation. In the case of the opening of a district SSA office, for example, it would be possible to plan well in advance the approach, the stories, and the events to accompany the ceremony.

But, this kind of special event can also be a fast-breaking development which requires hasty mobilization, such as the first Presidential visit to social security central headquarters in Baltimore. The occasion was the Fifteenth Annual Awards Ceremony for social security employees in the fall of 1966—in itself a special event, but made even more memorable by the fact that President Johnson chose it as the occasion for a major policy address. Hence the heightened excitement—and the need for meticulous planning.

SSA received its first indication that the President might appear at the awards ceremony about a week before the event. It was a mere 48 hours before the ceremony, however, that this commitment was confirmed—barring, of course, unforeseen circumstances which would affect the President's schedule. As tenuous as the original possibility of the President's appearance was, SSA officials had to plan as if it were a certainty.

A visit by the President is the ultimate in special events, involving arrangements for the White House press corps—representing the major syndicates, networks, and newspapers—as well as for the local press. Other problems include such diverse items as loudspeakers, seating arrangements, security measures, bad weather plans, itineraries, and photographic coverage.

The SSA office of information began preparing background materials for the press and other media representatives, arranging for hostesses, and planning coverage of the event by its own staff for later use.

A special event of this magnitude serves many purposes, but central to all of them is the element of public attention which places the information office in a key position in all of the arrangements, even those which are the primary concern of other units. Although someone else will have the platform built, they will ask information: where, and how high? Someone else will rent the chairs—but will ask information: how many, and what kind? Someone else will provide telephone lines, but will ask information: what classes of lines, and where will the terminals be placed?

Information must answer where the television cameras go, and where they will get electrical power. The information officer will be responsible for seeing that the loudspeakers are placed so that everyone may hear, but still avoid feedback into the television, filming, recording, and radio microphones. He will catch hell if the crowds are not controlled and if arrangements for invited guests, high school bands, printed programs, and emergency medical facilities go wrong.

In the case of the President's visit, every one of these matters had public relations implications.

Up to the last minute, there was a great deal of behind-the-scenes activity to assure that no detail had been overlooked. Carpenters worked around the clock to ready the speakers' platform. To accommodate the 25,000 guests and observers, a parking lot was transformed almost overnight into an outdoor auditorium, complete with a huge "Welcome Mr. President" banner.

Another special highlight of this special event was the participation of Dave McNally, who had only a few days earlier pitched the winning World Series game for the Baltimore Orioles.

The background of that story well illustrates the important contributions an alert field organization makes to special events. Some years before, an Oregon field representative had noted that McNally, then a fledgling baseball pro, had received social security survivors benefits for most of his youth because of the death of his father. The SSA field representative passed along the information to the central office, and it was filed away for future use. Now McNally was a national baseball hero. With an assist from the Orioles' public relations representatives, the SSA secured his cooperation, and on the bright blue day of the awards ceremony, the young man was in the front row of dignitaries on the podium.

"Contrary to some rumors," the President said solemnly, "I am not here to scout Dave McNally for the Washington Senators."

Among other kinds of special events that evolve regularly and can be planned well in advance are anniversaries and statistical milestones.

One example of such a successful human interest special event, planned around a statistical milestone, involved a retired Indiana public utilities employee who began to receive retirement benefits just as the total number of Americans receiving benefits each month reached 20 million.

He was William J. Kappel, who retired at the end of March 1965 after 42 years of employment with the municipally owned Fort Wayne city utility system.

Working closely with the SSA's district office in the Kappels' home town of Fort Wayne, the agency told the story of this middle-class midwestern family through news releases, photo stories, and radio and television interviews. The climax of the story came in a White House ceremony when President Johnson presented Mr. Kappel his first social security check.

The Social Security Administration's goal in this special event, as in all others, was comprehensive coverage, not only on the day of the White House ceremony but in the succeeding days and weeks. The film that was made, the press releases that were written, and the photos that were taken were used in magazine articles, newspaper columns and features, television and radio shows, publications, and talks to community groups.

Local stories also are important. Almost every government organization has some kind of field arm. Social Security's extensive field organization—some 700 district and branch offices throughout the United States—is an invaluable asset in the agency's public information activities.

For one thing, its decentralized staff and facilities help it to fight the natural inclination to believe that Baltimore and Washington form the center of the world from which the holy writ on social security emanates. In actual practice, it is the data the agency receives daily from its eyes and ears in the field that, to a significant degree, set the direction and the pace of its public information program.

After the advent of medicare, one staff assistant in the office of each of our eight regional assistant commissioners was given special training and responsibilities in public information. One of these responsibilities is to apprise Baltimore of situations in their regions which might deserve special attention.

Each social security district manager and each field representative keeps in touch with the newspapers, broadcasting stations, magazines, and other communications outlets in the area he serves. They bring national social security stories to the attention of local editors and identify local tie-ins.

They initiate and carry out most actions without the help of the professional staff in Baltimore. Most of these local "human interest" stories reach the central office in the form of clippings from the local newspapers. Just as a good newspaperman has a "nose for news," SSA likes field people to have a "sense for special events." Sometimes a local item turns out to be the basis for a national project.

Such was the case when a field representative in California found that one of the contestants for the title of Miss California was receiving social security benefits because of the death of her father. Further study showed that not one, but several of the contestants were SSA beneficiaries. None of these beneficiaries was selected as Miss California, but the district office was alert to the mathematical possibilities of there being at least one beneficiary among the 50 Miss America contestants at Atlantic City. This germ of an idea, brought to the attention of the central office, resulted in a color film about Debbie Molitor, Miss South Dakota of 1966—her life on a midwestern college campus, the Miss America pageant in which she participated, and, of course, the part social security was playing in her life.

But not all special event ideas come from the field. In 1956, for example, Victor Christgau, then director of our Bureau of Old-Age and Survivors Insurance, asked about the number of people 100 years old or older receiving social security benefits. Mr. Christgau was slated to speak at centennial ceremonies in his home town of Austin, Minnesota, and he thought this would be an interesting statistic to work into his remarks. The SSA had no idea; but social security records are kept on magnetic tape for use by computers, and employees did find a tape from which this information was secured. There were, at that time, 31 beneficiaries 100 years of age or older. In 1967 there were 2000.

As a result of Mr. Christgau's inquiry a decade ago, the Commissioner of Social Security now sends greetings and best wishes to every beneficiary who reaches 100 years of age. The district offices often deliver this greeting in person, and if the beneficiary is willing, they often invite the local press to be present. Also, if the beneficiary is willing, he is interviewed, and the story of his life is recorded in a continuing series of books called *America's Centenarians,* which is published by SSA. The seventh volume has been printed.

All of these centenarians were past 67 when the social security law was enacted.

In addition to the SSA's field organization, several other considerations should be mentioned to fill out the background against which this agency makes use of special events.

First is the fact that the chief information officer is directly responsible to the Commissioner of Social Security. This close working relationship does much to facilitate the internal coordination and planning which are necessary for the success of special events.

Second is the fact that the SSA does not have a "special events specialist" per se in the central office. The absence of an employee with that assigned function is not an oversight, but stems from the fact that such a position does not lend itself to a particular set of skills that would likely be possessed by one person. In fact, the "campaign" nature of a special event requires a marshalling of many diverse skills—press, audio-visual, publications, and national and community organization specialists.

Third, central office has the physical facilities and staff resources for the in-house production of special public information material—movies, television and radio spots, posters, and exhibits. One of the very real advantages in having these facilities is that SSA can often cut production costs. Its expenses in connection with the Miss South Dakota film, for example, were about $2500; commercial production would have cost about $18,000 to $20,000.

Economic considerations aside, the availability of these audio-visual and graphics facilities results in a better product and allows greater speed of reaction to fast-breaking events than if comparable services had to be contracted on the outside. The very process of procurement can be time-consuming. Moreover, time is saved by using staff personnel who are familiar with SSA programs and with the requirements of the project. Outside consultants are retained to avoid too much subjectivity.

The ingredients for a useful special event depend in large measure on the type of program to be illustrated. The "special event" is more than just a happening; it is a composite of the happening, the message, the people who need to be reached, and the media.

Special events are one of the most useful and effective tools in public information. The director of any Government public information program can be reasonably well assured of getting an excellent return on his investment of hours and dollars in special events—in terms of increased public understanding if he makes sure in advance that an adequate budget is available, trains his people to use special events, and uses each event to get the important program messages into as many media as possible.

Preparing Promotional Campaigns

BERNARD POSNER
DEPUTY EXECUTIVE SECRETARY
PRESIDENT'S COMMITTEE ON EMPLOYMENT
OF THE HANDICAPPED

Promotional campaigns are initiated for a variety of reasons. A government agency wants its employees to become more cost-conscious. Another wants to recruit young lawyers. Still another wants to inform the people of the benefits of a new law. And another agency wants to eliminate prejudice against Eskimos, improving their chances of finding jobs.

These are four examples among the scores of promotional campaigns conducted each year by agencies of the federal government. Each campaign in its own way attempts to implant ideas, to change people's attitudes or actions. Each campaign must have a well-conceived plan of attack, a kind of "generalship" not entirely unrelated to what might be found on a battle field.

The promotional campaign is government's megaphone. It is one way of claiming attention over the "great, blooming, buzzing confusion" that is America, as John Dewey put it. Someone estimated that the average American is beset by more than 1500 different promotional messages and appeals and exhortations each day. Little wonder that government agencies need to raise their messages above the babble.

There are no flash formulas for successful promotional campaigns. But there are a number of rules that can minimize failures even though they cannot guarantee success. One factor, however, eludes all rule-making: imagination. A campaign above all must be imaginative.

Accepting the limits of imagination and creativity, there are at least ten important rules, the "ten commandments of promotional campaigns," which ought to be followed, and here they are, with examples and illustrations from past government efforts.

First, the objective of the promotional campaign must be clearly defined. This deceptively simple commandment probably is the most difficult of all. The objective must give direction to all promotional efforts. If the objective is too broad, the campaign will be shapeless; if it is too narrow, it will be confining. A proper objective takes much thought. When formulated it should be put into writing and kept near for ready reference. It is the campaign's navigation chart, the road map.

For example, the agency that sought to recruit young lawyers might stress job security of government employment—but young lawyers may not be interested in security. Or it might emphasize bigness of the legal department—but young lawyers may not want to become engulfed by bigness. A better approach might be: come to work where the action is; the agency's legal department is deeply involved in social programs having an impact on the America of today and tomorrow. This approach—almost a challenge—might cause many young lawyers to look twice.

William Ruder and David Finn, heads of one of the largest public relations companies in the country, Ruder & Finn, Inc., wrote an article for *Management Methods Magazine* in which they observed that "fifty percent of new public relations programs undertaken during the past five years have ended in failure. . . . The vast majority that didn't succeed suffered from one common shortcoming: they lacked the vital direction provided by a long-range goal." Thus to have a clearly defined objective is a primary rule.

Second, research should be conducted on the nature of the audience to be reached. A promotional campaign attempts an audacious deed: to reach the minds of people. How can it possibly succeed unless we have some notion of what is passing through people's heads in the first place?

This does not necessarily mean spending large fortunes for attitude surveys. It does mean remaining alert for all sorts of clues to current attitude patterns. One way is to watch for news items, editorials, magazine articles, and anything else giving indications of attitudes. For example, the agency seeking young lawyers might learn much about aspirations of present-day law students from reading campus law newspapers.

Another way is to make use of an agency's field offices, which usually keep much more sensitive fingers on the public pulse than do headquarters offices in Washington, D. C. To learn about attitudes of veterans, the Veterans Administration once asked its contact offices in all parts of the country to query every tenth veteran who walked in the doors. The questions were uniform: income, employment, marital status, use of VA benefits, and so on. The results provided a perceptive profile of the American veteran.

Research can help set the objective or change the direction of promotional campaigns. A processor of boned chicken asked a government agency to help find out why sales were slumping.

The agency found the food had been promoted as a delicacy, fit for affluent tables. Yet closer analysis disclosed that the biggest market was among the disadvantaged; when the chicken was mixed with rice, a little went a long way. The processor switched its campaign. Sales have gone up ever since.

Virtually every agency has a staff of statisticians. They can give valuable advice and guidance on attitude measurement. They can help design samplings and other statistical aids to an understanding of the nature of the audience.

Third, the specific "public" must be carefully identified. People tend to align themselves into specific groupings with common interest, problems, and outlooks.

This brings up the question, to whom should a promotional campaign be directed? A top-of-the-head answer, "the general public," in many cases is wrong. Instead, specific publics ought to be reached. They should be listed and placed in order of priority. These are clearly defined targets. We can aim at them with a rifle, hitting them one by one. We no longer need to blast away with a shotgun, hitting nobody in particular.

Obviously, there are some broad-based campaigns that warrant promotion to the vast undifferentiated "general public." Take out the shotgun and blast away. But even here, keep the rifle handy. Be sure to find individual publics that should be reached on an individualized basis.

Consider the campaign to eliminate prejudice against the Eskimos. What publics should be reached? Employers? Yes, but that is only the beginning. Who is involved in hiring practices? Owners of business and industry who establish policy, personnel managers, industrial physicians, line supervisors, union shop stewards, safety engineers—all these are individual publics to be reached by rifle shot campaigns.

That is not all. What about rank and file workers who have a great deal to say about whom they will or will not accept in their ranks? They must be reached.

And what about the Eskimos themselves? They have certain responsibilities when they enter the labor market—to equip themselves with usable skills, to develop satisfactory work habits, to build good records of reliability. They must be motivated to do these things.

Even this is not all. What about educators, vocational counselors, rehabilitation specialists, and all the others who have regular contact with the Eskimos? They must be encouraged to give the proper guidance to job-seeking Eskimos.

The only way to develop a comprehensive list of publics to reach is to know thoroughly the practices and problems of one's agency, and to know thoroughly the nature of all the diverse groups to reach. There is no substitute for knowledge.

Fourth, a related commandment is to use campaign ammunition on the opinion molders. Most of us are other-directed. We really are not the independent self-starters we pretend to be. The one person we mistrust is ourselves. We may bluster in the presence of wives and children, but a still small voice asks: "are you sure you're right?" So one eye should be kept in the direction of the folks whose opinions we respect. When they nod, the people nod; and when they frown, the people frown. They can be spokesmen to spread the message in terms that will be heeded.

In many cases, opinion molders are the leaders of the community—editors, ministers, teachers, bankers, labor leaders, and business leaders. But not always. Certain publics may have their own opinion molders drawn from the most unexpected places. For example, an automobile manufacturer found that opinion molders for the auto-buying public were gasoline station repairmen; they were the ones listened to with respect. A processor of canned soup learned that opinion molders for the public of newly wed housewives were mothers and/or mothers-in-law; they were the ones who knew soups from A to Z.

Fifth, the proper medium to reach the people must be selected. Media are the voices to the publics. Many media are at our disposal, each with strengths and weaknesses. Consider media the keys of a mighty organ. With a proper combination, we can produce glorious chords; or, with improper mixtures, ear-splitting dissonances.

In terms of promotional campaigns, at least three elements should be sought. First, we want the element of repetition, of telling our story until it works its way into the minds of our publics. Second, we want the element of selectivity, of effectively reaching individual publics. Third, we want the element of detail, of conveying our message in enough depth so that people know exactly what we are talking about. No single medium gives us all we want. So we blend them for a proper mix.

The following check-list of media may help in reaching a blend.

Newspapers. Excellent for reaching specific publics through special sections (women's, business, real estate, and sports). Since the press prints news, and since we cannot possibly generate news about our campaign with rapid regularity, newspapers perhaps cannot provide the degree of repetition we would like.

Television and Radio. Strong on repetition, through public service spot announcements, news items, and interviews on guest-participation shows. But television and radio cannot communicate a message in detail. Television and radio paint with broad brush strokes, not fine lines.

Magazines. Not much repetition. Most magazines do not repeat articles on the same subject for many issues. But they provide an extra impact through reprint possibilities, permitting an article to be converted into a direct mail piece. Most magazines (except for the general ones) aim carefully for specific publics.

Direct Mail. Expensive—every single item costs postage. Direct mail can reach specific people with little waste circulation. But the direct mail piece must be unusually imaginative, for it is in competition with a great many other pieces, each clamoring for attention. Studies show that the greatest effectiveness comes with several mailings, not just one, adding more postage costs.

Carcards. Most carcard space is available without charge to public service campaigns. But of course the printing is not free. Carcards have an unusually high recall rate; in Washington, D. C., more than half of all bus riders recalled carcard messages they had seen a month earlier.

Billboards. Space is available for public service campaigns, again free except for printing. Ten years ago, outdoor advertising people recommended a maximum of eight words on billboards; today they recommend five. People drive faster.

Annual Reports. What happens to an agency's annual report? Is it filed and forgotten? It need not be. It can be the fountainhead of numerous news stories for both general and specific audiences.

Newsletters. A booming new medium, read by busy (and not

so busy) people who want capsule information. So far there are 3000 newsletters in America—including a newsletter on newsletters.

The next three media have something in common: person-to-person impact. Most communications authorities contend it takes more than mass media messages to change a person's mind; the mass media can create awareness, but somewhere along the line must come a person-to-person confrontation of some kind.

Exhibits and Displays. These can be arranged at conventions and conferences of the specific publics to be reached. Exhibits should be manned by knowledgeable persons who can chat with passers-by. This gives a double impact: the drama of the exhibit itself and the personal confrontation of the person manning it.

Speeches. The speech is a communications medium too. It gives person-to-person confrontation with an audience—plus. If a speech is worth delivering, it is worth merchandising. A news item can be written about it, not only for the daily press but also for specialized publications that might be interested. This double impact can be achieved for nearly every speech.

Meetings and Conferences. These are means of reaching particular audiences on a person-to-person basis. If meetings become two-way streets, allowing for feedback as well as for presentations to audiences, they become much more valuable in the total communications efforts.

These are by no means all the media at one's disposal. There are many more. The key to their use is the blend, the creation of harmonious chords.

Sixth of the ten commandments, a theme or slogan should be developed for each campaign. Pity the poor public, asked to remember so much about 1500 promotional messages each day. The only help it can get is a theme or slogan that can serve as a quick shorthand reminder of the message. If nothing else is remembered, at least the theme might be.

The theme should be ubiquitous. It should be seen and heard everywhere—on the airways, in the press, on exhibits, on carcards and billboards, and it should be most carefully conceived, since it epitomizes the heart of the promotional message. It should say enough to stand on its own feet.

For 20 years the President's Committee on Employment of the

Handicapped has used as its theme: "Hire the Handicapped; It's Good Business." This slogan may win no literary prizes, but it has its merits. Its overtones create an impact on employers more forceful than many words. "Look, Mr. Employer," they imply, "nobody wants you to hire the handicapped through charity. We do want you to know that if you give them an equal chance to compete for work, their skills and abilities can contribute to your good business." The American business community has responded to this theme. It has been used for two decades, and as far as the President's Committee is concerned, it will be in use for many more.

Seventh in our list of ten commandments, the campaign should be paced for its most effective impact. A promotional campaign is a more-or-less steady outpouring of material, with the hope that over a period of time an impact will be created upon audiences. It is also a whirlwind effort to reach people's minds in a hurry, a kind of mental blitzkrieg. It should be both.

The ideal promotional campaign should proceed at a somewhat steady pace, with an output of messages to all media suitable for reaching the publics. But at regular intervals, there should be a peak period of intensified effort, a time to pull out the stops and blast away at full volume. These peak periods lend heightened "visibility" to the campaign.

A steady promotional pace is needed, but it lacks the change of pace that brings added attention. The heightened all-out period of visibility lacks the steady follow-through that never lets audiences forget. The two go hand-in-hand.

One of the greatest masters of pacing was President Franklin D. Roosevelt. He once wrote to an old associate: ". . . The Public psychology and, for that matter, individual psychology cannot, because of human weakness, be attuned for long periods of time to a constant repetition of the highest note in the scale. . . . People tire of seeing the same name, day after day, in the important headlines of the papers and the same voice, night after night, over the radio. . . ."

The visibility device of the President's Committee on Employment of the Handicapped is a special week established by Act of Congress, National Employ the Physically Handicapped Week, early in October of every year. The mere creation of this week does not guarantee stepped-up promotion. Rather, the week becomes a peg upon which to hang all kinds of special attention-getting activities: awards ceremonies, open house at sheltered workshops for the handicapped, speeches, employers' conferences, a heavy outpouring of mass media publicity, posters, and billboards.

That same week also happens to be Fire Prevention Week, National Newspaper Week, National School Lunch Week, National Y-Teen Roll Call Week; and it is also part of Country Music Month, Fish 'N Seafood Parade, Garden Appreciation Month, Let's Go Hunting Month, National Congress of Parents and Teachers Enrollment Month, National Indoor Games Month, National Restaurant Month, Pizza Festival Time Month, and many more.

Each of these visibility periods is directed to a different mix of publics. Each serves as a peg for special events without too much overlap. There is room for all in the vast country of America.

Eighth among commandments, the timing of a campaign must be carefully considered. When does it begin? When does it end? Why? Generally, the longer the campaign, the better the chances of reaching the minds of the publics. But there are times when short campaigns are warranted—such as recruiting limited numbers of people.

Usually, campaigns ought not to be conducted during the Christmas season; the mass media are so loaded with advertising that they do not have much room for public service publicity; and also, people's thoughts are elsewhere. Yet some campaigns are held only at Christmas—for instance, those of a charity nature.

Timing depends upon the audiences to be reached. For school-going young people, a campaign should run from late summer to fall. Promoting water safety at the beach is a summer campaign.

Timing also depends upon the psychological depths of attitudes and opinions to be changed. It has taken not just years but decades for the President's Committee on Employment of the Handicapped to change public attitudes about the capabilities of the handicapped. It would not take nearly that long for an agency to convince its employees to become more cost-conscious, or for another agency to recruit young lawyers fresh out of law school.

Many hard and fast rules about timing do not exist, but it is one of the crucial elements that must be considered in planning any promotional effort.

Ninth, cooperation of other groups and organizations should be sought. No one can possibly conduct a successful promotional campaign alone. A campaign is a time for teamwork, for joining forces with like-minded groups and organizations.

One of the early steps in planning a campaign should be to list all the groups and organizations that possibly could be counted on for support. Campaign functions can be assigned for each, to make the campaign a group activity.

National Employ the Physically Handicapped Week is an example of cooperation, top to bottom. Consider TV-radio coverage alone. The Veterans Administration prepares public service TV and radio material. The National Association of Broadcasters mails it out and urges member stations to use it. The Advertising Council also promotes its use. Local officials of public employment offices and vocational rehabilitation agencies take time out to call on TV and radio stations to make certain the material will be used and to offer their services for special programming (guest interviews, audience participation shows, and the like). Usually, one or more leading industries will produce a TV public service film for showing during the week and afterwards. Organizations concerned with various categories of the handicapped produce their own TV and radio material urging jobs for the people they serve. The National Association for Retarded Children, for instance, promotes employment of retarded adults during the October week.

These cooperative efforts involve just two media, TV and radio. The story of cooperation could be repeated again and again with the other mass media, with a national writing contest for high school students, with speeches before audiences of employers, with exhibits in town squares, with every possible sort of special event.

Groups and organizations working together create what chemists call a synergistic reaction; the end result of their combined efforts is many times greater than the sum of their individual inputs.

Tenth, the results of the campaign should be measured. After the thunder has faded, there comes a time to sit back and wonder: "What happened? Did it work?" So some system of measuring the campaign should be set up.

Some quantitative measure can be easily gained: the number of spot announcements on TV and radio, the column-inches of newspaper publicity, the number of magazine articles, the number of posters displayed, the number of speeches made and the size of the audience.

Another way to measure effectiveness is to start with clearly identified objectives and to see how close the campaign comes to reaching them. If the guideposts are visible, one should be able to tell how far he has succeeded.

How would we measure the four campaigns mentioned at the beginning? The agency that wanted its employees to become cost-conscious, and decided to ask for two money-saving suggestions from each, need merely measure the volume of suggestions and estimate their savings. The agency that wanted to recruit young lawyers would simply glance at its employment figures. The agency that sought to educate people about a new law affecting them could measure the rate of applications for benefits. And the agency that wanted to eliminate prejudice against the Eskimos would watch their employment rate.

Even at best, however, measuring devices for campaigns are often not entirely reliable. Who can tell whether Eskimos entered the labor force because of the effectiveness of our campaign or because of a severe shortage of workers? Or who can tell whether people applied for benefits because of our educational campaign or because of advice they might be receiving from an outside organization? Or whether young lawyers came to work for the agency because they listened to the campaign or because of publicity resulting from a law suit involving the agency? Or whether people became cost-conscious because our campaign told them to or because of a government-wide increase in cash awards for money-saving ideas?

We can develop promotional skills to the utmost. We can live faithfully by the "ten commandments of promotional campaigns."

We can follow all the established rules, and even make up rules of our own. Yet we never can be sure we shall succeed. For the promotional campaign is one of the most difficult tasks on earth —the task of reaching the minds of human beings.

We may try to probe man's brain, but brains are not dormant, waiting to be probed. Human minds are active, vigorous, ever-changing, aggressive. Human minds refuse to respond as pieces of machinery; they refuse to be type-cast. That is the greatness of the human race. And this is the reason why our best efforts at creating promotional campaigns may not always succeed, no matter how skillfully we plan them.

We would not have it otherwise, would we?

7. Public Information and the Mass Media

THE mass media of communications are the most important means of government information. Without the mass media, the government's voice could not possibly reach the 200 million people with whom it must communicate in modern society. Newspapers, magazines, radio, television, books, and movies play the key role in public information.

There is a traditional antagonism between the public information officer and the newsman, even though most information men used to be newsmen. This is not necessarily unhealthy, for it produces a tension that keeps both sides alert. *Wayne Phillips,* Director of Public Affairs at the Department of Housing and Urban Development, discusses this problem in "Information and the News Man."

Mr. Phillips is eminently qualified to do so. In addition to his ten years as a front-page reporter for the *New York Times,* he has worked for the *Denver Post, Watertown* (Mass.) *Sun, Boston Globe,* and *San Francisco Chronicle.* He has taught journalism at Columbia University and the University of Denver.

While radio and television have risen to dominant roles in mass communication, government has not yet taken full advantage of these new media for public information. *Harry C. Bell,* Radio and Television Officer for the Department of Health, Education, and Welfare, laments government's neglect of the electronic media and points out ways in which the public information office can take better advantage of "Broadcasting for Instant Impact."

Mr. Bell came to the government from the entertainment and broadcasting industry. For many years he was employed by the Music Corporation of America as a theatrical agent, artist's manager, and sales director. He was President of B/B Management Corporation, Nirene Productions Corporation, and Caliope Music Corporation; Vice President for Radio and Television of International Talent Associates; and Director, Sales and Development, Gotham Recording Corporation.

Motion pictures also offer new means to give drama and impact to governmental messages and information. The government has been using films for training purposes for half a century, primarily for military training, but a new wave of young movie makers is joining government to use "Motion Pictures for Dramatic Effect." The problems and prospects are described by *Charles Glazer,* Motion Picture Producer for the Veterans Administration.

Mr. Glazer was educated at Boston University, where he received a B.S. and M.S. in the School of Public Relations and Communication. Prior to joining the government, he served as editor at the Harvard University Film Study Center. He has written, directed, and produced many award-winning films during his government career.

Although not so instantaneous or dramatic, books and magazines play an important role in government information. They provide more detailed information and give it a permanence that none of the other media can achieve. *Roy Hoopes,* consultant to the Department of Health, Education, and Welfare, describes the use of "Magazines and Books for Permanent Impression."

Mr. Hoopes has had wide experience in both the magazine and book field. He has held editorial posts on *Time-Life* International, *Pathfinder, Hi-Fidelity, National Geographic, Democratic Digest,* and *Washingtonian* magazines. He is the author of ten books and dozens of magazine articles. His latest books are on government subjects, *The Complete Peace Corps Guide* and *The Peace Corps Experience.*

MEDIA RELATIONS . . .

Information
and the Newsman

WAYNE PHILLIPS
DIRECTOR, DIVISION OF PUBLIC AFFAIRS
U. S. DEPARTMENT OF HOUSING
AND URBAN DEVELOPMENT

THE relationship between a government public information office and the press is sometimes as complicated as the relationship between landlord and his tenants, and that has been called the second most passionate relationship known to man.

Unlike the quality of mercy, which eases landlord-tenant ties, relationships between government public information offices and the press are often strained. They are also, like all other human relationships, a product of the personalities involved, much more than the issues.

As a rule public information officers are former members of the press; frequently they have worked longer as members of the press than they have as information officers. So between them and the members of the working press there is always the question:

"Why did you go to work for the government?"

The question has the same nagging quality as that devilish advertising slogan we've all seen:

"Is it true blondes have more fun?"

Some reporters regard their craft as I once did, as a "calling"— in the old puritanical sense of an ordained occupation. They regard those who have left the craft for other pursuits as somehow akin to fallen priests. And they wonder not only why they did it, but whether they might also find it tempting.

They sense some of the obvious things—usually higher pay, a more comfortable office, perhaps more regular hours—whenever they come into a government public information office. They are forever nagged by a reporter's consciousness that he can never be anything but an outsider, a spectator. And they wonder what it would be like to be "on the inside"—to *really* know the answers to the questions they are exploring.

And every so often this anxiety breaks into the open, as it still does for me today—nearly seven years after resigning from *The New York Times*—when a former colleague will ask:

"Do you ever regret leaving the newspaper business?"

Which is a little like asking a man:

"Do you ever regret leaving your first wife?"

The reply one offers depends on what kind of a day it's been. In any event, the question has no persuasion because you sure aren't going back.

Some of the younger and more ardent reporters consider a government information officer as a personal affront.

305

They feel he has sold out for material gain.

They feel he is a paid propagandist who could not speak the truth if he wanted to.

They feel their mission in life is to expose him and those he works for.

Relationships with these reporters are apt to be difficult. The best way to get along with them is to have as little to do with them as possible. They need solitude to enjoy their self-righteousness.

Fortunately, most reporters come to at least tolerate a government public information officer as a fallen angel—someone who could not quite make it in the newspaper business, but nevertheless may be performing a useful function where he is.

This is much better, because it is easier to get along with the fellow who feels sorry for you than with the one who resents you.

And it is even possible to progress, over a period of time, from this relationship to one of mutual respect. This, of course, is the relationship all public information officers strive to achieve.

It requires, first of all, a capacity for candor on both sides. This means an understanding that some things are for attribution and others are not.

A public information officer need not regard it as part of his responsibility to defend stupidity or malice. And he should recognize it as part of the responsibility of the press to expose stupidity and malice when they become matters of public interest. I have no hesitancy about being candid with reporters about things like this—providing I know the reporter is not going to force me into a position of having been publicly critical of the organization I work for.

The growth of mutual respect between a public information officer and a member of the press also depends a good deal on the technical competence on both sides.

When I was a newspaper reporter I thought all my colleagues were great reporters. It was not until I had to fill in on city desks and had a closer look at some of the work of my colleagues that I realized how far short of the mark some of them fell.

There is very little a public information officer can do with an incompetent reporter except try to be sure that everything the reporter gets is in writing. And even then the information officer is living dangerously.

When I was a newspaper reporter, on the other hand, I thought all government public information officers were incompetent. And now that I have been a government public information officer for a while I know that is not true either.

To be any good at all a public information officer must first of all be available—and that means at any hour of the day or night.

In this pressure cooker we call Washington, D.C., that can be a major problem. On an average day in HUD we receive in the Division of Public Affairs in Washington more than 60 telephone calls from reporters. It might be possible for one man to take all those calls—but he would certainly have no time to dig out the answers to the questions he would be asked.

Consequently the calls have to be fanned out among a half dozen press officers, each specializing in a particular area of department activities. And behind each of those press officers is a backup man or woman to assist in digging out answers.

Despite strict prohibitions against the transferring of calls, and insistence on giving top priority to the handling of press calls, I still occasionally hear of a horrible incident when a reporter could not reach a press officer or could not get a straight answer when needed.

During the day, whenever I am away from my office, I carry a telephone paging device with me so I can be reached in an emergency.

On nights and weekends our press lines have automatic answering devices giving the home telephone numbers of duty officers who are available to answer queries. But even so, the system has been known to break down.

Once last year, just to see how good a job we were doing in handling press queries, I had checks made with every reporter who had called HUD in the course of a week to find out if he had any difficulty in getting the information he wanted.

It was a disastrous experiment.

Most of the reporters promptly called the press officers they had talked with and told them I was checking up on them. All I accomplished was the aggravation of my own staff. A good press officer must also be able to make some kind of sense out of the day to day activities which he is reporting to the press. Because he often is, in fact, the only reporter covering his department or agency on a regular basis.

Urban affairs is today and has been for some time an area of major news significance. HUD produces an enormous amount of news—more than 6000 news announcements a year, most of them of purely local interest, true, but still many of national significance. Yet there is not one reporter for any newspaper or news service who is consistently assigned to cover HUD.

Our press officers therefore have to function as reporters—keeping in day-to-day contact with the operating officials in the areas for which they are responsible and writing news releases that are in fact news stories reporting the activities in those areas.

Several years ago I read a comment by a former White House official to the effect that he was constantly amazed when he picked up the afternoon newspaper on his way home to read what a sensible, rational pattern the fragmented chaos of the day could assume.

That is the job of the reporter—to make an irrational world make sense to the spectator. The public information officer has the same job—to make it make sense to the reporter.

He must be able to detect and try to understand the patterns of policy behind myriad scattered decisions. He must be able to describe those decisions and bring them together in aggregates to get some sense of their significance. He must be able to reduce them, also, to their impact on specific people in specific places— so he can show what policies mean to people and how they shape their lives.

This is the interpretive reporting we used to study about when I was a student in journalism school—a kind of reporting that grows more important every day as the volume of detail to which we are subjected spirals further and further beyond the capacity of the mind to absorb. It is the kind of reporting that for some reason is rarely found today outside of the *Wall Street Journal*.

It is not enough, however, for the public information officer to be a generalist. The reporter must of necessity assume that role, because he must move from one area of public interest to another rapidly and effectively, trying to skim the cream of significance without confusing the reader with irrelevant detail.

The public information officer, though, must understand the areas of government activity for which he is responsible as thoroughly—or more so—than the operating officials in that area. He cannot do his job if he is nothing more than a switch point in an information system—a point where the reporter is told "Go here, go there, go somewhere else, but don't ask me."

He must be able to take the question of the reporter and pursue the answer with the same tenacity he hopefully used when he was a reporter, until he understands—for example—how a mortgage is put together or how an urban renewal project is processed.

He is not expected to know the answer to such questions the first time he is asked, of course. But he is expected to have enough sense to say he does not know what he does not know, and enough energy to dig out the answer so he will know the next time it comes up.

He also should be able to recognize and know the use and the value of the significant detail.

The public information officer who compiles meticulously all the facts of a complex government undertaking and then callously inflicts it on a reporter is not helping anyone. He is like an artist painting a brick wall who feels compelled to draw the outline of every brick—until a viewer's eyes swim in confusion.

The information officer should, instead, be like the artist who by a cross-hatching here and there suggests the brick of the wall. He should be able to select from a mass of fact those details that are significant and illustrative, which in a news story can give the reader the picture succinctly and clearly.

The relationship between the public information official and the press in regard to the head of the government department agency for which he is responsible is a very delicate one.

Representatives of the press feel, and rightly so, that they should have ready access to the top official of any government department or agency. Those officials, on the other hand, have only limited amounts of time that they can give to the members of the press.

The public information official has the job of trying to strike some reasonable balance in these demands.

Without having done any real time and analysis study, my guess is that Secretary Robert Weaver devotes from 20 to 30 percent of his working time to public information activities of one kind or another—speeches, press conferences, interviews, radio and television appearances, and meeting with public interest groups. I think that is a very substantial amount of time to take from a man who also must oversee the administration of a major government department. Yet I am constantly fending off the complaints of members of the press who feel he does not give them adequate attention.

The public information official also has to realize—and the reporter should recognize—that it is the boss who controls the situation, and not he.

Secretary Weaver makes the public appearances that he wants to make, sees the members of the press that he wants to see, and holds the press conferences that he wants to hold—not the ones I want. I channel requests to him and replies from him. I make recommendations that may or may not be accepted. And I make the arrangements he wants.

Contrary to some popular literature, most men in government are their own image makers. And this has been true of every man I have worked with. They think—and rightly, I think—that they know more about the kind of image they want to project and how to project it than any public information officer. And if they do not have that kind of ego and self-confidence, they have no business in public life.

Many of the same qualifications apply to the speeches and statements of government officials. Most of them are thoroughly literate men with minds of their own and very little patience with the scribblings of their staff.

Far too much has been made in this city of the role of the ghost writer—to the point, sometimes, where I think the impression is given that public policy is being made by public information men.

It is part of a public information officer's job to write routine speeches and statements for public officials. But every *major* policy speech or statement Secretary Weaver has delivered in the past seven years was written by himself—personally, in pencil, on white, blue-lined pads. He spends hours writing and rewriting those statements to be sure they say exactly what he wants them say—not what some public information officer wants him to say.

I have stressed aspects of the personal relationship between the public information officer and members of the press. I have said very little about the mechanics of the public information office —press releases, press conferences, and such matters.

That is not because I think the mechanics are unimportant. The mechanics of handling telephone calls or delivering press releases can make or break the effectiveness of a public information office. But it is because I think the personal relationship is of overwhelming importance once those mechanics have been worked out.

The best organized public information office in the world cannot do a thing without a solid and healthy personal relationship between those who work there and the members of the press.

The ability to produce and distribute 6000 press releases a year, as we do, is no small task. But it is a meaningless task if they are dropped in the mail and forgotten. That is like casting seed in the desert and hoping that somewhere, somehow some of it will find a place to take root.

The ability to handle 60 press inquiries a day, 300 a week, 1200 a month, 62,400 a year—as we do—is meaningless if they are all "Hello, Goodby, and Good Luck." If that were the case, we might as well set up a switchboard with recorded messages.

The effectiveness of HUD's public information office and of any other public information office depends on the number of reporters who feel that they know somebody at HUD who they can call and who will get them a prompt, straight answer to a question.

Beyond that everything else is secondary.

Broadcasting for Instant Impact

HARRY BELL
RADIO-TV OFFICER,
OFFICE OF PUBLIC INFORMATION
U. S. DEPARTMENT OF HEALTH,
EDUCATION, AND WELFARE

THE importance of radio and television to the success of government information programs cannot be overstated, for these electronic media can disseminate more information to more people in less time than any other form of communication. Oral and visual messages can provide almost instant comprehension about complicated subjects even to somewhat apathetic audiences.

Radio and television transmit a staggering volume of news and information on an infinite variety of subjects every 24 hours to millions of Americans who like their news digested, compacted, and sandwiched between variety shows, "Peyton Place," and endless commercials. In short, radio and television have changed the pattern of communication in America. But too many government information officers are still almost exclusively wedded to the printed news release, designed for the newspaper editor.

Many radio and television stations are on the air 20 to 24 hours a day seven days a week and must have a volume of interesting and diverse material on which they can build programs to fill their scheduled air time. Their need is the information officer's opportunity. A well-planned television special can reach an audience of 10 to 50 million people. A two- or three-minute public service segment on one of the regularly scheduled television entertainment shows can reach as many as 25 million viewers. These audiences are vitally important to the government information program, and they must be reached if government programs are to be known and understood by the majority of our citizens.

A quality government publication with a good distribution system may reach 200,000, or 300,000, or possibly 400,000 Americans. It may even be read by a fair percentage and kept on the bookshelf for reference. Publications are desirable and necessary. But few publications from government agencies reach mass audiences with impact. Use of electronic media to supplement all other communication efforts is essential. And in most cases, the electronics media should rate first priority in time, talent, and budget.

Few government agencies have designated radio and television officers to work with broadcasters on a day-to-day basis. As a result, government misses many excellent opportunities to place its officials on discussion programs and to cooperate in the produc-

315

tion of "specials" on a wide range of subjects in the public interest. Broadcasters need someone within every large government agency who knows the electronic media and is able to develop imaginative ideas. When rapport has been established, the radio-television officer has set half the stage; the half that remains—changing internal attitudes about the use of radio and television by government—can be much more formidable. It is a strange paradox that government officials can spend so much time watching television, and so love to see themselves on it, and yet fail to give administrative support for use of the electronic media to describe agency programs for those who pay for them—the intended recipients, the American people.

How does one set up a radio-television unit? How does one find the people to make it go? What are the best guidelines?

The electronic media are the best hunting ground for talent, and many media people would welcome the chance to serve their government if given the invitation. The radio-television officer is a salesman. His job is to sell his agency's program and program people to the broadcast industry in terms of audience interest. To do his job effectively the radio-TV officer must make himself well known to the program people within his agency in order to gain their confidence and assistance. And he must make himself known to broadcast producers, directors, and commentators for the same reasons.

One of the secrets of success is matching the interests of the government official with the interests of the producer of a radio or television show. Such matching is always challenging; it is sometimes impossible. But every radio and television officer in government must learn the game. The personality of the official, the current importance of what he wants to say, the convictions of the producer, and sometimes the nature of the show's sponsors, are some of the elements that enter into the matching game.

Rick Rosner, associate producer of the popular Mike Douglas Show on CBS, is extremely sensitive to the subjects that will register with his afternoon audiences across the country. He insists on a preview of subject matter, including a telephone conversation with the key official who is to appear, before he will set dates or suggest the interview to Mike Douglas. There is no question in my mind that Mr. Rosner's attention to detail and his study of audience reaction and interests have made important contributions to the success of the show.

Within a government agency, the radio-TV officer usually discovers that it is easier to persuade his top official to appear on a given show than it is to convince some of the official's protective assistants. Once past the barrier of protectionism, the radio-TV officer must still relate audience interest to what his top spokesman wants to say. Usually a bit of compromising regarding style and approach is necessary on both sides.

In any event, personal contact is absolutely essential in dealing with radio and television producers. Telephone calls alone are not enough. And this contact must be equalled by internal persuasion within the government agency.

When I first recommended that former Secretary of Health, Education, and Welfare John W. Gardner appear on the Mike Douglas Show, I knew that he had a keen personal interest in promoting useful activities for older Americans. I also knew that a significant percentage of regular viewers of that show were oldsters at home or housewives who could offer suggestions to their parents and relatives. Mr. Gardner's appearance, Mr. Rosner advised me a few weeks later, generated more mail than almost any other one-time guest appearance on the Mike Douglas Show up to that time.

It does not always work out so well. On another occasion I had booked Wilbur J. Cohen, then HEW Undersecretary, to appear on the Merv Griffin Show in New York. We were to take a plane at 4 P.M. and do the interview on film at 6:30. At 4, about the time we were to drive to the airport, Mr. Cohen was called to the White House. Fortunately, Bob Shanks, producer of the show, was understanding of our problem and arranged a new date. This experience convinced me that the "no-show" problem in Washington is a very real one because of uncontrollable conditions. The radio-TV officer working with producers (especially those away from Washington) must go out of his way to identify the problems of transportation and possible last-minute cancellations to avoid embarrassment and worse.

Betty Groebli, who conducts a popular talk-show on WRC radio in Washington, told me that I was the first information person who had ever called on her in her office when we met in

April 1967. This was difficult for me to believe then, but I have heard other radio and television personalities and producers make this statement many times since.

The radio and television officer must enjoy not only a close personal rapport with his agency's officials, but a close working relationship with his agency's total information activity. The editors and writers within the information program must have confidence in the officer's reliability and expertise before they will include him in their activities and project planning.

The fact that radio and TV men in government are new on the scene seems to promote a tendency on the part of other information personnel to isolate them from important stories. Keeping the broadcast specialist in the dark until the eleventh hour minimizes radio and TV coverage. No responsible radio-TV officer would "play favorites" or break deadlines, for he shares the same burdens as his colleagues. And he seeks the same general objectives. He is not likely to jeopardize the confidence of his fellows and the respect of the media he serves by releasing information prematurely to any source. But in order to be effective he must be fully informed. He must act in continuity with other information efforts. And he knows this. Thus the information chief in any agency must assume responsibility for keeping the radio-television officer alerted to upcoming events and problems. Total impact absolutely requires the imput of the broadcast specialist. The information chief cannot afford to give him anything less than an equal voice in information planning and implementation.

There are many ways to develop a story for broadcast. But there is only one rule to follow: know the media; know the subject. Hard news goes to the news editor with emphasis on film and taping possibilities. Notice of news conferences and briefings must include comment on what is to be discussed, its significance, and the names of the principals who will make statements and answer questions. No broadcast editor is likely to assign a crew on a wish and a prayer.

Special productions and documentaries require patience and careful nurturing if they are to be developed at all. Nothing can replace thoughtful homework and preparation. The producer will be interested in the full development of ideas, not grand pronouncements.

Listings of broadcast programs and personnel are readily available. The radio-TV officer's job is to study these programs, know broadcast editors, producers, and commentators, and see them regularly with constructive plans and imaginative ideas. He must establish himself as the person they can and should call when they have a question about the agency's activities, desire an interviewee for a discussion program, or wish to arrange an interview with an agency official in his office. The radio-TV officer must accommodate the small requests willingly and graciously if he expects to foster a lasting rapport with the media.

Within the agency, he must also build rapport with his information colleagues and program heads and constantly search for news and news leads. As a new member of the information team, he must take the initiative in his internal relationships. Without active inside news sources there is little of substance for him to convey to media representatives.

The radio and television officer can be of special help in developing news briefings. He can coach officials, prepare visuals, and arrange the room in advance for the convenience of cameras and recorders and to the best advantage of the principals who will conduct the briefing. As a member of the planning unit for such events, he will also have input regarding approach and content as well as timing and staging. And in preparing agency officials, he can present the same kinds of tough questions he believes broadcast reporters may ask.

One broadcast media asset often overlooked is the one- or two-minute film or tape recording preceding or following testimony to a Congressional committee or the delivery of an important speech. A brief statement, well written and well read, can be used almost immediately. The millions of viewers and listeners who see and hear the summary statement will not only be promptly and adequately informed, but may well be motivated to read more about the matter in the morning newspaper. Contrary to some opinion, I believe that radio and television stimulate newspaper readership. All media are supplementary. One medium does not and cannot replace another, especially if both are geared to current needs and attitudes.

In staging events, the radio and television officer must give practical consideration to equipment, power sources, chairs, tables, and all that is necessary, for he will be held accountable for any awkward or embarrassing moments caused by the failure of equipment to function or the appearance of a wrong number on a chart.

When it has been decided that an agency will have a news briefing, and after the item appears on the city wire, the radio-television officer can begin to make personal calls to broadcast news and others who may have an interest in the upcoming event.

Everyone is seeking the same air time. The agency with a hot story is going to get good coverage. After that, time will go to the agency that has prepared its presentation thoughtfully and thoroughly.

The government is still print-oriented; procedures and thinking are still geared to newspapers and pamphlets, and information people generally are just now beginning to appreciate that the radio and television officer can and should play a very large role in the overall information function. The radio and television specialist cannot do his job without the assistance and close cooperation of the print people in information. And he cannot do any portion of his job without the confidence of the people who administer programs.

If the information radio and television specialist has done his homework, knows his program, knows the people within the program, knows what the camera could see and the recorder could hear if they were turned on the program, the program will get broadcast coverage. If the radio-TV officer has made himself visible and available to the broadcasters, they will seek him out. What government urgently needs are more experienced radio and television specialists in the information ranks. Indications are that most information chiefs agree. And to the extent they agree, government information efforts will improve.

ELECTRIC MEDIA . . .

Motion Pictures for Dramatic Effect

CHARLES GLAZER
MOTION PICTURE PRODUCER
U. S. VETERANS ADMINISTRATION

I N 1908 a United States Department of Agriculture entomologist
started making movies of insects, and by 1912 a tiny motion
picture operation was hidden in an attic near the Department.
But James Wilson, who was Secretary of Agriculture at that time,
felt that movies were "the work of the devil," so it was not until
he was secretly filmed making a speech before a group of corn
club boys, and was later tricked into viewing the film, that his
attitude was reversed and the motion picture unit could come
out of hiding.

Since that inauspicious beginning, motion pictures have come
to be widely used in government public information programs.
Today, the Department of Agriculture Motion Picture Service is
one of the largest civilian film production units in the government; it makes 90 films a year for its own use and for other government agencies. This figure is dwarfed by the Department of
Defense whose mammoth appetite for training and information
films is only partly satisfied by the production of 4000 films a
year. The United States Information Agency makes 300 films a
year, but, with one notable exception (the film of President
Kennedy's funeral), these are not shown in the United States.
Other large film producers or sponsors are HEW, which produces
about 160 films a year, and NASA, which makes about 180.

Almost every major element of government has sponsored or
felt the need for a motion picture. Although films represent large
budget items, the cost per viewer and the effectiveness of the medium for putting across complex ideas make them economically
practical and highly desirable. Some information officers may
solve funding problems by stimulating cooperation among other
agencies which have similar interests. For example, the Veterans
Administration produces shared-cost films with the President's
Committee for Employment of the Handicapped.

The information officer who has acquired the responsibility
for the production of a government film soon finds he has an
awesome task. He may contract the film to a private producer;
he may use government film production facilities; or he may
split up the production between government and private con-
tractor.

The problems of contracting a film to a private producer tends
to discourage the uninitiated. But to streamline procedures, pro-

posals have been made to establish an office within the General Services Administration to advise prospective government film sponsors on the courses of action available with respect to outside contracting.

Contracts are generally of two types: call contracts and open bid. Call contracts are made with individuals and identify the type and quality of work each producer can provide. The sponsor thus has a list of qualified producers from which to make a free selection.

The open bid contract allows any film producer to offer a proposal. Unfortunately there must be a very strong tendency to stress lowest bid rather than quality. It is not unusual for the high bid to be ten times more than the low bid because there are so many intangible elements in film production.

A judgment based on cost alone is illogical and dangerous, yet contracting officers too often process film bids without consultation with information specialists. They cannot make the proper judgments and the end product reflects this lack of expertise.

For example, the motion picture script is one of the most misunderstood and misused items in government film production. Too often it is written to be read rather than heard. It is judged as a piece of literature, rather than a living part of the film. After being written and rewritten, after every nuance of the narrative is inspected, the script passes from desk to desk and sometimes from committee to committee collecting initials as it goes.

However, a motion picture script is not like the blueprint of a building where every dimension and type of material is spelled out and followed precisely. The contracting officer who treats a script like a blueprint begs serious trouble. When I was assigned my first government film to direct, I was handed a script and told, "This is your bible. Follow it exactly." But there are many versions of the bible, I told myself.

In the process of transferring words on a piece of paper to pictures and sound, change is inevitable and desirable; change is essential. The ability, courage, and judgment to make changes are assets to the film maker.

A technical advisor who had just been through his first experience in motion picture production told me: "I've discovered that a film is born three times," he sighed. "Once when it is written. Again when it is directed. And once more when it is edited."

As a motion picture is developed, new insights unfold before the camera which call for on-the-spot changes. A director must improvise and stay alert for unanticipated ways to illustrate ideas. A new breed of director who writes as he directs is making an appearance on the cinema scene.

In many instances, I prefer to work from a narrative outline of the film rather than from a finished script. The outline gives me precise knowledge of the concepts in the film but offers wide latitude in its cinematic presentation.

Although last in the film-making process, editing is the key to success. The editor selects and relates the scenes and sequences which the director has put together. The editor builds and shapes the final product.

The film or television script which places the visual in one column and the sound in another can mislead the inexperienced reader as to the real relationship of narration to picture. Good film narration should not be simply part of an illustrated lecture. Words and pictures should be interrelated like counterpoint in music. Thus the writer must work with the director in developing the sequences and with the editor in shaping the final dialogue or narration.

The effectiveness of a film is not necessarily nor usually related to cost alone. Good film makers can do an effective job of putting across complicated ideas with low-budget techniques. The basic criterion in judging if one has received his money's worth is simply whether the finished product does the job it was designed to do. This is not to say that the use of color and more costly techniques are not highly desirable and in some instances essential to achieve total effectiveness.

Interesting and useful motion pictures require real thought, effort, and time. Part of the effectiveness of the cinematic communication depends on the director's viewpoint and the skill and perception of the cameramen. Like a fine painter, the cameraman must convey ideas, not simply images or reflections. The quality and cost of a film are the aggregate of the number of "shots" that make it up and the art and skill with which they are put together.

Other factors that bear on the cost of a film are the quantitative and qualitative use of actors, synchronous sound, music, art work, animation, and special effects.

In producing films within the government one falls prey to a maze of rules and regulations which are utterly incompatible with the problems of film making. A vivid impression I have is sitting in a room with other government film executives explaining why I had not gone through regular procedures to purchase a few relatively low-cost lights. I explained that some lights had gone bad during production and that many people were being held up in a busy government office. The quickest way out of the predicament was to run to the nearest store and purchase the lights. Nevertheless, regulations were regulations and I was told this should not have been done.

"How can I make films under these circumstances?" I asked.

"Actually," was the nervous reply, "you really can't make films in the government."

Everyone has heard stories of how bureaucratic rules cause inefficiencies. Fortunately, there are also many instances when courageous government employees "interpret" these rules for the ultimate benefit of the program and the taxpayer.

During the production of a certain film, I found that we needed a man to design and supply costumes. We searched the area diligently until we found one person who could do the job, but procedures required that we obtain the special services on bid which would take at least a month to consummate. I picked up the phone and explained that I was supposed to complete filming in a month . . . that a large sum of money was involved . . . that this film had the interest of many government agencies. Our business official thought for a moment. "Well, this is sort of the grey area. But you could hire your man as an art director under our talent contract." So the problem was solved.

Film production personnel often perplex government program officials whose budgets pay the way. A writer friend of mind was asked by a top official of a large agency, "Why is it your film people think they are something special?" What he could not appreciate was that creative specialists cannot operate under the same rules and regulations as clerks and typists. No art medium can exist under guidelines that are too rigid.

Before a film is made into an "answer print" (final), an edited "work print" and sound track are run for the production crew (and usually a committee of all concerned). This large group usually includes individuals who have only a cursory knowledge of the background and objectives of the film. Some do not consider the film as a whole, but only their special interests. No good film was ever produced by a government committee, but this does not discourage committee members from trying.

So we have the committee—the deadly committee, renowned and often rightly so for fouling up the effectiveness of government operations of every kind. If all the suggestions of a film committee are adopted, the film's carefully built structure is destroyed. If it is produced, bored audiences will rate it as "another typical institutional film."

This destruction by committee need not be if creative specialists would be more assertive. The committee can be reasoned with and cinematic values can be saved if the facts and ideas are presented in an organized, persuasive way to the committee.

Some fine films have come out of the government and the USIA is giving young film makers a green light for innovation. So the quality of government films should continue to rise. For instance, "A Year Toward Tomorrow"—the dramatic story of young VISTA workers produced for $63,000 by the Office of Equal Opportunity, earned a Hollywood "Oscar" as the best documentary film of 1966.

Many agencies have area or state representatives through which information films and spot announcements are distributed to television stations; this is better than sending films directly from a central point in Washington. Smaller government units often get assistance from the larger agencies in the distribution of their films.

There are 31,000 film titles on a wide variety of subjects deposited in government film libraries. Of these, 25,000 belong to the Department of Defense and 6000 to civilian agencies. Many of these films are available on free loan from the individual agencies and cooperating state and private libraries. Efforts are being made to consolidate the cataloguing of all government films.

Millions of feet of out-takes from completed films and scenes from unedited films are stored by the government. These scenes are available to motion picture and television producers. The motion picture is an effective information tool. And films are regularly approved by almost all government units. The question is whether the quality and usefulness of films will be upgraded. The answer depends on the resourcefulness and performance of film specialists and the cooperation and understanding of top agency officials.

THE PRINTED PAGE . . .

Magazines and Books for Permanent Impression

ROY HOOPES
CONSULTANT, OFFICE OF PUBLIC INFORMATION
U. S. DEPARTMENT OF HEALTH,
EDUCATION, AND WELFARE

I T is often said that in the age of television, people of our global village are reading fewer books and that the magazine industry is dying. The number of people who read magazines regularly might be small compared to the number of people who watch television regularly, and the swing of advertisers to television because of its cheaper cost-per-thousand has hurt the general consumer magazines. But the general magazine business is very healthy and specialized magazines are healthier than ever.

It is also true that the number of Americans who read books does not compare favorably with some other countries—Great Britain, for example. But the book industry in America is thriving, thanks in part to more young Americans entering college every year. More books—including books on public affairs—are being bought and read in America than ever before.

For government information officers, the message about the media is obvious: modern, television-oriented information and public relations men will make just as big a mistake if they ignore magazines and books as the mistake made by the old-style, newsprint-oriented media men who ignored television.

The simple fact is that there will always be a publishing industry. A great many people—not necessarily the educated only —absorb information effectively through the printed page and do not feel they really know something until they have read it. The educated, reflective opinion makers and thought leaders often prefer the printed page to television as a source of information because it offers material in greater depth and can be filed away for future reference. Finally, certain things can be accomplished with magazines and books that cannot be accomplished through television and the daily press, which make them indispensable tools of the information officer or the public relations advisor.

The most difficult problem in dealing with magazines is their variety. Their audience, philosophy, and contents are as varied as their size, shape, and frequency of publication. Some weeklies, fortnightlies, monthlies, quarterlies, and even annuals are edited for a mass audience, some for men, some for women, some for a specialized audience. Some are news magazines, some thought and opinion magazines, some designed strictly for entertainment— and many for a combination of purposes.

331

The first thing any media man must know is the nature of the magazine he is dealing with. He should know the general field as a part of his basic professional knowledge as well as a doctor knows the instruments in his black bag. If he gets a query from a magazine with which he is not familiar, he should obtain a copy and study it carefully to get a feel for the kind of material its editors are looking for and what they are likely to do with it.

All magazines have two things in common—a deadline and a lead-time. In the magazine business there are several deadlines— the date on which information is due, the date the writer must pass the material on to his editor, the date the magazine must have the copy to the printer, and the date the magazine actually goes to press. The most important deadline for the information specialist is the date on which the editor must have the manuscript.

Magazine deadlines do not come every day, as they do on newspapers, but they are just as pressing. If a newspaper deadline is missed the item can usually be used the next day, but if a magazine deadline is missed, often it is too late to use the material. Despite the obvious need for deadlines, some government information officers ignore them, much to the irritation of many who cover Washington for the nation's magazines. *Life* has its deadline on Wednesday, *U.S. News* on Friday, and *Time* and *Newsweek* on Saturday.

The information officer must also be aware of lead-time—the interval between the magazine's closing date and its appearance on newsstands or in mail boxes. *Time* and *Newsweek* close on Saturday and are on the newsstand the following Monday. Other weeklies do almost that well. The fortnightlies—*Saturday Evening Post* and *Look,* for example—have longer lead-times, around three weeks as a rule. Monthlies run anywhere from a month and a half to more than three months.

An information specialist trying to interest a magazine in a story must consider the publication's lead-time. Newsworthy items should go to the publications with the shortest lead-times. If they are given to monthlies which won't hit the newsstands for weeks, the story can be lost.

Interviews with Washington officials on live political issues usually do not fare well in magazines with long lead-times. The political climate can change overnight and the rush of events can undercut thoughts and opinions on sensitive political issues.

Editors of magazines with long lead-times are acutely aware of the problems caused by newsworthy exclusives or statements by prominent public figures on changing political issues. Editors of monthlies are primarily interested in articles on long-range trends or on problems or developments which will be of concern to their readers for some time and are unlikely to be altered by events which might take place within one, two, or three months after their closing dates.

Profiles of personalities can be of special use to monthlies, but most editors will not be interested simply because an official has an important job. A profile based on a man's personality should reflect his unusual personal characteristics. The profile based on his job should show the man's involvement in projects, programs, or issues of importance to readers. The ideal profile portrays a man who is an unusual personality involved in an extremely important job.

Most information officers dealing with the publishing industry spend their time either in direct response to editors' requests, or in trying to interest editors in an article, an interview, or a book. Let us consider the editor's requests first.

When a request comes from a writer or editor, seriously developing an article, every attempt should be made to get him in touch with the experts or officials working in the area in which he is interested. Whether or not he asks for it, he should be sent a package of all printed publications relating to his subject. This will give him background material, which, at the very least, will help assure that names are spelled correctly.

In responding to a request, the information officer should curb the temptation to make the article or book come out the way he would prefer it. Naturally, he is going to try to point it in the direction he would like it to go and correct false information. But if a project takes an unacceptable form, he must not try to reshape it but should try to find another writer to develop the project in another way.

Above all, no information officer should try to persuade a writer that everything is perfect. If mistakes have been made, the agency should admit them. If the author is a good reporter, he is going to find them out sooner or later anyway. Most magazines are fair in their approach to government operations. It is much better to be candid with their writers.

Information officers should never close the door to a writer or a publication. It is to their advantage to be in communication with the media at all times. If the doors are closed, the writer may well end up working with inaccurate sources.

Finally, if a damaging article is scheduled for publication, there is no need to panic. The agency should not start feeding its rebuttal to Drew Pearson, as some agency information officers have done on occasion, or start threatening the editor with hints that friends on Capitol Hill or in the White House can make it tough for him or his magazine. The best approach is to try to obtain an advance copy of the article as early as possible and have the agency's rebuttal ready on publication day. If the article is built on misinformation and a faulty interpretation of the facts, as was a recent article in a national magazine attacking Social Security, an agency can, as the Department of Health, Education, and Welfare did, issue a press release pointing out the errors in fact and interpretation. The agency might also write a letter to the editor explaining its position, which most magazines will publish.

It is surprising how quickly a story will die, even one which shows the agency caught red-handed. Because so much is thrown at the reading and viewing public, it is difficult to catch interest and hold it. This works to an agency's disadvantage when it is trying to convince the public of a need for one of its programs. But it can also work to its advantage when it wants to divert attention from its mistakes.

Perhaps the most important aspect of the information man's job is attempting to place stories about his department and its officials in national magazines. The first question most information officers ask is: should the story be an exclusive—do I have the right to provide what is essentially public information to only one publication?

Information will usually be released to the press—including the magazine press—in the form of a press release that is not exclusive and is marked for immediate release. But these stories are of little use to most magazines, especially fortnightlies and monthlies. Magazines generally want exclusives, and the information officer should sometimes try to provide them. The officer should play fair with his exclusives, and not favor one magazine continually. If an agency has a big story, it might develop different angles for different magazines. But competing magazines should be advised that their rivals are working on a different angle.

When a magazine writer goes to work on an assignment, some information officers occasionally succumb to the temptation of getting double coverage by hinting to another magazine that its competitor is working on an important story. This is bad business. If a magazine is working on a story either suggested by an agency or originated by the magazine, the agency's information officer should remain silent.

Let us assume that an agency has developed material which would make excellent background for a magazine piece. Perhaps a long-range study has been completed, and although its findings are not sensational enough to interest the daily media, they contain considerable material of national interest. "This would make a perfect magazine piece," everyone agrees at the Monday morning information staff meeting. What should be done?

First the information officer should learn everything about the project by reading the full report, learning how it originated, and why, and discussing its broad, long-range significance with senior officials. Next, he should develop in his own mind a magazine-type newspeg. In doing so, he should ask himself is this *really* significant, and why? If he cannot convince himself that the material is significant enough to warrant a magazine piece, he is not going to convince a skeptical magazine writer who must, in turn, convince a skeptical editor.

After mastering the material, the officer must decide which magazine he wants to approach. A good story can be directed toward almost any general interest magazine, but some stories seem tailor-made for certain magazines. He should know almost by instinct exactly what magazine would be most interested in a story developing in his office. He should also follow closely the personnel changes in the upper echelons of the magazine world because a change of editors at one of the major magazines often signals a change in editorial direction.

Having picked his magazine, he should prepare a package for the magazine's writers or editors. The most important ingredient in the package is an outline or synopsis of the article. In most cases, a two-page, double-spaced outline is enough to tell the story. However, some magazines like longer treatments, the *Reader's Digest,* for example. It also helps at *Reader's Digest* to begin the outline with a human interest lead, and sprinkle it with relevant quotes and anecdotes.

In addition, the officer might want to include some detailed background material which the editors can study. In some cases, it may be useful to include photographs that help portray the significance of the story.

To attract the editors prompt and careful reading, the best approach is through personal contact. When it is necessary to approach a magazine cold, the information officer should go to the article or text editor. He should not press for a decision based on a verbal presentation.

Once the proposal is in the hands of the proper editor, the information officer should fight the temptation to phone the next day and ask: "What do you think of that idea I gave you?" It will take most magazines two or three weeks to respond. If the initiator has not heard from the magazine in three weeks, he may then follow up.

Once an article proposal is accepted, editors or their writers will begin to shape the material. The head of the agency should agree to give time to interviews to state his views on the subject. The agency's information unit should be put on stand-by to assist the magazine in developing the story.

The information officer will also want to place byline articles by the top men in his department—agency head, secretary, or assistant secretary. Generally speaking, magazines will not be interested in bylines of lower rank staff officials and will prefer to assign their own writers. Occasionally they will be tempted with an article bylined by a well-known Washington name. Top government officials cannot accept fees for these articles, and such savings might appeal to a less prosperous magazine. The larger magazines will usually prefer to pay a fee for the article, which might be donated to charity or, sometimes, be paid to the ghost writer. Senators and Congressman can accept fees and usually are quite eager to do so, especially in an election year.

The information officer can usually provide an interview with the agency head—either an informal, background interview or a formal interview to be published as such in a magazine. Tait Trussel, managing editor of *Nation's Business,* urges that government information officers "should try to arrange more interviews with top editors and the head of their agency or department. These should just be informal get-togethers and not organized for the purpose of selling anything. Just a discussion about some of the problems and issues in your man's area, which can be a two-way street. The government official will often learn as much as the editors."

An increasingly popular journalistic technique is the formal interview. Most magazines publish them occasionally, and at least two magazines—*U.S. News* and *Playboy* publish them regularly.

U.S. News has been publishing interviews since the late 1940s. "In choosing persons to be interviewed," says Carson Lyman, *U.S. News* managing editor, "we watch for someone in the news or someone who speaks with authority on a subject in the news, or whose views on a public question are in themselves news."

An individual picked for an interview in *U.S. News* is usually invited to the magazine's office, where he is interviewed by several staff editors. It is a spontaneous, conversational interview not based on a set of prepared questions. It is taped, and a transcript of the interview is sent to the interviewee, who has complete freedom to make alterations or corrections in the copy.

Playboy interviews are longer (one recent interview ran 62⅓ columns, or an equivalent of nearly 21 pages, and took 13 hours to complete), and the interviewee must be well known. Charles Percy, Ronald Reagan, Robert McNamara, John Lindsay, Robert Kennedy are some of the men it has sought for interviews.

Playboy expects the writer to dig deep into the man's public record, go over his major speeches, his writings, and his career. The writer is asked to prepare about 100 questions, which are sent to the magazine. The interviews are usually taped, although a stenographer is sometimes used.

Working with the full transcript, the interviewer puts together a finished manuscript, usually editing, cutting, and pasting to eliminate duplication and organize the final interview into a natural, conversational flavor and narrative. The completed manuscript is gone over again by the editors, who may ask for additional, follow-up questions. After the final interview is edited, it is sent back to the interviewee, who is free to correct typographical errors and quotations out of context. No deletions or additions can be made, except to update passages that have been overtaken by events. Occasionally, however, an afterthought may be added, but *Playboy* reserves the right to challenge it with additional questions.

"We strive for interviews," says Murray Fisher, *Playboy's* senior editor, "that probe beyond a man's prepared public opinions to question the often *un*questioned premises on which he bases his most private and personal beliefs. This requires space—more by three or four times than any other magazine devotes to dialogs of this nature—but we think the end result is a genuine reflection of not only the way the man thinks but what makes him think that way."

In-depth interviews can be useful in getting the views of top officials across to the public. Interviewees should be well-briefed and should not go into a session without having done homework. To prepare, the information officer should write out the tougher questions he thinks will be asked and give them to the interviewee a few days in advance.

Dealing with the book publishing industry is similar to dealing with magazines. The writer working on a book may not know much about the subject at the start, but he will know much more about it than most agency employees when he completes his research. Authors of books thus often speak with authority.

A book is likely to have much more impact when it is published than a magazine article. It may be widely reviewed, discussed on TV, and often might be the subject of stories in the news magazines and newspapers. Its essence may appear in a magazine at the time of publication. A single magazine article rarely makes this splash—although if it is on a controversial subject, it may lead to a book.

When an information officer is trying to develop a book idea, he should find an author and sell him on the idea before approaching the publisher. About half a publisher's time is spent trying to find authors to make books out of good ideas. Publishers will be more disposed toward an idea if it comes in the form of a proposal for a book by an established writer.

Author candidates are reporters, magazine staffers, free-lance writers, or agency employees who can be persuaded to take time off to do a book. Authors need assurance that there is sufficient material which the information officer should place at his disposal. If the author can be given a researcher, so much the better. A good, solid book discussing an agency's work is worth its weight in gold, and a few weeks of a bright young researcher's time is a sound investment.

It is only a short step from persuading an author to do a book to actually subsidizing the book by offering to pay the author (or agreeing to buy copies in advance from the publisher). It is, however, an important step, and one that should be considered carefully.

The information officer approaches a publisher and agrees to buy a certain number of copies in advance—perhaps several thousand copies at a 50 percent discount. The publishers are assured of selling at least another couple of thousand to libraries and the trade. Thus a breakeven sale is assured. With any luck, they can sell a few more and make a little profit.

Most publishers do not publicize this kind of arrangement, but at least one veteran told me that "all publishers have done it at some time or another." Of course, some publishing houses specialize in a "rarity" operation and produce few books not underwritten, and some are even profitable. I know of at least one book authored by a Congressman and supported by an agreement (to buy several hundred copies) which sold very well and is still bringing the author royalties.

Although men holding elective office are free to enter into such arrangements, it is not done by top appointed government officials (except with their own money) because it would mean buying books for promotional use at the taxpayer's expense. There are legitimate exceptions. The Peace Corps supported the publication of *The Peace Corps Reader,* which it gives away as a recruiting handout. But it clearly states that it was published for the Peace Corps. The United States Information Agency has also entered into such arrangements, which have been criticized severely primarily because there was no mention on the books that they were published with the support of the USIA and some copies were sold in the United States, although they were intended for distribution abroad.

I recommend staying away from all subsidy arrangements if they involve buying books with public funds. However, I do think it would be legitimate for any agency to try to develop a book, and then offer it to a publisher with the understanding that royalties would not have to be paid to the author.

Most men in top administration jobs do not have the time or inclination to work on a book while still in office, even if much of the work is done by a research-writer assistant. The time for the government servant's book is after he leaves office, when he has more freedom and can speak more frankly.

The most important thing the government public information officer can do to prepare himself to deal with the publishing industry is to work at least two or three years on a magazine or for a book publisher. The experience will give him a better appreciation and understanding of the editor's problems, more confidence in dealing with them, and help generate more respect for his agency.

Bibliography

BOOKS

Barth, Alan. *The Government and the Press*. Minneapolis, 1952.
———. *Government by Investigation*. New York, 1955.
Castberg, Frederick. *Freedom of Speech in the West; a Comparative Study of Public Law in France, the United States, and Germany*. Oslo, 1960.
Cater, Douglass. *The Fourth Branch of Government*. Boston, 1959.
Chaffee, Zechariah, Jr. *Free Speech in the United States*. Cambridge, Mass., 1946.
———. *Government and Mass Communications*. Chicago, 1947. 2 volumes.
Cohen, Bernard D. *The Press and Foreign Policy*. Princeton, 1963.
Commission on Freedom of the Press. *A Free and Responsible Press; a General Report on Mass Communication*. Chicago, 1947.
———. *Freedom of the Press, a Framework of Principle*, by William E. Hocking. Chicago, 1947.
Cooper, Kent. *The Right To Know; An Exposition of the Evils of News Suppression and Propaganda*. New York, 1956.
Cornwell, Elmer E. *Presidential Leadership of Public Opinion*. Bloomington, Indiana, 1965.
Cross, Harold L. *The People's Right to Know; Legal Access to Public Records and Proceedings*. New York, 1953.
Doob, Leonard W. *Public Opinion and Propaganda*. New York, 1948.
———. *The Right of the People*. Garden City, N.Y., 1955.

341

Eberling, Ernest J. *Congressional Investigations; A Study of the Origin and Development of the Power of Congress to Investigate and Punish for Contempt.* New York, 1928.

Eek, Hilding. *Report on Developments in the Field of Freedom of Information Since 1954.* New York, 1961.

Gerald, J. Edward. *The Press and the Constitution, 1931–47.* Minneapolis, 1948.

Hey, Herbert W. *Congressional Demands for Executive Information.* Chicago, 1956. [M.A. thesis, University of Chicago (on microfilm).]

Hiebert, Ray Eldon (ed.). *The Press in Washington: Sixteen Top Newsmen Tell How the News is Collected, Written, and Communicated from the World's Most Important Capital.* New York, 1966.

Johnson, M. B. *The Government Secrecy Controversy, A Dispute Involving the Government and the Press in the Eisenhower, Kennedy and Johnson Administrations.* New York, 1967.

Johnson, Walter. *The American President and the Art of Communication.* Oxford, England, 1958.

Kelley, Stanley, Jr. *Professional Public Relations and Political Power.* Baltimore, 1956.

Ladd, Bruce. *Crisis in Credibility.* New York, 1968.

McCamy, James L. *Government Publicity.* Chicago, 1939.

McCormick, Robert R. *The Freedom of the Press Still Furnishes That Check Upon Government Which No Constitution Has Ever Been Able To Provide.* Chicago, 1934.

McGeary, Martin N. *The Development of Congressional Investigating Power.* New York, 1940.

Michael, George. *Handout.* New York, 1935.

Mollenhoff, Clark R. *Washington Coverup.* Garden City, N.Y., 1962.

Newton, Virgil M. *Crusade for Democracy* (the Tampa Tribune). Ames, Iowa, 1961.

———. *The Press and Bureaucracy; An Address.* Tuscon, Ariz., 1961.

Nimmo, Dan D. *Newsgathering in Washington: A Study in Political Communication.* New York, 1964.

Pinón, Tiana Antonio. *The Freedom of the Press: A Critical Evaluation of the Totalitarian and Liberal Theories.* Manila, P.I., 1960.

Pollard, James E. (ed.). *Laws of the 48 States Bearing on: I. Definition of "Newspaper." II. "Open Meetings" of Public Bodies. III. Definition of Public Records.* Columbus, Ohio, 1957.

———. *The Presidents and the Press.* New York, 1947.

Raymond, Allen. *The People's Right To Know* (a report on Government news suppression, prepared for the American Civil Liberties Union). New York, 1955.

Reston, James B. *The Artillery of the Press.* New York, 1967.

Rivers, William L. *The Opinionmakers.* Boston, 1965.

Roston, Leo C. *The Washington Correspondents.* New York, 1937.

Rourke, Francis E. *Secrecy and Publicity; Dilemmas of Democracy.* Baltimore, 1961.

Shils, Edward A. *The Torment of Secrecy.* Glencoe, Ill., 1956.

Siebert, Frederick S. *The Rights and Privileges of the Press.* New York, 1934.
Summers, Robert E. (comp.). *Federal Information Controls in Peacetime.* New York, 1949.
————. (comp.). *Wartime Censorship of Press and Radio.* New York, 1942.
Wiggins, J. R. *Freedom or Secrecy?* (Revised edition.) New York, 1964.
Young, Kimball, and Raymond D. Lawrence. *Bibliography on censorship and propaganda.* Eugene, Oreg., 1928.

PERIODICALS AND OTHER ITEMS

Abelson, P. H. "Partisan Attack on Research." *Science,* 156:1315 (June 9, 1967).
"Access to Official Information; a Neglected Constitutional Right." *Indiana Law Journal,* 27:209–230 (Winter, 1952).
Alsop, S. "Does the Washington Press Lie?" *Saturday Evening Post,* 240:16 (July 15, 1967).
Archibald, Samuel J. "5 U.S.C. 22—Relic of 1789." *American Society of Newspaper Editors Bulletin,* 404:1 (Dec. 1, 1957).
————. "Government Secrecy: The Lid Remains on Many Matters Wholly Nonmilitary" (condensation of an address). *Wall Street Journal,* 154:16 (Oct. 22, 1959).
————. "The Game of Ghost." *Columbia Journalism Review,* 7:1 (Spring, 1968).
"Backgrounder: Off-the-Record Information Being Opposed." *Newsweek,* 69:71 (May 22, 1967).
Bagdikiam, B. H. "News Managers." *Saturday Evening Post,* 236:17–19 (Apr. 20, 1963).
Bateman, J. Carroll. "Techniques of Managing the News (Practiced by the White House From George Washington's Time to the Present)." *Public Relations Journal,* 19:6–9 (August, 1963).
Beckerley, J. G. "Government Control of Technical Data." *Confluence,* 5:147–157 (July, 1956).
Beetle, David H. "It's Your Government—But How Much Can You Learn About What Is Going On?" *Monitor: The Voice of Industry in New York State,* 47:7–11 ff. (March, 1962).
Bingham, Worth, and Ward S. Just. "President and the Press." *Reporter,* 26:18–23 (Apr. 12, 1962).
Boner, J. Russell. "Conflict of Protection: SEC Blackout of Some Corporate News Not Always a Safeguard for Investors." *Wall Street Journal,* 165:14 (February 4, 1965).
Burns, J. M. "Between Presidents and the Press." *Saturday Review,* 49:25 (Sept. 3, 1966).
Campbell, A. "Not for Attribution: State Department Briefing on Aggression from the North: The Record of North Vietnam's Campaign." *New Republic,* 152:7–8 (March 13, 1965).
Campbell, E. "Public Access to Government Documents." *Australian Law Journal,* 41:73 (July, 1967).

"Candor, Credibility, Confidence: Techniques of Feeding Misinformation." *Nation*, 201:429 (Dec. 6, 1965).

Cater, Douglass. "News and the Nation's Security." *Reporter*, 25:26–29 (July 6, 1961).

"Cold War in Washington: President and the Press." *Time*, 85:38 ff. (March 5, 1965).

Collins, Philip R. "The Power of Congressional Committee of Investigation to Obtain Information From the Executive Branch: The Argument for the Legislative Branch." *Georgia Law Review*, 39:563–598 (May, 1951).

"Comments on Proposed Amendments to Section 3 of the Administrative Procedure Act." *Notre Dame Lawyer*, 40:417 (June, 1965).

Cormier, F. "Johnson and the Press." *Saturday Review*, 49:70–72 (Sept. 10, 1966).

Cowell, F. B. "Government Departments and the Press in the U.S.A." *Public Administration* (London), 9:214–227 (April, 1931).

Crawford, Kenneth. "Gap Prone: Need for Government Information on Bombing Policy." *Newsweek*, 70:39 (Sept. 25, 1967).

———. "LBJ and the Press." *Newsweek*, 63:18 (Feb. 17, 1964).

"Cutting the Red Tape: Freedom of Information Act." *Newsweek*, 70:88 (Sept. 18, 1967).

Davis, K. C. "Information Act: A Preliminary Analysis." *University of Chicago Law Review*, 34:761 (Summer, 1967).

"Did You Hear That? Concerning A. Sylvester's Alleged Statement that Press Should be Handmaiden of the Government." *Nation*, 202:668 (June 6, 1966).

Donnelly, Richard C. "Government and Freedom of the Press." *Illinois Law Review*, 45:31–56 (March/April, 1950).

Eller, J. N. "All Washington's A Stage." *America*, 112:847 (June 12, 1965).

"Executive Privilege: Public's Right to Know and Public Interest: A Symposium." *Federal Bar Journal*, 19: iv (January, 1959).

Featherer, Esther J. "The Moss Committee, 1955—," University of Missouri School of Journalism, Freedom of Information Center Publication No. 110 (October, 1963).

"Fog in the Channels (United States Government's Management of News and Regulation of Information)." *Economist*, 209:561–2 (Nov. 9, 1963).

"For Attribution: Washington Post Challenges 'Background only' Government Information." *Time*, 89:56 (May 19, 1967).

Friedman, L. M. "Disclosure of Information: A Coin With Two Sides." *Public Administration Review*, 17:10–13 (Winter, 1957).

Fuller, Lon L. "Governmental Secrecy and the Forms of Social Order." In Carl J. Friedrich (ed.). *Community*, Nomos II (New York, 1959). Pp. 256–268.

Golden, L. L. L. "President and the Press." *Saturday Review*, 48:65–66 (May 8, 1965).

Goldschmidt, Maure L. "Publicity, Privacy, and Secrecy." *Western Political Quarterly*, 7:401-416 (September, 1954).

Graham, Philip L. "Public Administration and the Press." *Public Administration Review*, 13:87–88 (Spring, 1953).

Green, Harold P. "Atomic Energy Information Control." *Chicago Bar Record,* 38:55–62 (November, 1956).

———. "Information Control and Atomic Power Development." *Law and Contemporary Problems,* 21:91–112 (Winter, 1956).

Hennings, Thomas C., Jr. "Constitutional Law: The People's Right To Know: Extent of the Right of the Executive to Withhold Information from the Public; Arguing That the Right to Withhold Information Is a Very Narrow One." *American Bar Association Journal,* 45:667–700 ff. (July, 1959).

———. "A Legislative Measure To Augment the Free Flow of Public Information." *American University Law Review,* 8:19 (January, 1959).

Hughes, E. J. "Plaguing Fictions of Politics." *Newsweek,* 70:15 (July 24, 1967).

"Information and Secrecy." *Commonweal,* 74:164–165 (May 12, 1961).

Kelley, Stanley, Jr. "P.R. Man: Political Mastermind." *New York Times Magazine,* pp. 10 ff. (Sept. 2, 1956).

Kennedy, John F. "President and the Press"; address, April 27, 1961. *Vital Speeches,* 27:450–452 (May 15, 1961).

Knebel, Fletcher. "Kennedy Versus the Press." *Look,* 26:17-21 (Aug. 28, 1962).

Kraft, Joseph. "Politics of the Washington Press Corps." *Harper,* 230:100 ff. (June, 1965).

Kramer, Robert, and Herman Marcuse. "Executive Privilege: A Study of the Period 1953–60." *George Washington Law Review,* 29:623–717 (April, 1961); 827–916 (June, 1961).

Krock, Arthur. "Press Versus Government: A Warning." *Public Opinion Quarterly,* 1:45 (April, 1937).

Latimer, J. Austin. "The Power of Congress to Subpena Members and Documents From the Executive Branch." *South Carolina Law Quarterly,* 7: 379–393 (Spring, 1955).

"'Lights! Cameras! Action!' The LBJ News Conference." *U. S. News & World Report,* 59:66–67 (Sept. 20, 1965).

Lippmann, Walter. "President and the Press." *Newsweek,* 65:15 (March 1, 1965).

McAllister, Dale. "Executive or Judicial Determination of Privilege of Government Documents?" *Journal of Criminal Law and Criminology,* 41: 330–335 (September/October, 1950).

MacDougall, P. "Open Meeting Statutes: The Press Fights for the Right To Know." *Public Management,* 45:33-37 (February, 1963).

Mamana, J. M. "FDA's Obligations Under the 1966 Information Act." *Food Drug Cosmetic Law Journal,* 22:563 (October, 1967).

Manning, R. J. "Foreign Policy and the People's Right to Know (Address). *Department of State Bulletin,* 50:868–877 (June 1, 1964).

———. "Journalism and Foreign Affairs," address, July 9, 1962. *Department of State Bulletin,* 47:185–190 (July 30, 1962).

———. "Journalism and Foreign Affairs (Address)." *Department of State Bulletin,* 50:541–549 (Apr. 6, 1964). Same, with title "Press and the Government." *Vital Speeches,* 30:453–457 (May 15, 1964).

Marks, Herbert S., and George F. Trowbridge. "Control of Information Under the Atomic Energy Act of 1954." *Bulletin of the Atomic Scientists,* 11:128–130 (April, 1955).

Mitchell, John J. "Government Secrecy in Theory and Practice: 'Rules and regulations' As an Autonomous Screen." *Columbia Law Review,* 58:199–210 (February, 1958).

"Modernizing Federal Publicity." *Public Opinion Quarterly,* 1:87 (1937).

Moss, John E. "The Crisis of Secrecy." *Bulletin of the Atomic Scientists,* 17: 8–11 ff. (January, 1961).

————. "Moss Attacks Government News Control," address. *Aviation Week,* 77:112 ff. (Dec. 10, 1962).

Mundt, Karl E. "Government Control of Sources of Information." In *Annals of American Academy of Political and Social Science, Communication and Social Action.* (Philadelphia), 250:26–31 (March, 1947).

Nelson, B. "Unplugging the Muted Trumpet: Senate Says, NIH, Blow Your Horn." *Science,* 154:491 ff. (Oct. 28, 1966).

Newman, James R. "Control of Information Relating to Atomic Energy." *Yale Law Journal,* 56:769–802 (May, 1947).

"News and National Interest." *Christian Century,* 78:611–612 (May 17, 1961).

"News versus Security." Excerpts from a debate between the President and the press. Views on either side are brought together in dialog form; all of the statements have previously appeared in print. *Columbia Journalism Review,* 45–47 (Fall, 1961).

"Panel Discussion on Freedom of Information Act at Midyear Meeting." *American Bar Association Section of Taxation Bulletin,* 20:43 (April, 1967).

Parks, Wallace. "The Open Government Principle." Applying the right to know under the Constitution; secrecy and the public interest in military affairs. *George Washington Law Review,* 26:1–77 (October, 1957).

Paul, J. "Access to Rules and Records of Federal Agencies: The Freedom of Information Act." *Los Angeles Bar Bulletin,* 42:459 (August, 1967).

"People's Right To Know Reviewed." Access to public records discussed by H. Gross, A. J. Lazaraus. *National Municipal Review,* 43:213–15 (April, 1954).

Peterson, C. P. "Legislatures and the Press." *State Government,* 27:223–225 (November, 1954).

Pollard, James S. "The Kennedy Administration and the Press." *Journalism Quarterly,* 41:3–14 (Winter, 1964).

"The Power of the Executive to Withhold Information From Congressional Investigating Committees." *Georgia Law Review,* 43:463 (June, 1955).

"Propaganda Activities of Big Government Under Scrutiny." *Congressional Digest,* 30:131–160 (May, 1951).

Reston, James B. "The Press, the President and Foreign Policy." *Foreign Affairs,* 45:553–573 (July, 1966).

Rogers, William P. "Constitutional Law." The papers of the executive branch, right of the executive branch to withhold documents and other materials from Congress. *American Bar Association Journal,* 44:941–944 ff. (October, 1958).

Rolph, C. H. "Abuse of Official Secrets." *New Statesman,* 51:441–442 (Apr. 28, 1956).

Rourke, Francis E. "Administrative Secrecy, a Congressional Dilemma." *American Political Science Review,* 54:684–694 (September, 1960).

————. "Secrecy in American Bureaucracy." *Political Science Quarterly,* 72: 540–564 (December, 1957).

Scher, Jacob. "Access to Information," recent legal problems. *Journalism Quarterly,* 37:41–52 (Winter, 1960).

Sigma Delta Chi. "Advancement of Freedom of Information Committee," report. In *Sigma Delta Chi, annual report,* 1957, 1958, 1959, 1960, 1961, 1962.

Spitzer, Carlton E., "Public Information in Government Policy." *Public Relations Journal,* 24:24–26 (February, 1968).

Strout, Richard L. "Government by Leak." *New Republic,* 136:8–10 (Jan. 21, 1957).

Sullivan, J. "Public's Legal Right to the News." *Shingle* (Philadelphia Bar Association), 16:248–250 (November, 1953).

Sylvester, Arthur. "Government Has the Right to Lie." *Saturday Evening Post,* 240:10 ff. (Nov. 18, 1967).

Sypher, A. H. "You Can't Fool All of the People Even Some of the Time." *Nation's Business,* 54:31–32 (February, 1966).

Tebbel, John. "What News Does the Public Believe?" *Saturday Review,* 45: 43–44 (Mar. 10, 1962). Discussion, 45: 78-79 (Apr. 14); 72–73 (May 12); 48 ff. (June 9) 1962.

"Trial by Press Release." *Nation,* 199:83 (Sept. 7, 1964).

Tugman, W. M. "People's Right to Know." *State Government,* 27:225–226 (November, 1954).

Uretz, L. R. "Freedom of Information and the IRS." *Arkansas Law Review,* 20:283 (Winter, 1967).

Waples, D. "Publicity Versus Diplomacy," notes on the reporting of the summit conference. *Public Opinion Quarterly,* 20:308–314 (Spring, 1956).

Wiggins, James R. "Do Public Officials Withhold the News Because They Do Not Trust the Public?" *The Quill,* 42:10–11, 24, 26 (November, 1954).

Index